"*Amoskeag* is, quite simply, a marvel of evocation. No one who has watched a rich and lively interview die between tape recorder and transcript can feel anything less than awe before the taste, skill, and immense labor on the part of the authors and editor which make this book a triumph of selective intelligence in the service of historical truth. Enhanced by memorable illustrations from the great Lewis Hine classics of young children with ancient faces, to family snapshots, and including the fine architectural photographs of coauthor Langenbach, *Amoskeag* is far more than a valuable collective biography. Without ever reducing the representative to the symbolic, its transparent art frees the few to speak for the many, and by extension, for each of us."

—The Nation

"There is much valuable information about the inner workings of mill and community, the interlocking of family and factory, the forms of 'interdependence and sociability' fostered by textile manufacturing in the work experience itself. Workers speak in their own voices, as subjects in their own right."

—New York Times Book Review

"Each interviewee (managers included) is the sum of a life-time of memories; each shows, in word and portrait, evidence of being the end product of unnumbered different griefs and joys. A reader is smitten with a sense of how harsh the workers' lives were, and how deep the strength which led them to accept the inevitable . . . These veterans of industrial armies come off with impressive dignity." *—Washington Post Book World*

"The lives recorded here really do breathe—attain, indeed, considerable cumulative impact before the end . . . For many, working in the mills was a genuine experience of human solidarity, not merely a trial or a period of fearful exploitation—a time when the sense of community may have been as vital a fact or feeling of weariness or want . . . People knew they were in it together; in the place, the job, and the general human circumstances."

—Atlantic Monthly

"The quiet, shattering accounts of the workers' endless labor leave no doubt as to who was doing what to whom . . . This is a memorable chorus of real and forgotten voices."

—*Kirkus Reviews*

"A splendid and substantive book."

—*Los Angeles Times*

"An intensely human, thoroughly researched portrait of early-twentieth-century life and labor at the world's largest textile mill."

—*Library Journal*

"*Amoskeag* offers an unique approach to the history of American industrialization and the social life of its workers. It reveals the exciting potential of social history derived from a combination of written and oral sources . . . Perhaps it is that Hareven and Langenbach let the mill people speak so freely throughout the work that makes the story so believable. The illustrations alone are worth the price. *Amoskeag* is the best of the new social history." —*Richmond News-Leader*

"The doffers, wavers, spinners, dyers, and bobbin girls who provide the oral history that makes up the guts of *Amoskeag* speak plainly and poignantly . . . *Amoskeag* is a memorable book. I find myself going back to it from time to time, to spend an hour in the weaving rooms, the machine shops, the warm, crowded kitchens of the tenements . . . touching, interesting, informative."

—*Barron's*

"[The authors] interviewed generations of workers at every level—from owners and executives down to the least skilled. They have caught the recollections of workers who went on strike and workers who did not. [The] photographs make the place very real to the reader, and the speakers help trace all sorts of social change—most notably, the steady decrease in docility over the past century."

—*The New Yorker*

Amoskeag

► *Tamara K. Hareven*
and Randolph Langenbach

Amoskeag

Life and Work in an American Factory-City

 Library of New England

University Press of New England

Hanover and London

Published by arrangement with Pantheon Books, a division of Random House, Inc.

Printed in the United States of America   5   4   3   2   1

CIP data appear at the end of the book

Grateful acknowledgment is made to the following for permission to reprint previously published material:

Association Canado–Américaine: Excerpts from *Le Canado-Américain*, November 10, 1913, published by the Association Canado-Américaine, Manchester, New Hampshire. By permission of Mr. Gérald Robert, President General.

Sampson & Murdock Company: Maps of Manchester, 1911, from *The Manchester Directory*. Copyright 1910 by Sampson & Murdock Company, Boston.

Acknowledgments for photographs may be found on page 395.

We are grateful to Robert Perreault and to Elizabeth Lessard for alerting us to errors in the first edition of this book.

Frontispiece: The lower canal, 1968.

To the people of Manchester, New Hampshire—
past and present

► *Acknowledgments*

Over the many years involved in the making of this book we have incurred debts too numerous to count.

We are deeply grateful to the people interviewed for this project, who opened their homes to us, who shared their life stories with us, and who so wisely taught us about their world. In addition to the people included in this book, we would like to thank the hundreds of people interviewed, whose stories are equally significant but which, because of the shortage in space, were not included in this book. Among these, we are especially grateful to William Sullivan, Gordon Osborn, Charles Parsons, Saul Greenspan, William Zopie, Roland Gagnon, and William Langois, all of whom enlightened us on different aspects of textile production and management. We would like to thank especially those who were intensely involved with this project, who allowed us to interview them several times, and who handled our recurring enquiries with patience and understanding: F. C. Dumaine, Jr., Dudley Dumaine, Alice and Marcel Olivier, Thomas Smith, Lewis and Virginia Erskine, Ora Pelletier, Cora Pellerin, and Bette Skrzyszowski and Mary Dancause and their families.

This book could not have been realized without the support of the following foundations and organizations: The National Endowment for the Humanities, The New Hampshire Council for the Humanities, The Norwin and Elizabeth Bean Foundation, The New Hampshire Charitable Funds and Trust, The Cogswell Trust in Manchester, New Hampshire, the Rockefeller Foundation, the Textile Workers Union of America, and the National Endowment for the Arts for support of Randolph Langenbach's photography.

We are extremely grateful to our chief interview and research assistant, Robert Perreault, as well as to Ron Petrin, and Sally Boynton; to Denise Perreault, Agnes Gotboud, Wanda Fisher, Jean Evangelauf, and Sidney Ellis for transcribing; to Jean Evangelauf for assistance in research and editing; to Ronald Grele for consultation on interviewing methods; and to Laurel Rosenthal, Judy Campbell, Karen Roche, Lynn McKay, Gloria Solari, and Connie Ickes for efficient and dedicated typing. The secretarial pool at Clark University, and especially Theresa Reynolds, invested an enormous effort in the many retypes of the manuscript. We are also indebted to Howard Litwak for assistance in researching and editing the manuscript.

The Manchester Historic Association housed the oral-history project during its first stage. We are grateful to the director, Virginia Plisko, and librarian Elizabeth L. Lessard for their continuing help and for permission to publish the photographs owned by the Manchester Historic Association. We also greatly benefitted from the assistance of the Association Canado-Américaine in Manchester, particularly from the valuable information from Mr. Gérald Robert, president of the Association. Mr. Robert Lovett of the Baker Library, Harvard Business School, has generously assisted us with information; and Dr. Thomas Leavitt, director of the Merrimack Valley Textile Museum, has provided support and guidance throughout the project. Clark University has generously helped with support for part of the tape transcription and with sabbatical leave. I [Tamara Hareven] am also extremely grateful to the Radcliffe Institute, where I was a Fellow during the completion of this book; and to the Rockefeller Foundation's Center for Scholars in Bellagio, Italy, where we worked on parts of this book while scholars in residence. I am also indebted to the Center for Population Studies, Harvard University, where I am currently a Fellow; and especially to William Alonso and Dale Cohen.

Transformation of the four-year oral history into this book would not have been possible without the encouragement and guidance of André Schiffrin, who creates books rather than just publishes them.

Two people have contributed enormously to the creative and insightful shaping and editing of this book: Joan Rosenstock of Cambridge, Massachusetts, and Tom Engelhardt of Pantheon Books. Both gave generously of their time beyond the call of duty. We are indebted to them for their patient struggle with thousands of pages of text and for their cheerful dedication to this laborious process. The expert copyediting of Donna Bass, who did much more than just copyedit, and the skillful and friendly management by Wendy Wolf, at Pantheon Books, have shuttled the manuscript through its final stages.

We would also like to thank all our friends and colleagues who have taken an active interest in this project and whose scholarly advice was extremely valuable, especially David Montgomery, John Modell, and Stephan Thernstrom; and our New Hampshire friends, for their hospitality while we were working on this project, John and Mona Brooks, Joseph Scannel, and Father Paul; and Edward and Ann Langenbach for support and encouragement.

—Tamara K. Hareven and Randolph Langenbach
Cambridge, Massachusetts
Spring 1978

► *Contents*

Part Four

The World of Work   111

Part Five

Families   237

Part Six

Strike and Shutdown   293

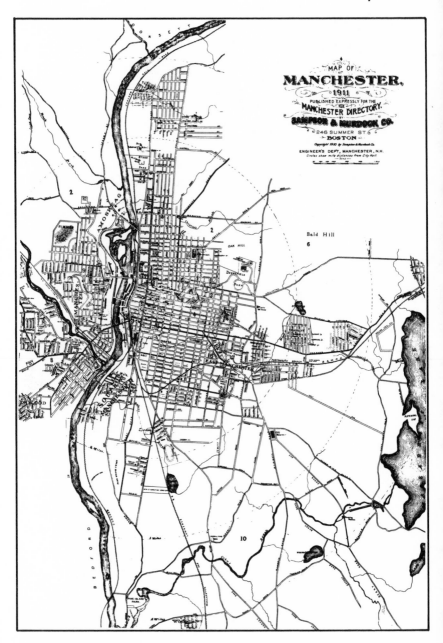

Map of Manchester, 1911

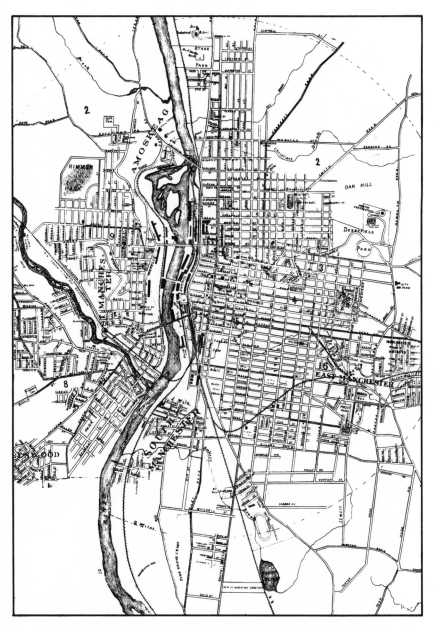

Detail from the map at left. The Amoskeag Mills, indicated by heavy
black lines, are located parallel to the Merrimack River.

► *Part One* ◄

The Setting

The river façade, 1967

River façade view

Upper canal weir, 1969

The mills along the upper canal, 1968

The Coolidge Mill, 1975

The Mechanic Street gate to the millyard, 1969

To many people, the view from Interstate–93 as it passes through Manchester, New Hampshire, seems to typify America's nineteenth-century industrial experience. The solid walls of red brick factories, which flank the Merrimack River for over a mile on one side and half a mile on the other, continue to captivate the viewer's attention despite their dilapidated state. To some, these buildings of the Amoskeag millyard are grim reminders of the "dark, satanic mills" and their exploitation of men, women, and children. To the former Amoskeag employees, who spent the better part of their lives in the mills, these empty shells are constant reminders of the all-encompassing industrial and social worlds in which they once lived.

It is the front of the millyard, facing the city, that dramatically underscores the architectural and social designs behind the Amoskeag. The front wall along the canal is pierced by archways, bridges, and wrought-iron gates. Encased in it is the conspicuous bay window, which marked the agent's office, the symbol of the Amoskeag's immediate center of control. A large cluster of boardinghouses, constructed in the style of federal townhouses and owned by the corporation, faced the solid wall of mills. The resulting design resembled a walled, medieval city, with the millyard fostering that same sense of enclosure.

The most striking aspects of the Amoskeag millyard were its organic unity and visual continuity, products of over seventy-five years of almost continuous construction by the corporation's own engineers and craftsmen. It was a rare example in the United States of a large-scale, long-term, co-ordinated approach to urban design. Even the bricks used in later additions were carefully matched in color to those of the earliest buildings.

The millyard was open at each end, with tree-lined canals and railroad tracks running through its entire length on two different levels above the river. Instead of a long, straight avenue, however, a gentle curve softened the rigor of the design, dividing the millyard into identifiable spaces. These carefully designed and meticulously maintained spaces were a supreme expression of the unbounded confidence of the Victorian Age, a confidence rooted in the belief not only in continuing material progress but in the ability to overcome almost any social problem in the headlong rush for industrial improvement. The bell towers, which were deliberately aligned with the city streets so as to be visible from all directions, were the most prominent expression of the corporation's sense of pride.

Amoskeag means "abundance of fish" in Penacook Indian dialect. The Indian dwellers in the northern New England region looked upon the Amoskeag Falls as a source of pure water and excellent fishing. Two centuries later, the fathers of the Industrial Revolution in American harnessed the water power of the same falls for the operation of their textile machinery.

By any standard, the Amoskeag was a giant. At its peak, in the early twentieth century, it was the world's largest textile plant, employing up to seventeen thousand workers. It encompassed approximately thirty major mills, each of which would be equivalent to an entire textile mill elsewhere. Combined with numerous related buildings, these mills covered a total of eight million square feet of floor space, an area almost equal to that contained in the World Trade Center in New York City. The Amoskeag housed a total of seventy-four separate cloth-making departments, three dye houses, twenty-four mechanical and electrical departments, three major steam power plants, and a hydroelectric power station. The Company was almost totally self-sufficient in its operations and carried out all of its own design and construction, even of the largest mills. For a time, it also manufactured locomotives and Civil-War rifles, as well as textile machinery.

The Amoskeag Company founded the city of Manchester and dominated it over the entire century of its existence. There was hardly a person in Manchester between 1838, when construction began, and 1936, when the mills shut down, whose life was not in some way affected by the Company. To the people who lived and worked there, the Amoskeag was a total institution, a closed and almost self-contained world. The Company's policy of corporate paternalism penetrated almost every aspect of the workers' lives. The Company viewed the employees as its "children" and expected loyalty in return. Many of the people in this book did develop a strong identification with the corporation. Most took pride in their work and in the fame of the Company and its products. They were not indifferent to the aesthetic quality of their environment nor to the institutional grandeur it conveyed. The subsequent physical deterioration symbolized to them the disappearance of their own world. As one former worker observed:

> It's too bad to see so many beautiful buildings in ruins and to think that so many people earned their living there. Today, everything is falling down. If our old parents, who worked so much in these mills, if they'd come back today and see how these mills are, it would really break their hearts.

Even now, forty years after the final shutdown, many of the workers still call themselves "Amoskeag men." Yet, despite their close identification with the Amoskeag, they were painfully aware of its hold over their lives.

> It seemed like you were locked in when the Amoskeag owned the mills. If you told the boss to go to hell, you might as well move out of the city. The boss had the power to blackball you for the rest of your days. The only way you could get a job there again was if you disguised yourself. Some of them did that. They would wear glasses, grow a mustache, change their name. . . . It was either that or starve to death.*

Many of the people in this book are just one or two generations removed from the Industrial Revolution. Some heard firsthand accounts of this early industrial development from

---

* Interview with William Moul, who was a weaver in the Amoskeag mills.

their parents. In their own lives, many experienced the wrenching movement, from isolated village life in Ireland, Poland, Quebec, or even rural New England to a large, ethnically diverse, boisterous New England industrial town; and from the natural rhythms of farm work to the speed and rigid time schedules of the industrial world.

Most of these people preferred the industrial city to the "lost," mythical, rural community which, today, is often idealized for its harmonious and wholesome way of life. They had a realistic view of industrial life, with all its difficulties and exploitation; and they accepted the modern world into which they had been swept. In adapting themselves to it, they also modified it, wherever possible, to fit their own needs and traditions. The deep attachment that many formed to their work transcended daily routines. They developed an identity as industrial workers, and some approached even routine operations with the perfectionism of craftspeople.

Contrary to the prevailing popular idea that large factories and the urban environment cause individual anomie and social fragmentation, most of these people had a highly developed sense of place and formed tightly knit societies around their kin and ethnic associations. Despite their hardships and the conflicts they experienced, they shared the feeling they so frequently expressed about their lives in the mills: "We were all like a family."

The Amoskeag Manufacturing Company and Manchester, New Hampshire, the city it had planned and developed starting in 1837, were products of the new industrial order launched in New England by a closely knit group of Boston-based entrepreneurs. The newly created town, strategically located by the Amoskeag Falls on the Merrimack River, was deliberately named after Manchester, England, already famous as the world's largest textile city. Half a century later, Manchester, New Hampshire, emerged as the site of the world's largest textile factory, yet it managed to avoid some of the environmental problems of its English namesake. "None of the manufacturing towns in New England pleased me as much as Manchester, in New Hampshire," wrote a British traveler in 1902. "Unlike its great-grandmother, it has clean air, clear water, and sunny skies; every street is an avenue of noble trees. . . . Perhaps the handsomest, certainly the most impressive, buildings in Manchester are the Amoskeag and Manchester Mills."

Manchester was modeled on the factory town of Lowell, Massachusetts, founded two decades earlier and developed by the Boston group. These entrepreneurs established the headquarters of their prospective new company in Boston, where it remained throughout the corporation's life. During the 1830s, the Boston associates purchased the water power for the entire length of the Merrimack River, New England's second-largest river, and assembled a 15,000-acre plot across the Amoskeag Falls as a site for the planned city. The development of the city's real estate was never entirely divorced from the Company's operations. Control of the land on which the city grew gave the Company control over the city's development during the entire century of the Company's existence. A new industrial city was thus superimposed upon the rural countryside, a reluctant neighbor of the rapidly expanding corporation.

Manchester's urban plan reflected the social program of its Boston developers. Like Lowell, Manchester founded a community of young women working together in the mills and living together in boardinghouses, within the social system of corporate paternalism—a philosophy of benevolent control—which treated workers as the "corporation's children" and which permeated all aspects of life: the organization of work, the strict management of the boardinghouses, the founding of charities, and the endowment of churches. In the mid-nineteenth century, when the majority of the labor force consisted of young, unmarried women from rural New England, the Company also regulated their behavior after working hours in order to reassure their parents. The boardinghouses were closed and locked at 10:00 P.M., church attendance was compulsory, and alcoholic consumption was prohibited. However, Manchester never achieved the fame of Lowell as a city of mill girls.

This so-called utopian period came to an end for most of the planned New England industrial communities shortly before the Civil War. Irish immigrant families willing to work for lower wages replaced the mill girls, and speculative housing gradually replaced corporation boardinghouses. Lowell, the "glorious" city of spindles and mill girls, became an ordinary industrial town. Manchester headed in the same direction but with a difference: while management had become fragmented among many small factory units in Lowell, it was consolidated in Manchester. With T. Jefferson Coolidge as treasurer, the Amoskeag Company, during the last two decades of the nineteenth century, began to annex those mills which had originally been constructed as separate corporations, though founded by the Boston Associates and managed by overlapping directorships. Thus, by 1905, the Amoskeag Company had become, along with the physical expansion of the millyard, the only large textile corporation in the city, with the exception of the Stark Mills, which were annexed in 1922.

To encourage the development of business and private housing in Manchester, the Amoskeag auctioned off land to private buyers for stores and residences and, at the same time, endowed churches and certain social clubs with land, all according to a master plan conceived in the 1830s. The plan went beyond a mere layout for streets and houses to include an elaborate set of restrictions and rules that controlled the nature of the private development. The deed restrictions included limitations on the number and size of the houses in the residential areas ("to avoid overcrowding") and even on the types of materials allowed for the construction of buildings in the commercial areas. These plans and restrictions were followed in subsequent developments during the entire history of the Company.

As the corporation grew and consolidated production under one centralized management, the city itself expanded and diversified. Yet more than two thirds of Manchester's employment opportunities remained dependent on the Amoskeag Company. In fact, until the 1930s, no new industry could be established in Manchester without the Amoskeag's permission because the Company controlled practically all the available industrial land. This explains in large part the recurring pronouncements by the people in this book that "the Amoskeag was Manchester."

The Amoskeag's control of Manchester was different, however, from that of the Pullman Corporation in Pullman, Illinois, or of southern mill villages. Manchester was not a company town in the usual sense of the word. There was no company store; about 15 percent of all the workers' housing was owned by the corporation. By the beginning of the twentieth century, Manchester was a lively city full of private shops, movie houses, and dance halls. It had grown into one of the largest cities in New England, boasting a population of fifty-five thousand. After 1900, two shoe factories opened in Manchester, as did the 7-20-4 Cigar Factory. Most of the cigar workers were Belgian, and few of their relatives worked in the Amoskeag. The shoe factories, on the other hand, fulfilled an important backup function for the Amoskeag workers. Many families tried to make sure they had at least one member working in the shoe factory so as not to be completely dependent upon textile employment. In general, however, Manchester's occupational diversity was clearly limited.

The Amoskeag Company's control over the economic life of the city gave it great influence over its political life as well. Amoskeag overseers and other officials served on the board of aldermen; and management retained close ties with the police force, which proved a most useful connection during the ensuing strikes.

While the Amoskeag bestowed certain advantages on the city, it also exacted heavy tolls. This was particularly true for workers and their families during the long and bitter strike of 1922 and during the subsequent period of the corporation's decline, when employment opportunities became progressively scarcer. The shutdown of the mills in 1936 was a devastating blow to the whole city.

Absentee management and remote control also had their impact on the spirit of both the mill and the city. Symbolically, at no time did Manchester residents own a significant portion of the stock. The Amoskeag Company was managed by a board of directors, many of whom were prominent Boston financiers but few of whom had more than small investments in Amoskeag securities. Most had little familiarity with the Amoskeag plant. The treasurer, the man almost solely in charge of the management of the Amoskeag, ran the mills out of the Boston office. Consequently, most of the workers and managers in Manchester had limited contact with the treasurer.

In Manchester, the agent—a local, salaried official—had charge of executing, and to some extent planning, most aspects of production, as well as handling all matters concerning personnel and labor relations, but he answered to the Boston office. The Amoskeag Company was unusual in that it had only six agents in its entire history. Three of them were from three generations of the same family: the Straws. The longevity and loyalty of its agents were one of the major pillars in the Amoskeag's phenomenal sense of continuity. Ezekiel Straw, who later became governor of New Hampshire, first became agent in 1856, having worked as an engineer for the Company since

The spinning room of the Coolidge Mill when it opened in 1909. With over 100,000 spindles, this was one of the largest spinning rooms in the world.

1838. He set the pattern for corporate paternalism, which his son, Herman, later retained adapted to a newly arrived immigrant labor force. Most of the people in this book were contemporaries of Herman Straw and his son, William Parker Straw, and spent the major part of their working lives under their regimes. Herman Straw, whose tenure as agent represents the peak period in the Amoskeag's development, retired as agent in 1919 but continued to act as a consultant for the Company until his death, in 1929. William Parker Straw failed to command the same loyalty and respect as had his father, particularly during the period of the corporation's decline and the labor struggles of the 1920s. To most workers, the Straws were the Amoskeag. Some workers even thought that the Straws owned it. F. C. Dumaine, who followed T. Jefferson Coolidge as treasurer in 1906, did not really enter the employees' lives until the nine-month-long strike of 1922.

As the Amoskeag was emerging as a major modern corporation during the second half of the nineteenth century, the original composition of its labor force was also undergoing a transformation. By the 1850s and '60s, Irish family groups were gradually replacing the New England mill girls as the basis of the Amoskeag work force. Despite the Amoskeag's initial reluctance to allow them into the city, Irish canal and railroad builders eventually followed the construction route that led through most New England towns. By 1860, the foreign-born constituted 27 percent of Manchester's population; and of the 5,480 foreign-born residents, 3,976 had come from Ireland.

The Amoskeag also began to absorb German and Swedish immigrants in small numbers, mainly as skilled craftsmen. In addition, the Amoskeag imported from Scotland many skilled textile mechanics and dye experts, sometimes to teach various skills to the local workers. Approximately eighty "Scotch girls," who were skilled gingham weavers, were brought to Manchester after a thorough search and recruitment in different villages around Glasgow. The Scottish community in Manchester also drew less-skilled immigrants, who joined their relatives to work in the Amoskeag.

Starting in the 1870s, French-Canadian immigrants, driven from rural Quebec by land scarcity, depleted farms, and poverty, began to enter the labor force of the Amoskeag mills. One of the interviewees, repeating her father's deathbed admonition, expressed the despair shared by many Quebec farmers: "When I'm gone, don't keep this land. *Sell it.*" By 1900, the steady recruitment of French Canadians into the Amoskeag had significantly altered Manchester's population. Quebecois priests, who had earlier resisted their parishioners' immigration to New England, now succumbed to that stream of migration and proceeded to establish parishes in their new locations; the first French parishes were founded in the 1870s and 1880s.

The Amoskeag Company, like other New England companies, soon concluded that the French Canadians were the ideal labor force and proceeded to recruit them systematically. By the end of the nineteenth century, mill agents from New England had become a well-known phenomenon along the Quebec countryside. The editor of the New England newspaper *Le Travailleur* testified before the Massachusetts Bureau of Labor Statistics about the pervasiveness of this practice.

> I have a letter from an agent of the Boston and Maine Railroad who says he is ready to testify that since two years, no less than one-hundred superintendents or agents of mills have applied to him for French help, one mill asking for as many as fifty families at a time.*

The Amoskeag had a special advantage in the recruitment of French Canadians because of its location on the railroad route between Montreal and Boston. In addition, the Amoskeag's advertisements in Quebec newspapers, including elaborate descriptions of the fine working conditions and attractive opportunities, accompanied by photographs of the millyard, were all designed to attract farmers as well as industrial workers. The typical advertisement read as follows:

> More than 15,000 persons work in these mills that border on both sides of the river. Their wages allow them comfort and ease and all seem to be content with their lot. It is true that the larger company to which they sell their labor treats them as its own children. . . . [The article here proceeds to enumerate the welfare activities of the Company.] That is the reason why the Amoskeag Company has never had any trouble with its employees. It treats them not as machines but as human beings, as brothers who have a right not only to wages but also to the pleasure of life. . . . Its employees work not only to earn a wage but to please their employers, who know how to treat them well. It has resolved with justice to itself and its workers the problem of the relations between capital and labor.**

This migration to Manchester was part of a larger French-Canadian influx to other New England industrial towns. Man-

---

* *Massachusetts Bureau of Labor Statistics Thirteenth Annual Report: The Canadian French in New England* (1882), p. 17.

** *Le Canado-Americain*, November 10, 1913.

chester was exceptional, however, in the size and cohesion of the French-Canadian community that developed on its West Side from the late nineteenth century. Even today, this section of the city is often referred to as Little Canada. By 1910, French Canadians comprised 35 percent of the Amoskeag's labor force and 38 percent of the city's population.

The fact that management recognized the French Canadians as a "docile," "industrious," and "stable" labor force made them especially welcome. They were particularly well suited to textile work because of the large number of children in their families. By contracting with one worker, the Amoskeag frequently could bring an entire family group into the mills, with the likelihood that additional kin would follow later—with their own large families as well.

Their emergence as a critical segment of the mills' labor force by no means gave the French Canadians a position of power, though they did fill a significant portion of the skilled and semi-skilled jobs. The ranks of overseer and second hand were still confined, by and large, to native-born Americans, English, Scottish, and second-generation Irish, with an occasional sprinkling of Germans and Swedes. By the time the French Canadians might have had a chance to enter supervisory ranks, the Amoskeag was already on the decline, heading toward shutdown. As a result, the French Canadians drew their strength from sheer numbers. In many workrooms, the bosses were forced to learn some French in order to maintain smooth operations.

Later immigrants, particularly Greeks and Poles, who came in smaller numbers, never achieved the same strength and influence. Poles started coming to Manchester, first from other New Hampshire and New England communities, and later directly from Poland. In 1902, the 850 Poles in Manchester founded their first parish. By 1920, the city's Polish population had grown to two thousand, with Poles comprising approximately 10 percent of the Amoskeag's labor force. The Greeks began to appear in Manchester around the turn of the century; and by 1920, they constituted as large a proportion of the Amoskeag's labor force as did the Poles.

These newer immigrants did not benefit from the advantages the French Canadians had gained. Although, by 1910,

the bosses had become accustomed to speaking or understanding some French, most of the Poles and Greeks had to depend
upon translators. They were also more firmly locked into the
lowest skilled and unskilled jobs. Tensions between different
immigrant groups frequently led to name calling and occasionally to fights in and around the mills.

In response to the new ethnic diversity of the work force, in
1910 the Amoskeag launched a corporate welfare and efficiency program. The paternalistic measures were devised to
attract additional immigrants to the city, to socialize them to
industrial work, to instill loyalty to the Company, to curb labor
unrest, and to prevent unionization. The Amoskeag was by no
means unique in its introduction of these programs: between
1910 and 1917, a significant number of industrial concerns
were maintaining a variety of company welfare programs of
various types. Most of these programs shared the same goals as
the Amoskeag's. In giant corporations, such as the Amoskeag,
corporate policies of welfare and paternalism had their own
economies of scale. Large corporations could afford such policies, with less cost per person than in smaller outfits. The
Amoskeag's program, for example, compares with that of the
Ford Company. This is no coincidence, since close personal ties
existed between F. C. Dumaine and Henry Ford. The architectural distinction of the Albert Kahn–designed Ford Highland
Park plant played a role in Ford's policy, just as the maintenance and refinement of the Amoskeag's much older millyard
continued to effect the morale of its labor force. Despite these
similarities, the employee welfare program in the Amoskeag
was distinct from those of other companies in its continuity
with the Amoskeag's nineteenth-century paternalistic traditions and in the emergence of an Amoskeag "spirit," which
served both for workers and management as an important
source of identity.

The efficiency program, inaugurated simultaneously with
the welfare program at the peak of the corporation's expansion,
introduced an employment office, intended to centralize the
hiring process of all workers and keep a systematic record of all
hirings, firings, and reasons for leaving. The employment office
was management's effort to control the size and diversity of the
departments in the mill and to curb labor turnover. Having a

personnel file in the employment office for each individual worker also helped keep a check on the worker's background and activities. The employment office thus fulfilled the dual function of centralizing hiring and helping screen out unwanted workers, especially blacklisted workers and "agitators."

The welfare program, vivid in the memories of most workers, touched their lives in numerous ways. It included a textile club, a textile school and a cooking school, and a dental service, as well as a limited superannuation plan.

The Amoskeag Textile Club, founded under this program, developed a variety of social and recreational activities. It organized annual dinners and picnics for the employees and their families, sponsored a shooting club and a baseball team, put on musicals and plays once a year, held Christmas parties for the workers and their children, and published a semi-monthly magazine, the *Amoskeag Bulletin.* The textile school, which was affiliated with the club, offered technical training in different skills. Reaching out to the workers' families, the Amoskeag Company established a playground, and sponsored a visiting nurses' service. As an incentive to greater work stability, the Amoskeag also introduced a home-ownership plan, offering house lots for sale to workers who had been in the Company's employ for five years or longer. These workers could pay off half the mortgage for a dollar. After another five years, they could liquidate the balance for another dollar. The Company also helped workers secure loans from a local bank for the construction of a house.

The majority of the laborers, mostly French Canadians, were less exposed to the Company's welfare programs than were the workers in more highly skilled or managerial positions. Language had a great deal to do with this. Most of the French Canadians, Poles, and Greeks could not understand English, so in their social relations, they tended to remain among their families, friends, and members of their ethnic clubs.

One of the Amoskeag's most important contributions to its workers' welfare was undoubtedly the rental privileges in corporation tenements.* The "corporations," as the workers called

* The word "tenement" did not have the negative connotation then that it has today. It referred simply to housing which was rented from the corporation. The people were "tenants," the house was a "tenement."

them, were three-to-five-story attached brick houses strung along the streets leading down from the center of the city to the millyard. These substantial and attractive structures, with high ceilings and hardwood floors, were originally built as boardinghouses for the first mill girls. Some of this company housing was subsequently remodeled into family tenements, while the rest continued to serve as boardinghouses for single workers. The rent, which amounted to about $1.00 per room per month, was always substantially lower than the market rate for the rest of the city. The buildings were carefully kept up by the Amoskeag's maintenance crews. To qualify for occupancy, workers had to have large families with more than one member working in the mills. Their names were kept on waiting lists for many months—sometimes years—before their turn came.

Although many of the narratives in this book mention the corporations, it is important to remember that by 1910, only about 15 to 20 percent of the Amoskeag's labor force lived in them. Other workers rented city housing, and a significant number owned their own homes. Residents in the corporations experienced a different relationship with the Amoskeag and a different way of life from those who lived in private housing. The corporations were closely integrated with the millyard, a situation that many workers preferred. Workers walked to work, and their family members could see the millyard through the tenement windows. Working women were able to leave their children at home and to run across the bridges to nurse or check on them during breaks. Children growing up in the corporations were also more closely involved with life in the mills and spent more time in the Amoskeag's playground. The texture of the neighborhood was also different in the corporations. Unlike the situation in the rest of the city, different ethnic groups mixed in the corporations. Residents in the corporations generally developed a closer identity with the Amoskeag, while those living in the ethnic neighborhoods were more involved with their churches and neighborhood activities.

Were the Company's paternalistic policies successful in forestalling labor unrest? In an otherwise turbulent industry, except for minor activity during the 1880s, the corporation's paternalistic programs and the overall Amoskeag "spirit" effectively discouraged unionization in the Amoskeag until the First World War. The United Textile Workers of America (UTW) made their first inroads into Manchester in 1917, a time when labor shortages coincided with high demand for production, both due to the war effort. The union formed several locals among the skilled textile occupations. Union membership, although small, was drawn from strategic positions in the mill. In 1919, the UTW organized the first strike to occur in the Amoskeag since an 1885 strike led by the Knights of Labor. The strike halved production in the Amoskeag. Because the mills were working primarily on war orders, the secretary of war dispatched an arbitrator, who granted the workers their demand for a 15 percent pay increase instead of the 12 percent the Amoskeag had offered. The strike was settled within five days, but in the process, the union added five thousand new members to its rosters.[*] The union's foothold in the corporation remained limited, however. The main concession that it succeeded in obtaining was the formation of an adjustment board to be run jointly by representatives of management and labor. Overall, the union was not very successful in the Amoskeag. The corporation never conceded a closed shop, and the workers were not allowed to collect union dues in the workrooms.

Despite the UTW's slow emergence in Manchester, one event succeeded in galvanizing a large majority of the Amoskeag's workers against the corporation. That was the announcement, issued in February 1922, of an increase in working hours and a 20 percent wage cut. Similar wage cuts were being made in most of the New England textile cities at the same time and were precipitating strikes. The Amoskeag strike of 1922, which ensued in response to the announcement, was the first long-term general strike in the Company's history and marked the turning point for both the workers and the mills.

The events leading to the strike, as well as its disastrous consequences for the mills and the city, can be better understood in the context of the Amoskeag's continuous decline from

[*] Daniel Creamer and Charles Coulter, *Labor and the Shut-Down of the Amoskeag Mills* (Philadelphia: The WPA, National Research Project, 1939), pp. 191–92.

the post–World War I period until its final shutdown in 1936. Ironically, the seeds of the Amoskeag's decline were hidden in its success. While its enormous size was a factor in its durability, its growth to this extraordinary capacity must itself be interpreted as a sign of its impending decline. In an effort to save on the cost of making each yard of cloth, the Amoskeag had added spindles, only to discover that the textile industry had too much productive capacity for the market and that it would be the New England mills that would lose in the long run.

Although the Amoskeag made the greatest profits in its history during World War I, industrial demobilization followed; and the Amoskeag, along with most other New England textile corporations, began to experience a gradual decline. Southern competition, antiquated machinery, inefficiency, and high labor costs were all factors. The Amoskeag gradually curtailed production, tapered its labor force, and cut wages. Many workers were fired, others were laid off temporarily, and still others had to join the reserve labor force.

This growing job insecurity drastically changed the work atmosphere and the pace of production in the mills, adding to the demoralization that followed in the wake of the strike. While during the pre-strike period many of the workers had left the Amoskeag on their own accord in search of better jobs, in the post-war period, most workers left because they were laid off or dismissed. By the 1920s, a period of prosperity in the United States, the workers in the Amoskeag were already rehearsing for the Great Depression.

During the decade following the strike, the Amoskeag tried to keep labor protest under control by establishing a company union as a substitute for the UTW, which had officially ceased activity in the Amoskeag. In reality, the company union, or, as it was called, the Plan of Representation, was initiated by the corporation as an agent for the negotiation of wage reductions. Although the corporation gave the impression that the workers supported it, it was actually imposed on them. When the plan was brought before the workers for a vote, a majority of the cotton and worsted operators rejected it. They were "persuaded," however, to accept it after a temporary shutdown of the cotton division. The Plan of Representation was in effect for ten years, a period during which the employee representatives were forced to vote a total wage reduction of 40 percent, while the cost of living declined by only 20 percent.

The workers voted to abolish the Plan of Representation in June 1933 after a dispute over wages; and the United Textile Workers Union reemerged in the mill, openly taking command of a strike in 1933. Unlike its predecessor in 1922, this strike was marked by violence, which necessitated the calling out of the state militia. During these last years before the shutdown, in an effort to reduce costs, the corporation, unable to lower wages any further, used the technique of speeding up machinery. This imposed an even greater burden on the workers and thus a greater strain on labor relations.

Arbitrary layoffs continued, and management disregarded the principle of seniority in discharges and layoffs. On September 4, 1934, the Amoskeag workers joined a national general textile strike, which was called off after three weeks without significant results. From that point on, the arena of labor protest shifted from organized strikes to sit-down strikes in the various departments. These continued until the final shutdown.

In September 1935, the Amoskeag shut down operations, with the proclaimed intention of reopening. In December of the same year, the corporation applied for reorganization in the New Hampshire bankruptcy court. In July 1936, the master of the court ordered liquidation of the Company's assets. The Amoskeag's shutdown in the midst of the Depression destroyed the economic base of a city of 75,000.

Most of the people in this book were caught up in that shutdown and in the Depression. The sudden disappearance of their source of subsistence and the extinction of their world of work set them back by at least one generation. Most of them lost their jobs, their life savings, and the possibility of career advancement for themselves and their children.

The life histories of these people were thus deeply intertwined with the corporation's economic fluctuations over the past three quarters of a century. The first generation of workers migrated to Manchester before the turn of the century, at a time when the corporation was at the peak of its development, when the mills were prospering and labor was in demand.

These people formed strong attachments to the mills, and their identities were deeply anchored in the Amoskeag. Most of them married and raised their children while working there. The sociability that surrounded their work experience tended to mellow the bitterness of the subsequent decline.

The generation that started work shortly before the strike knew an entirely different Amoskeag. The beginning of their work lives coincided with insecurity in employment, wage declines, and increases both in work loads and labor/management conflicts. Unlike the previous generation of workers, for whom the employment office did not exist, they faced the employment office with trepidation. Many had to accept temporary jobs and anticipate long periods of unemployment; nor could they rely on the mills for the future employment of their children.

The third generation of Amoskeag workers began work shortly before the shutdown. For them, the Amoskeag was a place where one was lucky if one could "buy a job." They were hurt more profoundly by the shutdown because they were caught in it before they had had a chance to learn skills or to experience orderly work lives. They entered adulthood during a time of job insecurity and unemployment. After the worst of the Depression had subsided, they still had difficulty achieving economic stability.

Job insecurity was the overriding theme in the lives of all three generations: first, in the rural communities, which they had left behind; and then in the industrial environment to which they migrated. To achieve economic security, they were prepared to work extremely hard and to sacrifice the schooling of their children. Their goals were simple but often difficult to realize: to hold down stable jobs, to own their own homes, and to raise their children to work in higher-status jobs. Many had to postpone this last dream until the third generation because they depended on the labors of their children to stay above the margin of poverty. Most of them never achieved stability in their own work lives; some thought they found it, at least temporarily, but lost it with the decline of the textile industry. Their children and grandchildren were about to achieve it when the shutdown of the mills, in the midst of the Depression, deprived them of their chance.

Despite declining wages and increasing job insecurity, they

preferred the industrial world to farm life, whose drudgery and isolation they never forgot. In Manchester, they were part of a network of New England industrial communities, so that in times of need, they could seek alternative jobs in other towns. These people confronted economic insecurity with hardened realism. They were prepared to face disaster as a normal part of life. But their fatalism did not make them passive. They struggled to improve their lot—or at least to keep from slipping backwards. The remainder of the time they rolled with the punches.

► *The Interview*
Process

This book evolved in stages. Randolph Langenbach was
initially attracted to Manchester by the integrity of the architectural and urban design of the Amoskeag millyard, and he
soon began to document the relationship between architecture
and social organization in the growth of a planned industrial
town.* Tamara Hareven was interested in the ways immigrant
workers adjusted to industrial life, particularly as it affected
family and work patterns.** In 1971, she began a large-scale
project to reconstruct the life and work histories of three thousand former workers in the Amoskeag, whose combined experience spanned three generations and reached back into the
second half of the nineteenth century.

The oral-history project evolved out of these two research
projects. At first, we interviewed only a small number of people
as a way of gaining insights into the experiences of those who
had worked in the Amoskeag and who, thirty years after the
shutdown, still had strong attachments to the mills. It was not
until 1972 that we decided to embark on systematic oral-history
interviews of former workers in the Amoskeag mills and of their
family members. This decision stemmed from our realization
that we were studying a disappearing phenomenon, a realization underlined by the death of our first interviewee, Mary
Cunion, an eighty-year-old Scottish weaver, and the demolition
of one of the finest structures in the millyard. We were intent

* Randolph Langenbach, "Amoskeag: An Epic in Urban Design," in *Harvard Bulletin* (February 1968): 18–28; and in a forthcoming book, *Corporation City*.

** Results of the research project will be published in a forthcoming book
by Tamara K. Hareven, *Family Time and Industrial Time*.

upon preserving this world, at least through historical documentation.

Most of these former workers, when approached, found it difficult to understand why we would seek them out and why we would follow the subject in such detail rather than just read about the Amoskeag in official company and town histories. They were particularly puzzled by our interest in their early lives and work routines. Even though the Amoskeag still meant a great deal to them, they could not grasp why their life stories were important to us. Consequently, at first not many people came forward voluntarily to be interviewed. We approached possible subjects primarily through informal networks rather than through advertisements. We followed up the kinship and friendship networks of the initial interviewees, asking them to recommend us to others they knew who had worked in the Amoskeag. We also contacted social and ethnic clubs, like the Knights of Columbus, the TKK (the Polish social club), and the Association Canado-Américaine. In addition, we frequented old-age clubs. We found a good number of interviewees in the lunchrooms of the Meals for the Elderly project and in the Smile clubs, where older people assemble to play cards and chess, and to do handicrafts. This group of retired interviewees was followed by a younger group who, until 1975, were still working in the Chicopee Mill in Manchester.

Our interview process changed considerably after the shutdown of the Chicopee Mill, on February 27, 1975. The last functioning cotton mill in Manchester, the Chicopee was housed in the former Coolidge Mill in the Amoskeag millyard. When it opened in 1938, it employed former Amoskeag workers and their children. With its small labor force and its concentration on one product—gauze for sanitary uses—the Chicopee bore little resemblance to the Amoskeag. It did, however, provide an important continuity with the Amoskeag in the lives of its workers, and its shutdown caused many of them to relive the shutdown of the Amoskeag on a lesser scale.

It was on the very day the Chicopee shut down that we met the loom fixers. Having been trained in the repair of machinery to a level of precision and skill similar to that of piano tuners, they were now assigned the task of breaking up the machinery and throwing it into junk heaps outside the building. The shutdown of the Chicopee had broken the routine of their lives and caused them to reflect on the meaning of their work lives in a way in which they would not have during a normal work period.

Interviewing gained new meaning with the opening of Randolph Langenbach's exhibit, "Amoskeag: A Sense of Place, A Way of Life," at the Currier Gallery of Art in Manchester during the fall of 1975. This exhibit of eighty mural-sized photographs traced the historical development of the architectural design and town plan of Manchester from its inception in the early 1830s. Many of the photographs were historic pictures which the Amoskeag Manufacturing Company had taken of its own workers, as well as photographs of child laborers taken by Lewis Hine during the first decade of the twentieth century.

The exhibit evoked an overwhelming response from former Amoskeag and Chicopee workers, some of whom visited the show over and over. On Sunday afternoons about five hundred former workers with relatives and friends would go through the exhibit. In a separate gallery room, visitors were able to listen to excerpts from our oral-history interviews, arranged together with appropriate photo images into a slide tape. "I never thought I'd live to see my husband's picture hung in a museum" was a typical comment. The former workers of the Chicopee whose portraits were displayed in the exhibit had become historical symbols. As soon as they realized this, it was no longer necessary to explain why their lives were important, why we wanted to interview them, and why we were writing this book.

We observed several rules throughout the interview process: prior to interviewing a former Amoskeag worker, we reconstructed his or her work history through the Amoskeag's individual employee files. As the interview progressed, we shared this information with the interviewee, who was frequently surprised that so complete a record of his or her own career had survived. When we found contradictions between what was said and what their work records reported, we pointed them out to the interviewee, and we correlated the information from other sources. In certain situations, the work record was particularly valuable in jogging people's memories, and often the mere mention of the name of the overseer enabled the interviewee to recall forgotten incidents.

All the interviews were taped. Those which were recorded in French were first transcribed in French and subsequently translated by Robert Perreault. The interviews conducted in English were also transcribed verbatim. We reorganized the narratives topically, without sacrificing the original style and language.

This volume represents only a fraction of the more than three hundred interviews gathered. Many fine interviews were not included here because of limitations in space. Others, although informative, were too fragmented to provide a coherent narrative. In selecting the interviews for the book, we were not concerned merely with the uniqueness of individual experiences. We were also interested in the variety of experiences and perceptions, as well as in the collective experience of these people as they lived through historical changes in a common setting. We wished to capture both common patterns and individual nuances. It was therefore significant to include conflicting narratives and perceptions of the same event, as well as to reiterate similar ones.

What is important in oral history is not merely the facts that people remember but how they remember them and why they remember them in the way they do. For example, a number of interviewees, when asked when they finished working in the Amoskeag, replied 1922. The work records of many of these people show, however, that they continued working into the 1930s and sometimes until the shutdown. This discrepancy comes from the fact that the strike of 1922 was such a shattering experience that the world they had known seemed to end with it.

Randolph Langenbach began photographing the Amoskeag millyard in 1967 and continued this documentary work over the following decade in an effort to record the millyard before its demolition under urban renewal. The photographs in this book are part of a collection of over two thousand negatives.

He took most of the portraits of the oral-history interviewees in 1976, with the exception of Mary Cunion, whom he photographed in 1969. Most of the people were photographed in their homes, during and following the interviews. Other photographs were taken in an empty Amoskeag mill on December 10, 1977, when WGBH TV filmed a documentary based on this book.

The old family photographs come from the interviewees' family albums, which they kindly made available to us. The historic photographs of the Amoskeag mills and of Manchester come principally from the unique collection held by the Manchester Historic Association of photographs taken by the Amoskeag Company itself over a sixty-year period, beginning in 1869.

A number of the old photographs of Amoskeag workers, especially of the children, were taken by Lewis Hine as part of his nationwide documentation of child labor. Hine took these pictures for the National Child Labor Committee. The vast collection is presently housed in the Library of Congress.

A brief description of the machines and the work process inside a textile mill will help the reader understand the experiences which the people in this book discuss. The Amoskeag Manufacturing Company housed two main divisions: one was dedicated to the manufacture of cotton, the other to the production of wool. Of the two, cotton was by far the larger, as Amoskeag's mainstay was cotton gingham, a fabric in vogue at the beginning of this century. Within each division, countless different types and styles of cloth were produced.

To understand the production process, it is important to distinguish between clothing manufacture and cloth making. Amoskeag did not manufacture clothing; it produced the cloth. This was sold to the clothing manufacturer, and the sweatshops in New York City and elsewhere busily stitched Amoskeag material into garments. Although many of the workrooms were hot and humid, the distinction between work in a sweatshop and that in a mill is significant. In piece-goods manufacture, all of the operatives sit at tables and operate various types of sewing machines. The room is filled with small machines and lots of people, each one performing a fixed and repeated task. In a mill, the machines are larger and are designed to do the work. The employee's job is to fill and empty (*doff*) the machine at regular intervals. The work can be arduous, but it tends to be more varied, and the worker is always moving about the room. Textile mill work depends upon the machines being filled with material and running properly. If such is the case, the operative can find, for a short while, some time to relax.

The following explanation details the making of cotton cloth; the process for wool is very similar. Here, the process is described as it was carried out in the 1920s, although at this level of detail, very little would be different today.

The raw material arrived in Manchester in large bales delivered by train. The freight cars were drawn up beside long rows of warehouses, and the fiber was then blown through a large tube across the river to the mills on the opposite bank.

First, the hoops holding the bale of fiber were cut. The bale was then thrown by hand into the *bale breaker*. This machine picked the compressed cotton apart and delivered it in hand-sized tufts onto a conveyor belt. *Openers* then repeated the same operation, breaking apart the tufts more thoroughly. From the opener, the fiber was transported to the *picker room*, where it was dropped onto the first of three *pickers*, whose function was to beat out the coarser impurities. In the three machines—the *breaker picker*, *intermediate picker*, and *finisher picker*—the cotton was whirled and pounded over grid bars by rollers armed with short spikes. It was then compressed into a continuous sheet called a *lap*.

From the picker, the lap was fed into the *carding machine*. Here, the lap passed between two surfaces covered with fine wire teeth designed to separate the individual fibers and thereby complete their cleaning. The material came off the *card* as an untwisted rope called a *sliver*, which was coiled into tall cans. For producing especially fine thread, a step known as *combing* was introduced after the carding in order to remove all but the long fibers.

Prior to spinning, the material passed through several intermediate processes, depending on the type and quality of the yarn. The first step was *drawing* (not to be confused with *drawing-in*), the purpose of which was to stretch the sliver so that the fibers ran parallel. The next operation was *roving*, which reduced the size of the fiber so that it could be spun. Roving was divided into three or four stages. The first, or *slubber*, gave the sliver a slight twist and wound it onto a large

Spinning frame

bobbin. The fiber is referred to as roving throughout the remainder of the process. Each of the other stages further
twisted and reduced the roving so that it had the strength to be
spun into thread. These stages occurred on machines called the
intermediate frame, fine frame, and *jack frame*.

From the jack frame, the roving was placed on the *spinning
frame*. The process of spinning is similar to roving except that
the amount of twist is much greater and the resulting thread
much finer.

With spinning, we end up with finished yarn. For certain
products, several strands were twisted together, a process
known as *twisting*. At this point, we arrive at the most familiar

stage of the textile process: *weaving*. Prior to placing the yarn on the loom, there were several steps necessary to get the yarn into a form in which it could be woven. The principle of weaving is to have the *warp*, the threads running the length of the cloth, placed parallel to each other, and the cross threads (called the *weft* or *filling*) passed back and forth over and under the alternative warp threads by the action of the *shuttle*. The weft was spun directly onto the bobbins, which were placed into the shuttle, so all of the preparatory work was concerned with the warp. The first operation was *spooling*, where the warp threads were wound onto spools. These were then placed on a large rack, called a *creel*, from which they ran through the *warper* and onto the *beam*, a large roller that was placed on the loom. However, before the beam was so placed, the threads had to be strengthened with a starchy substance, which was applied by a machine called a *slasher*.

The last stage before weaving was *drawing-in*, a process which, until recently, was always done by hand. The individual warp threads had to be drawn through the eyes in the *harness wires* in a certain order that would allow the loom to weave a particular pattern. The complexity of the pattern was determined by the number of harnesses used. Next, the threads were passed through the *reed*. Then the whole assembly—the beam, harnesses, and reed—was placed on the loom, where it was woven automatically.

During the 1920s, the weavers were tending anywhere from four to fifty looms each, the number depending on whether they had to change the weft bobbins in the shuttle by hand (notice the term *handloom* in the book). By then, most looms were equipped with automatic stop motion, which stopped the loom instantly if any thread broke. The invention of this device dramatically reduced the number of faults in the cloth and relieved the weavers of a great burden of observation.

After the weaving process, the cloth went to *cloth inspecting*, where it was inspected for faults, such as missing threads, and was repaired. For woolens, this process is known as *burling*, as little knots, or *burls*, of wool are picked out of the cloth. The unfinished cloth was then *bleached* or *dyed*. Most mills sent their cloth out for *finishing*, but Amoskeag had the necessary facilities on its premises. Besides bleaching or dyeing, the processes in the finishing department included *brushing*, *singing*, and *napping*, which removed the raised lint and prepared the cloth surface. White cloth was then bleached. If the cloth was to be colored, then dyeing was carried out. Sometimes, especially in wool, the raw stock, or yarn, was dyed before it was woven into cloth. From dyeing, the cloth was steamed to make the colors fast; then it was washed and sometimes starched and stretched on a *tenter frame*. From there it was automatically folded and packed.

For a more complete listing of terms from the world of textile manufacturing, see the glossary on page 391.

SOURCE: James Paul Warberg, *Cotton and Cotton Manufacture* (Boston: First National Bank of Boston, 1921).

First Generation

► **Mary Cunion**

Mary Cunion was born in southern Scotland in 1885. Her aunt, Susan Cunion, was one of the original "Scotch girls" recruited from Glasgow and its vicinity by the Amoskeag in the 1870s. The Scotch girls were expert gingham weavers who were selected by the Amoskeag agents on the basis of careful scouting and letters of recommendation from local ministers. Once established in Manchester, Susan sent for her nieces and nephew. Mary joined her aunt in 1900 and worked in the mills for most of the next thirty-five years. At the time of the interview, she still occupied the same corporation tenement in which she had lived since coming to Manchester. Shortly after the interview, she moved to the Maple Leaf Nursing Home, where she died in 1974 at the age of eighty-nine.

THE UNDERSIGNED HEREBY AGREE TO ENGAGE AS GINGHAM OR CHECK LOOM WEAVERS, WITH THE AMOSKEAG MANUFACTURING COMPANY OF MANCHESTER, NEW HAMPSHIRE, UNITED STATES OF AMERICA, FOR THE PERIOD OF TWELVE CALENDAR MONTHS, TO COMMENCE AND BE COMPUTED FROM THE 15TH DAY OF JUNE EIGHTEEN HUNDRED AND SIXTY-EIGHT YEARS, AND PROMISE TO DO THEIR WORK WELL AND FAITHFULLY TO THE BEST OF THEIR ABILITY, WORKING THE REGULAR HOURS, AND AT THE RATE OF PAYMENT CURRENT IN THE FACTORY, DOING THE SAME TYPE OF WORK. THEY ALSO PROMISE HEREBY TO REPAY BY MONTHLY INSTALLMENTS IN SUCH SUMS AS MAY BE AGREED UPON, THE AMOUNT ADVANCED FOR THE PASSAGE TICKETS, AND FOR WHICH THEY HAVE THIS DAY SIGNED TWO PROMISSORY NOTES AT ONE DAY'S DATE.

Mary Cunion, 1969

I spent my happiest times in the mills. Can you beat that? I came to this house from Scotland in 1900. My Aunt Susan had it, and I've lived in this same room ever since.

I was brought up in the south of Scotland in a place called Douglas. I wasn't very long in school there. They wouldn't give me more than grammar school. They were going to put me to work doing housework. Everybody had to go to work in those days. Here, they're men and women before they work at all. But over there, we were working when we were fifteen. They wouldn't let you stay in school because the people were poor, and they needed your help.

My father and mother, both of them were gone. My mother died shortly after I was born, and we scattered around. Tommy and I were the youngest, so we were boarded out in the south of Scotland, way out of Glasgow.

My brother John and my sister Susan and my brother Perkin came out to this country one by one. My Aunt Susan brought my sister, and later my older brother came here and settled in Boston. The ones that came out to this country never bothered their heads with the kids left on the other side. They were too darn glad to get away from there. But after a while, my sister Susan sent for me, and I sent for Tom. We just took what came.

Later on in life, after we came to America and I was much older, my sister and I had a hard time understanding each other, getting along. Our ways of mind were different; and, of course, the English was different here than it was over there. I was talking broad Scots, and Susan didn't like that. She was ashamed of me. But after a while she got me broken in, and I went to Bryant and Stratton Business College at night and got quite smart.

My Aunt Susan Cunion was in the first group that came out of Scotland. The Amoskeag sent for her. She was single. I'm her brother's child. We had nobody when we came here, and she got us work. She sent my sister Susan to school for a while, but after I came out we all landed in the mill.

My Aunt Susan could neither read nor write. My sister got her books and she studied a little, but she couldn't read or put anything down on paper. My aunt had been a weaver over in Scotland. The Amoskeag Company hired the weavers and

bought the looms, and they came together in the one boat.
They brought Scottish looms. That's what my aunt said, that
they came with the looms. A four-box, it was a four-box loom.*
My aunt and another woman, Sarah, came out together, and
they taught others in the mills how to use the new looms. Oh, I
worked on a four-box loom one time. They're very interesting;
you have to watch your colors so they don't run into one an-
ther.

My aunt once worked in Lowell [Massachusetts], but she
didn't like the place there, the people. In Manchester the mills
were in better order. When I came over here, I made my aunt
give up working in the mill. She lived right here on the third
floor. There's a little tenement upstairs. By then, she was an old
lady, over seventy years of age. Of course, she went way back.
She talked a lot about the Civil War. She died around 1932. I
wasn't a weaver then, but I wasn't here long before they made
me one.

When I came in 1900, we worked from six in the morning
till six at night. I worked solid. My aunt, she wouldn't allow
any gallivanting around. Even on the weekends I worked. But I
liked it from the start. The ups were all right, and the downs
were all right. I liked weaving. I liked watching the different
boxes. Sometimes when the loom would get out of order a box
would drop at the wrong time and spoil a whole warp; the
warp would have to be cut out, and you'd have to start all over
again. Sometimes a box would drop on account of the loom; it
wasn't your fault.

It's a very interesting job, weaving is. I think it's the most
interesting work a girl can have. In fact, you never really learn
it all. My Aunt Susan used to say that, and she was a weaver in
the old country before she came here. In your lifetime, there's
always something new, because every warp you get in is a new
one, a new color. Keeps your mind busy.

I was smart because I was young, but the old weavers had
it over you for perfection. You didn't mind getting a roll of
cloth back once in a while and getting a shamed face then, but
you can't stand that when you get older. For weaving you have

* A four-box loom is a loom that could operate four separate shuttles each
with a different color thread. This would allow for the weaving of plaids
without the manual change of the shuttle at each change of the weft color.

to be clever. The colors are hard on your eyes. We used to have warps in five or six colors. You had to watch your pattern. That's why I liked it, because it takes on your brain as well as your hands. I used to like it when I'd have a man for a partner because they were awful good for fixing the looms if anything happened. Oh, they're strong.

Weaving was the best thing in mill work. We didn't mind the noise—once you're in here you never mind; the only thing is when you happen to be out and go back in, then you hear the volume of all that noise. You never know it unless somebody comes to speak to you. They have to holler right into your ear. Sometimes they'd bring you a girl one day, and she wouldn't show up the next. Then they'd bring you another one, and she would show up for a day or two. That's how it was. The noise bothered them. They wouldn't put the time in long enough to get used to that noise, and it would chase them out. The menfolk wouldn't stay at all. But the noise was part of the job; it never bothered me.

Everything was clean in the mill. We had what they used to call sweepers right in the room. But it was hot and disagreeable. If the windows were open, some people, they'd catch a cold, and they'd have to wear a shawl. If somebody opened the window, cotton would go fly everywhere, and it would get in your rig, and we would start a fight about the window being open. All in a day's work.

In the mill there were three or four French wherever there was one English-speaking. They came down from Canada. They're good, sturdy citizens. They built up this city a lot, the French did. I got along with those French Canadians. They minded their own business. We had our little ups and downs, but we fought them out. No, I have nothing against the French. The Irish used to fight with them, though. Oh, yes, they fought in the mill. I saw them hitting one another with shovels and all that stuff. But they would be fired for it. Once the overseer would get wind of it, he'd fire them.

One day the Amoskeag fired me. I didn't watch the loom, and it was running away ahead of me. They fired me for that. I got another job weaving the very same day. I was young at the time, about eighteen. Aunt Susan used to get after me. She'd say, "You don't keep your mind on your work. Your mind's

The mill workers in 1878

somewhere else, and of course you get confused." If you were fired, you'd have to go to some other mill—Amoskeag had twelve mills, you know—but you'd find a job. You see, your old boss wouldn't hire you back right away. If he had a recollection of firing you, he wouldn't do it for quite a while.

At one place, I got mad at the overseer and I walked out, but I had a job waiting for me somewhere else. Those were the days when you could get work and get your choice of work. If we got mad at one overseer, we could just walk out and get a job somewhere else. Oh, those were the days!

I don't think I went back as a weaver after the big strike in 1922. When I came from the old country, I had started as a tie-over girl; and when I ended the weaving here, I went back on the tying-over. It's simpler, and it's paid by the day. The weaving is paid by the cloth you take off, paid by the yard.

In winter, it's very cold here, but at home we survived with those steam heaters on. We just stayed downstairs; we didn't go upstairs. That's how we got along. The boardinghouses, they weren't steam-heated any more than we were.* Every roomer had a little stove with a bundle of wood beside it, and he just threw on a log. The Amoskeag did not provide the wood; you had to buy it. It would take the cold air off, but you were never comfortable. You didn't expect to be comfortable. There are tenements that haven't got steam heat even now.

I used to work days weaving, and the pay I made at weaving paid for the business college. It was right up here on Elm Street. I went to Bryant and Stratton Business College way back when I was only fifteen or sixteen years of age. I studied shorthand, and I studied typewriting in a regular course. I took the course, and I got a diploma. Mr. Chase of the Chase Tea Company wanted to hire me for the stenography; but when he showed me the price he was going to pay, I said I couldn't do that. I said, "They pay three times as much as that with my board at the Amoskeag!" He didn't send for me again.

It was all right, the Amoskeag. I liked it very much, but I got stuck there. It was because of the money they were paying. I had to pay my board everywhere I went; I had no parents. I

---

* Mary Cunion refers here to the corporation tenement in which she lived. The tenement was divided into two self-contained apartments: one upstairs and one downstairs. Mary lived below, while her relatives lived above.

wish I had followed up the business-school course. I would
have been better off. Money isn't everything; your brain
counts, too.

If I had my life all over again, I wouldn't be in the mill. No,
I wouldn't be in the mill. I'd rather be outside. It wasn't long
till I did see where I was wrong. It was drudgery there; of
course, it paid well, but it's regular drudgery. But there was
always something coming up that I needed to work.

I made $10.00 in about four days. You didn't think too
much of the money in those days; you could buy a lot of gro-
ceries, prices were reasonable. Then we had boardinghouses.
The boardinghouses used to give meals. They were always on
one side of the street and the Amoskeag tenements on the opposite side. Those meals were very good, but you used to get
almost sick of them. It was the same thing all the time. Boardinghouses—they don't run them any more. Now everybody
makes their own meals.

We used to have three regular floors in the tenements, but
they used the attics, too, in those days. Mr. Anderson—he was
in the dye house—he had an attic up there. You couldn't get
him out of it. Cold, dark! But he was very happy and contented. He never grumbled. They haven't been allowed to use
attics for a long time. You had to carry up water if you wanted
it. If you wanted a hot bath, you had to start the fire in the
stoves and warm it, just a pail of water at a time. Hardships—
well, people today would call it hardships. Before we had hot
water in the pipes, I had my old stove, my coal stove.

The bathroom was up a flight of stairs. My brother didn't
mind that. The menfolk didn't mind it; they liked it. But it
took a lot of coal to get a bath up there. People were poor,
they didn't like to put out all their money in rent, so we just
put up with those things. But you won't find any young ones
putting up with anything today, oh, no! They have to have
comfort, and I don't blame them. When I worked for the
Amoskeag—when it was the Amoskeag—°and it was a tenement, they used to deduct $5.00 a month for rent. One dollar a
week. And we had the whole five rooms. You got no luxury,

° "When it was the Amoskeag" means: when the houses were owned by
the Amoskeag Company.

but you got a roof over your head, and you were darn lucky that you got that.

Payday was every two weeks. The paymaster used to come in the halls. He went in a row, and you had to behave yourself. If you didn't pay your rent, they'd find out what the trouble was, and you'd catch it. If you still didn't pay after a certain number of weeks, they'd put you out of the tenement. They used to do that—it was done everywhere. They didn't interfere too much with your behavior, though; that was your own business.

I've lived in this same tenement for sixty-eight years. Now I'm an old lady, eighty-five. I must be ten years out of work. My old radio is getting like myself, it's getting worn out. I still like this country, though. I liked it from the time I came. Nice dry air, nothing like Scotland. If you worked, you made a little money, so you didn't need to watch every penny, like over there. They were awful stingy over there with their pay. I went home on a visit after I was in this country five years, and I didn't like it at all. It rained every day. The trip was just a waste of money. My sister said, "Let's get back to civilized America!" I was glad to get back.

But ours was quite a history of hardships, too. The Amoskeag was just getting built up then—now it's gone down. It's been down for quite a while. The beginning came, and the flourish came, and now the end has come. It's just about the same with every business.

► *Mary Dancause*

Eighty-nine-year-old Mary Dancause was born in Manchester but spent her early childhood in Quebec. Unlike Mary Cunion, Mary Dancause saw working in the mill more as a way to support her family than as an independent career. Her work life was erratic, having to conform to her child-rearing responsibilities. She had six children, five of whom are still living. Her husband was a loom fixer in the Amoskeag. While working there, he developed a patent for which the Company subsequently claimed the credit. Some years after the Amoskeag shutdown, his crippling arthritis forced him to stop working. Because they still had young children to support, Mary had to go to work. She accepted a position as a maid in a resort hotel, a job she held until age seventy-nine.

We interviewed Mary in her little cottage in a southern suburb of Manchester. Her husband and his brothers had originally built the cottage as a clubhouse. Her married daughter, who was present at the interview, lives nearby.

My mother came from Canada all by herself. She was a weaver. One of her sisters had come to Manchester to work in the mill. My father was a widower, ten years older than my mother. She thought he looked nice with a mustache, so she married him and went back to Canada. He worked for a while with race horses. That was his job, but it didn't pay very much. So they returned to Manchester, and my mother worked in the mills. She worked at that Jefferson Mill, the one with the big clock, and I used to bring her her lunch in a big pail at noon. I think about that some days, and I can't believe it. She worked there for forty years. She made ACA Ticking, the cloth that makes pillow and mattress covers.

My father worked on a farm. He would clean up around, and in the summer he used to go and cut hay. Because he had been brought up on a farm in Canada, he knew how to do all these things. He also worked with two fellows in a saloon. They sold beer by the barrel, not like what you get now. They just took a little pail, believe it or not, and they would fill it and go on the street. You'd pay 10¢ and get a glass full of beer.

I was actually born in Manchester, on Orange Street, but I was raised in Quebec. My father's sister came to visit from Canada when I was two years old. I caught something from somebody else and got sore eyes. My parents couldn't take care of me. My mother needed money to pay her bills, and she was working in the mill. Another lady was taking care of me. So my aunt took me back to Canada until I was twelve years old.

After my parents had four new little ones, they wanted me back. A man they knew was going down to Canada, so they asked him to bring me back with him. Well, I didn't know this man, and I didn't want to leave, but what could I do? It was hard for my mother, working in the mill and taking care of the kids, so that's why they called me back. Oh, my God, I was only a baby when they sent me to Canada! I didn't recognize my parents because I was too young when I left them.

My parents also had one son in Canada, but they left him there. He was older than me. He lived with his grandfather and grandmother on my mother's side. They had a daughter, an old maid, and she brought him up. When my brother came back, my father didn't know him. He shut the door in his face! My father had just got up in the afternoon, and there was a knock at the back door. "We don't want nothing," Father said, and he banged the door. So my brother went around to the front. He rang the bell, and my father said, "It's you again." My brother said, "Wait a minute, can I talk to you?" He told him, "I'm your son."

When I came back, I took care of my sister. She was about three years old. I ran around with the mop sometimes, chasing her. She used to wet on the floor, just like a little doll. I had

Mary Dancause, 1976

two sisters and three brothers, five children to take care of, six days a week. In Quebec I never did anything much. Maybe I did the dishes, got the chickens. I never worked hard then. When I got home, to Manchester, and my mother didn't have a washing machine, I had to wash the clothes with my hands on a board. I had to do all the washing, cook the meals, and everything. I was twelve years old then. That would have been around 1900. It was the year President Roosevelt came on the train. I'll never forget seeing him.

I was so lonesome and I cried so much, you won't believe it. My mother would be working in the kitchen and I would be talking to myself: "I want to go back, I want to go back." I was homesick for Canada in the worst way. My family in Manchester was very poor, one chair for each person. My uncle in Canada, who owned a saw mill, always had a big house full of company, it was really jolly; but in Manchester, my father would come home, bang the door, and go to bed. That's all he did. One thing I'll never forget. The wall was very plain, and my mother had this big black cross on it, no statue, just a plain cross. I didn't talk English at all, and the kids made fun of me. Even now, I can't talk very good—no pronunciation.

When I was fourteen years old I started working in a boardinghouse, and I went to live there. They had a law in the mill, they wouldn't let you work that young. It was good, though, working in the boardinghouse. My future mother-in-law ran it. She had fourteen children! You don't see that any more. She brought up fourteen children. Anyway, she had good, good food. She always used butter. When they started to get the margarine, a young man came and told her to change. You see, he wanted to sell her the margarine. My mother-in-law couldn't talk English at all, so she said to her daughter, "Tell him to save his breath because I'm not buying that. Never, never."

She was in the kitchen at five o'clock every morning. The people who ate in the boardinghouse, most of them worked in the mill. It was on Stark Street. You eat and then go down the road, and there's your job. The mill workers came for breakfast at five thirty. I had to wake up at five o'clock to get ready. It was pitch black and cold in the winter. At noontime, they had quite a few come that worked in the stores: a barber, a meat cutter, one worked in an office.

My mother-in-law's cooking was good; every day it was something different. One day it was pork, another it was beef, another it was chicken. Then, come a holiday, it was her turkey. They used to make their own pastry, too. They had some bread from the bakeries in the morning. That was for toast. Then they'd have the homemade bread for noontime and supper. And soup—they made soup. Every day she had a different kind of soup. Once a week, they made those flapjacks in the morning. I think she used to make fifteen, sixteen pies on Friday. She made dessert all the time. She had a bunch of bananas on the table at night. They also made their own piccalilli. Oh, they had their meal! The food was cheap, of course. It was about 5¢ a pound of sugar and 12¢ a pound of meat.

When my mother-in-law finally gave up the business with the boardinghouse, everybody was upset. Some of them cried. Old people, they were so used to being there, it was like their home. They didn't want her to quit, but she couldn't do it alone any more. She got too old, too tired.

I met my husband in that boardinghouse. He had two brothers that lived there. My husband was four years older than me. He started work in the Amoskeag before my time. He used to clean the floor. Later he became a loom fixer. I was twenty-two when we were married. Before we were married, when I lived in the boardinghouse, I was just a worker. They were good to me, very good to me. They were paying me $3.00 a week as a waitress, and I used to clean the rooms upstairs, too, after the night meal was all done. Everything was cheap then. You paid 5¢ for a pair of stockings. Only 5¢. And a blouse was a dollar. My room and meals were free.

Years ago, a lot of people lived with their in-laws. It was cheaper; not only that, the elderly never went anywhere else to live. For five years after I was married, I used to have a room on the top floor in my mother-in-law's boardinghouse. As long as I was single and I worked there, I didn't mind living there; but after I got married, I didn't want to live there. We stayed because my husband paid the rent; but after the third child was born, I said, "If you don't want to leave, I'm leaving." So we moved out and went and lived in the same tenement my

sister lived in. We were four couples living in that tenement. I
suppose my husband still paid the rent for his mother's boardinghouse after we moved out. He was always good to his
mother, helped her a lot. He used to get the butter once a
week, big tubs of butter. That's heavy. And big boxes of
crackers—it was the whole case—and sugar by the barrel. He
would work in the mill and come at noon and eat in the
kitchen. Sometimes, after the boarders were gone, before we
cleaned all the tables, we'd sit and eat in the dining room. We
didn't eat as a family each day; but the holidays, a special time,
we would eat at the big table after the boarders were gone.

My husband and I used to go up to Lake Massabesic and
drink beer, walk around the lake. We started to go to the movies, 5¢ for a movie. A man would come on the stage and he'd
sing a song, a lover's song, and then they'd show the picture.
Saturday, at the Park Theatre, they had real actors. You'd pay
75¢ or a dollar, and you'd have the best seat. We used to go
there with another couple. In the summer, the girl I used to
chum with when I was single, we'd go across the river in a
buggy—there were no cars—and have a picnic, with bananas
and fruit. That's the good times we had.

The first job I had in the mill was spinning. I went to work
very young. We used to work very hard. To me, except for the
card room, it was the dirtiest job. The fuzz from the cotton was
terrible. We used to put another dress over, but the stuff that
falls on the floor, the cotton stuff, would get on my dress, in my
hair. Spinning was a terrible job; for me, it was the worst job. I
worked down there and I wanted to get out. Above the bobbin
there was a roller, and it would fall on the floor. I'd have to stop
the frame and clean all that, and in the meantime another
frame was doing the same thing, because it was full of cotton.
They gave me hell one time. I couldn't keep up. You fix one,
and two or three more would fall down.* Sometimes they'd
send another girl to help you. The bosses, they were pretty
good. They would tell you to keep going and make the work
better. I suppose I was too slow. Some girls were smarter than
me.

* She is describing the situation that occurs in spinning when a thread breaks.
The broken end has a tendency to get wound around the rollers, which
quickly get wrapped with a thick layer of yarn and fall off the machine.
Today a vacuum suction beneath each roller prevents this from happening.

I can remember that I went into a mill myself, for just fifteen minutes, back when I was in high school. I got a headache in those fifteen minutes. I then went to the shoe shop. They made good money there, but I couldn't stand it—I got sick from the smell. There were some rooms in the mill that didn't make too much noise, and we could talk. But in the weave room, where my mother worked, there the noise was terrible. It would shake and everything. I remember it was very hot and humid. They didn't open the windows much. If the wind came through, the thread broke and you'd have to tie it again.

I quit one day. About ten rollers had fallen on the floor, one here and one there. I was going crazy. I got my pay and I threw my apron into the garbage, I was so mad. I never went back again to spinning. I couldn't stand it any more. Years ago, people worked in the same mill; and if they got fed up, they would just go across the yard and get a job over there right away. Social Security, we didn't have that, so I started work again. I didn't want to starve.

My last job in the mill was on burling in the cloth room. I was working in the mill with that lamb on the roof.* They would bring in the big rolls of cloth. It was a sitting-down job, too. We would fix all the little knots to make sure it was all nice and even. Sometimes we'd miss the thread, but we'd go right along. It didn't pay too much—it was $12.00 for two weeks, that's all. I used to pay $5.00 for my room and board and 25¢ for a pair of stockings. In the cloth room we had a lot of fun. We used to sing. When you're young, it's fun.

I worked hard all my life. When the children were young, we got along pretty well. Only, when they closed the mill, we went a whole year without work, and we had four children at that time. They had to go to school. We had to eat. We lost our savings in the bank. I was so disappointed, I'll never put any money in the bank any more.

After my family was grown up, I worked at the hotel for 50¢ an hour, believe it or not. And I worked as a chambermaid after that. My husband was crippled with arthritis; he couldn't move his leg. I think it happened because he got cold. It was wet under the big looms when they ran them because of the

---

* She is referring to the weathervane on #1 Manchester Mill, which was a large ram on top of a tall pole located over the stair tower.

steam. He used to lie on the floor to fix the loom, so he'd be soaking wet when he got out from under. Those hard cement floors, they were bad. That was a dirty job. He worked hard. He was sick eighteen years, so somebody had to go to work.

He was so handy, everybody always wanted him to do something. I said, "Why don't you get like Albert [a carpenter]? You see that business? They make money." But he didn't want that. He probably knew there was security in the mills. The job was there, while with the carpenter job, you had to go looking for your work. A carpenter, half the time he didn't get paid. They would say, "Next time, next time, later." When Albert died, he had these papers out in the shed, and these papers said, "I owe him money." They never paid it. So what are you going to do? He never wanted to get out of that mill. Just a loom fixer, that's all he was.

We had bad luck when they closed the Amoskeag. They did a foolish thing, wanting the eight hours. I'll never forget that. They closed all the mills, and the cigar shop, the 724 cigar shop. My brother was working there. Those two businesses, that killed the whole of Manchester. People were never the same after that. I would never like to go back to those times. If someone said, "I can give you something to make you young again," I'd say, "Oh, no, I don't need that. I'm old, and I want to stay old."

► *Antonia Bergeron*

Antonia Bergeron was ninety-six years old at the time of this interview and almost completely blind. The interview took place in her small private room at the Mt. Carmel Nursing Home, with her daughter present.

Antonia had lived all her life on the East Side of Manchester, in the French and Irish neighborhood near St. Augustine's Church. She was a devout Catholic, and much of her life revolved around religious activities and French-Canadian women's orders connected with the church.

She started work at age fifteen, in 1895, and worked in the Amoskeag until the birth of her first child. Her husband worked as an edge trimmer at the Hoyt Shoe Company; her children also worked in the shoe industry.

In her old age, Antonia felt lonely and trapped in the nursing home. But she believed that she was better off than the other residents at Mt. Carmel because she was paying her own room and board. She died there in 1976.

I came here in 1895; and in 1900, when the century began, I got married. I was twenty years old on the first of October, 1899; and I got married on January eighth. Before that, I worked in the mills and I wove bags. We started by giving two weeks of our time for nothing to learn how to spin cotton. They gave us two [spinning] frames, and we had 20¢ per day. Then, when we were able to run an extra frame, they gave us 10¢ more. That made 30¢. I went up to 50¢. Then I left. I learned to weave. I wove those round [burlap] bags.

My father was on the farm in Canada. He wasn't very rich. He met my mother at Chicoutimi. It was a village at that time. She was a schoolteacher. After a few years of being married, he took her to a farm where there weren't even any roads. In order to bring flour for bread, they'd divide a bag of flour in half and put it on a horse's back. They spent their winters in a log camp when there wasn't any farming. They had nothing. Don't think my mother didn't find it hard in log camps. I still remember the camps. I remember when they built a house. There was the floor; it was round wood. Then they'd trim the wood, make it flat. And you'd wash the floor on your knees, with brooms of spruce needles. You'd boss the kids with them. You know how those needles are sharp. They made good, strong lye by boiling ashes from the stove. We made soap with it. We'd put it in water to wash the floors. Misery, you know, was made for people; it's not for the dogs. I had a dog, and he never had any misery. He'd lay down under the stove and he was fine.

My ma said that right after I was born, she went out to pick potatoes. In those days, they'd pass by with a horse and plow—back and forth—and the women would pick the potatoes. They'd dig with an axe, and rake until they'd find some more. All the children helped. When I was growing up, I also picked potatoes. We'd put them on the ground in a pile so they could dry. At night they'd pick them up to put them in the cellar.

We were thirteen children; I was the seventh. I went to a small school in the village with only about ten children. My mother taught school there. That's why we were more advanced. My mother started us. We could read fluently, and we could spell. Now they don't spell any more; they don't do anything. When you spelled "table," you had to say " 'tā,' *t, a,* 'ble,' *b, l, e.* Table" [laughs].

After I finished high school, as they called it, the inspector came and said, "If you want to teach school, you'll have to do model teaching first. I'll give you a small place, and you'll teach school to perhaps ten or twelve children. You'll start by showing them *ABCD.* It'll be very easy." But it was cold. In the morning, I knew that it was the schoolteacher who would have to get up and light the stove to heat the school before the children arrived. So when my neighbors from Lake St. John went to the U. S., I decided to go with them. I said to my father and mother, "You know, instead of teaching school here, I want to go to the U. S." Of course, it cost them a little to let me go (not money cost, but feelings cost), but they knew the people well and they had faith in me.

We had a lot of misery when we arrived in Manchester. I still remember the old lady where I stayed. Her daughters started working before us, so she gave them jam. But we didn't work, so she didn't give us any. Had I known that we'd have all that misery here, I'd never have come. If I'd only known what I knew after. But it was too late.

I didn't know anyone when we arrived; and in a few weeks, I owed room and board money. Then I met a woman who had taught me school in Canada when I was small. She worked in the mills here. She helped me, found me a job in the mills. After five or six months, I started to get my affairs straightened out. My mother came up later with my little brother and my little sister. She bought some secondhand clothes, an old stove, some beds and mattresses, and she set up housekeeping. My mother would go wash clothes in the convent all day. She also cleaned at St. Augustine's Church. They had just newly built the church at that time. She'd get a dollar a day. She'd come home at night with her hands all burned with lye.

As time went on, we'd have another person come up, and another, and finally the whole family was here. My father gave his land to one of his sons and came up to the States, too, but he didn't stay.

When we arrived, we lived on Spruce Street. There were Irishmen there. The Irish were naughty, you know . . . ah! We'd be sitting in the window, and it was so low, we were practically on the ground. We'd be there in the window, no screen, nothing, and the Irish would pass by and try to kiss us through the window. "Kiss me, Maggie!" We were scared. We didn't want to go out the door, the Irish would grab us. My brother Jean Baptiste was starting to grow up a bit. He said, "Let me go fix those Irishmen." There was a common there, not too far away. We called it Ireland Common. It was rotten with Irishmen. After Ma came we lived on Lake Avenue. After that, the Greeks arrived.

When I came here, there were several companies and many different mills. There was the Stark, the Jefferson, the Bag Mill, and there was what was called the *Mouton d'Or*.° The Manchester Mill made only wool. They didn't make cotton. We didn't yet speak of the Amoskeag at that time. Later, the Amoskeag started buying everything.°° They bought the Manchester Mills, too, wool and all. There were three rows of buildings. There were bridges that you crossed from one mill to another. There was so much room in the millyard that you could get lost.

When I was earning a dollar a day, it didn't take me long to get rid of it. For one thing, I had to buy a little to put on my back. You'd buy a piece of Indian cotton, 5¢ a yard. Ma had a sewing machine, and we'd make little dresses. Sometimes it was muslin, and we'd make ourselves little ruffles, and Lord, did we have trouble! Today I'm blind, and I can do better than I did at that time.

In the mills, especially in the weave room, we didn't talk much. There's so much noise, you can't hear. That's why I never learned to speak English well. I like weaving. I always liked it. And after I was married, I often went in when I had the time. My husband also started by weaving, but he didn't like it and he became a shoemaker. He had a good trade in the shoe shop, but he would sometimes loaf three or four weeks when the company took inventory. That was their excuse. But we still had to eat. At times like that, I'd go in to weave. My husband didn't say much. He'd say, "Why do you want to go to work? You have no reason to go there. Why do you want to give yourself misery for nothing?" He didn't like it much, but when you came home with $20.00 then, it was worth about what $50.00 is today. My husband would go to Kennedy's to buy butter for the week, the eggs for the week; he'd also buy cheese, tea, coffee.

When we first came here we worked six days a week. We'd start at 7 A.M. and work till 6 P.M., on Saturdays till 4 P.M. That made it a long day, but in the mills we had an hour to eat. When

---

° This refers to #1 Manchester Mill, which had a gold ram weathervane.

°° The Manchester Mills merged with the Amoskeag Company in 1902, and the Stark Mills merged in 1922. The other mills mentioned were always part of the Amoskeag Company.

The mill workers in 1878. The gold ram weathervane can be seen in the distance.

you work and you have a lot of ambition, the time goes by fast. You never felt you'd done enough. When you think you don't have enough money, you want to work to make more. We ran through the whole mill; you had to run all day. Today they no longer *work* in the mills. They don't earn their money. They get a lot of money, though. They've told me that they get big, big salaries.

At the Amoskeag Company, for a time the bosses were very fresh. The boss would chase the girls and slap their behinds, give them kicks in the rear end. They'd send them away, those

whom they didn't like, and not pay them. A little while ago, I
saw the second hand, Mr. L., on the street. He used to visit his
daughter, who lived upstairs from us. I recognized him. I said,
"Get out of the way or I'll run you over." I said, "When we
worked for you, you ran after us, you'd kick us. So if you don't
get out of the way, I'll run you down with the car" [starts
laughing]. The bosses were strict! Many times we were well
treated, though. We must appreciate what they did for us.
Just before the strike, the big strike that we had, my husband
had loafed about six months. No one in my family worked. My
daughter was married, and her husband didn't work. We were
twelve in the house to eat. I said, "I guess I'll go in and weave."
I went to the employment office. There was a Canadian man
[Boucher, the clerk in the employment office in charge of hiring French-Canadian workers]. He didn't even look at me. He
looked up in the air and said to me, "Madam, we have no place
for you. We're refusing people every day." I left without saying
a word. I said to myself, "Yes, I'm going to go see the super." I
went to the mills, and the super said, "Come tomorrow morning, and I'll give you some work. I'll make you a room girl." I
didn't much like that, but when you're hungry, you have to
take what you can get.

The second hands favored people because of nationality.
Sometimes we'd have German third hands who favored their
own people. At times you'd have to wait longer than others
because they had to start other work before getting to yours.
You'd say, "It seems to me that I went and got you for help
before so-and-so," and they'd say, "Oh, no, so-and-so came before you." That's what went on. But "real Americans," so to
speak, there weren't any working in the mills. The bosses were
Americans and Irishmen.

There were Germans who were bosses, too. The Germans
were more difficult. But after they like you they're OK. I
started weaving next to a German woman, and she didn't want
me there at all; but when I left for the family way, she cried
and gave me some nice gifts for the baby. After she started to
know me, I started becoming sociable, and I did a little work to
help her out. She was old, and I was young and fast. At noon
I'd sew for her. When you had a big run and a thread was
missing, you'd do it with a needle by hand. We had no right to

let a run pass through longer than half a yard. Well, I'd do a little sewing at noon. After that, we were very good friends, myself and the old German woman.

I came out just before the big strike. When the union went in, it didn't take long. The people went on strike. But there were some who weren't for that, so they had the militia there.° I didn't bother with it because I'd finished the week before. My baby was ill, and he died just when the strike broke out. So I stayed home, and my daughter went to work. It wasn't nice. They had the army to guard the doors. All the gates were watched so no one could enter. It was tough. I knew there would be trouble. Miss Richard was one of the heads of the union; she was a weaver. She told me, "You know, we're preparing a strike. We're going to have a big strike, and it won't be nice."

When the Amoskeag closed, oh my God! It was awful. Then there were a lot on relief. I never was because we were not affected. Everything went slack everywhere. Business fell completely. Before that, I remember we used to go to the Amoskeag store, at the corner of Bridge Street, and buy big packages of cotton, flannel. I used to go a couple of times a year and dress up all my children for school. Cotton dresses! They used to have beautiful cotton here. Flannel to make underwear for the children. I made them pajamas. It was always homemade stuff. Sometimes we'd make the trip for nothing. We didn't get a chance to be waited on; it was packed with people. We never had to buy anything already made, except for shoes and socks. Everything was made from cotton from Amoskeag.

° Here she is referring to the strike of 1933 rather than the strike of 1922.

Omer Proulx was born in Quebec in 1885, and Mary in 1894. Both had long work careers in the Amoskeag: Omer spent twenty-six years in the mills; Marie spent twenty-four. Both were at the mills when the shutdown occurred. Omer had advanced from a learner to a section hand, a considerable achievement. He temporarily left the Amoskeag in 1929 because "the pay was too small," but he returned within a year. Marie worked as a spinner, part of the time under her husband's supervision.

They were interviewed in their small apartment in a senior citizens' project in Manchester. Omer and Marie Proulx died within two months of each other, in 1975.

MARIE: In Canada, my father was a boss in the timber yard. In the summer, they would steer the wood on the river with poles. In the winter, he worked in the timber yard. That was his daily bread. He was on the road year-round, while we were working at home. So we lived well, we ate well, we weren't lacking anything, but we never had a father. One baby was born during the days that he spent away from home. Nine months without coming home! It was a long time for a woman. My mother was tired of seeing my father on the river and in the logging camps, and she said, "I'm always alone with the children. I'm sick and tired of this." He said, "Me, too. I'm tired of being on the road." So they decided to come to Manchester.

At that time we were six in the house. We had to help our

mother; she had everything on her back. My mother already knew of the life in the city of Manchester because she came here when she was fourteen years old and worked in the mills. At twenty-one years of age, she returned to Canada to get married, and she stayed.

When we came to Manchester, my father found work right away. He wasn't paid too much money—$1.10 per day. He went in on a floor of the Amoskeag, but he didn't work there long. He made friends, and his friends got him in at the Blood Machine Shop at the Amoskeag that same summer.

Omer was born in Canada. He was only a year old when he came here. He had parents who were five minutes here and five minutes in Canada. They raised their family like that. One was born in Canada and another was born in the U. S. Omer's father was a *habitant*,° but he always hated it. He never liked the land. He came to Manchester to pay off his land. I think he had three hundred acres.

I was twelve years old when I arrived here and started work. At age fifteen, I went to #4 Mill. We were there when we were married, and we stayed there. I was twenty years without going out of that room. I never went out to loaf, no! My husband was a frame fixer. For me it was a life of glory to work in the mills. Oh, did I like it! I liked it enough to miss it when I was all done. I finished in 1935. My little girl was born in 1933; she was two years old when I stopped.

I didn't know what it was like to have vacations. We didn't have them like they do today. We worked all the time. I started working from six to six. I did not find it a long day, not at all. I liked my work, and Omer was the same way. He'd go home and cry because he hadn't done enough. I worked a little spinning on wool. When I'd go to work overtime, it was to work on wool, because they didn't have any willing hands, and they'd ask me. I might as well have worked; I had no one at home.

When I started in 1906, we didn't need a pass from the employment office to work. All we had to do was show them that we were fourteen years old. Tall or short, it didn't matter; they'd just ask, "Are you fourteen years old?" OK. That's all. So that's how I went in to work.

° *Habitant* is the Quebec expression for farmer.

The Amoskeag Great Flag, made in 1916

When we arrived here, Papa said, "Well, now, my little girl, we'll no longer be around the house. We'll have to look out so that we'll work." I told him, "I'm going today with my cousin to the mills." She told me who the boss was. So I went and asked for a job. He saw that I was a Canuck [laughs], and he motioned to me with his hands: "Fourteen years old?" I said, "Yes." So he said, "OK, you'll start tomorrow morning." It was over with.

I had curly hair, and mother had never braided it; she always left it loose. So the next day when I went back to the mills with my curls, that old boss there took hold of my hair

and said, "Tie back." "Me?" I said. I asked why in French. So
he brought someone who spoke French, and he said that it was
too dangerous, that my hair could get caught in the straps of
the machinery. That has happened; not too many years ago
there was here in Manchester a woman that had all her hair
caught in the machine. So I had to tie my hair or roll it, and I
didn't want that—a little girl twelve years old with her hair
rolled in some manner. Neither did my mother want that. She
said, "She'll stay here if she has to fix herself up like that." But
Papa said, "Why don't you fix her like he said?" So she tied my
hair all in back. But the boss wasn't satisfied. He said, "Why
don't you put your hair in a cap?" There were some women
who had caps on their heads because the waste dirtied their
hair. I brought a woman's cap home and showed it to Ma. She
made me one, and the next day I wore it. I never had any
trouble after that. My father was never able to support a family of eight children on $1.10 per day. It was miserable at first.
Oh, were we miserable! Our old parents worked till their fore-
heads were sweating to try to have what we get for nothing
today. So I had to go work somewhere, and all there was were
the mills, there was only Amoskeag. I had to resign myself to
working there. I only got $8.40 for two weeks. It was not
enough for our expenses. We had to help our father; I was the
oldest one. Four dollars and twenty cents per week—I couldn't
go far with that.

OMER: And you earned $8,000 per day for the corporation.
We had figured that out. The spindles that you ran took $11.00
per pound. Marie had 125 spindles per frame, and she ran six
of those.

MARIE: A person who always wanted her work well done
there never sat down, never. You had to pick out your time to
eat, to have lunch and go for a drink, so as not to let your work
go down. If it fell down, you couldn't get it back up again. We
had a long way to run. A spinning frame was as long as from
one end of this house to the other. We had six frames like
that.

I lost my eyes at #4 Mill. That was a mill that had all sorts
of colors—for a while we had 101 colors. I had good eyes; and

when the boss noticed that I always found faults, he put me in front to look for them. Then there came a time when they needed a girl expressly for testing the cloth, so as not to leave any bad colors. I was thirteen years on that job as a yarn tester.

When you talked to the bosses, you had to be severe in your speech, but not too severe, or they'd put you out and you wouldn't have any work. At that time there were little majors among the bosses, like there still are today. There was only one company. Therefore we had to be a bit careful. One time, though, I wanted to take a rest from the spinning room. I had friends who worked on wool. So they advised me to go work with them. I did for two days; but when I went to the toilet, such a big cockroach fell on me that I passed out. It was as big as a thumb. I told the boss, "I'm not staying here any more. Give me my time, I'm leaving."

If a Canadian got a higher job, it was because he had Irish friends. Like Omer, who became a little boss, a second hand, because the big bosses liked him. He was very friendly with those guys—they advanced him because he was expert in his work. They knew he would make a good boss. We often were aware that people favored their own nationality. Greeks, for example, they were like you'd say *licheux*.° They did their work, but they'd earn their pay by licking—bringing a box of chocolates or something like that for the boss. If the boss liked to be licked, that person would be in favor. We were aware of that in your room, eh, Omer? Yes, we were aware of that many times. But I can't say that I was badly treated, and we went through many bosses when we were in the same mill.

The younger immigrants got up on their feet and went to school. Families that came in from the outside went to school. They learned the language, and they could fight for themselves more than the old people. Old people couldn't fight for themselves, and there wasn't any thought of advancing them either; it served no purpose. When Omer wasn't any older than fifteen, he was saying, "I'm going to have a white collar some day."

OMER: Fifty years ago, when I worked in the mills, it was to try out new things more than anything else. Weaving cotton

° French slang which means "to lick" or "butter up."

was just a small part of it. We'd try to develop new machines, to make more money. We spent years on the tying-over machine, for instance.

MARIE: Oh, Amoskeag worked hard to improve things. And they knew Omer was good at his work. It interested him. For months at a time he'd be working on his little toys [his inventions].

OMER: You have to like to do something before you can do it well. Say you get to college, get interested in something, and decide to learn it. So you end up by becoming a professor. It has to be in you to do something well. You have to love it.

MARIE: You have to want it. Amoskeag was serious about perfection. It had men to see to the bottom of things.

I didn't work for Omer a long time. I didn't like working for him. I was afraid. We knew the people in our room too well. There were some who said, "Why don't you ask to go upstairs with Omer?" But I was afraid there would be conflict. They'd say that I get sugar and the others get dirt. I didn't want that; I'd rather leave instead. There were misunderstandings; people were saying that someone was treated better than the others because the boss was a great friend. But Omer was not against it that I worked. He was proud of me. It was a joy, it was a joy to go to work.

OMER: Well, she loved it so much. Sometimes I'd say, "You can stay home." She'd go to work anyway, but we had no quarrels, nothing.

MARIE: Well, we weren't able to make it with one salary. Never on your life would we make it. That strike broke out [in 1922] because we wanted more money, and it was a mess. Of course, maybe the people were asking for too much, but I don't think so, because we worked almost like slaves.

When Amoskeag closed, I went back to work as a nurse's aide. I said to myself, "Was I ever awful for working in the mills so long and loving it, being neat like we are here!" But when I got my first paycheck, I found that I got from the hospital for one week what I would get in the Amoskeag in one day. I said to the nun, "I'll bring you one of my paycheck stubs to show you that what you're giving me for one week, I was making in one day." She didn't believe it. She said, "No wonder they closed their doors."

OMER: They had to close because of the strikes. The strikes that we had there, it cost them, oh, I don't know how many millions. Some of them would pass by and cut all the warps, and to fix them it cost $500. They'd throw bobbins on the floor and step on them and crush them. That bobbin cost 15¢. It would be full of yarn, and they'd twist it and take it apart and throw it on the floor.* That's why they went bust. No one worked for the Company after that. We all worked, but just in appearance. Apart from that, they didn't work for the Company. They worked against it.

MARIE: You know, there are malicious hands today, and there were some in former times. Mean people. It's mean to do things like that. Why cut a warp the whole length there? It was a great loss. Why do that? It's not necessary.

OMER: Of course not, but they held a grudge against the whole Company. They ruined everything. Everything! They broke everything. They found pieces of iron in the canal. Everything was broken. It would have been a loss again of a couple of hundred thousand dollars to repair it all. To have that cleaned up and start it up again, it cost too much, so they sold out.

---

* He is probably referring more to the strikes of the 1930s than to the strike of 1922. The strikes during the thirties were marked by more vandalism than the earlier strike.

Part Three

The
Corporation

► Frederic C. (Buck) Dumaine, Jr.

Frederic C. Dumaine, Jr., son of F. C. Dumaine, is the only one of seven siblings who has carried on with the Amoskeag's business to the present. He is currently treasurer of the Amoskeag Company, a holding company that was established in 1925 with the surplus capital his father had transferred from the Amoskeag Manufacturing Company during the 1925 reorganization. Among other things, the Amoskeag Company owns the Bangor and Aroostook Railroad, and has a major interest in the Maine Central Railroad. They also have a controlling interest in Fieldcrest Mills, one of the seven largest textile companies today. F. C. Dumaine, Jr., purchased Fieldcrest from Marshall Field in 1953.

F. C. Dumaine was born in 1866 in Hadley, Massachusetts, of poor parents. His father, a broom maker, died while he was still a child. After rising from office boy in the Amoskeag's Boston office to treasurer of the corporation in twenty years, he remained in control of the holding company until his death, in 1951, at the age of eighty-five. Buck was appointed treasurer of the company in 1939.

Buck was born in 1902. Like his father, he started as an errand boy in the Amoskeag's Boston office in 1913. He was apprenticed in the Amoskeag Company, worked in the mills as a young boy, and was groomed by his father for the Amoskeag business.

The management, call it what you want, Dad headed it. The most important man was the agent, Herman Straw, and before him Zeke [Ezekiel] Straw, Senior, his father. Herman Straw used to go out in the mills every day and would see at least one employee, no matter how far away from the office. It was a ritual with him. He knew enough about spinning, for instance, that if there were too many ends down on a frame, if a loom was running a bad pattern or it wasn't right in some way, he'd knock off the frame or loom, and the weaver or spinner would thank him for stopping it in time.

Herman Straw was one of the most lovable men you'd ever meet. His son, Parker Straw, was very shy and didn't mix easily. He didn't come by it naturally the way his father did. It may be that his problems started with the union. The competitors in the South paid lower wages, and he faced one strike after another. But rapport is the key. When you have a man that has IT, it filters down when he talks to his superintendents in the manufacturing division, the finishing or the dyeing, or the millwrights. If you don't have that rapport with your men, then all those little irritations begin. People start maneuvering around politically—"How will it improve my position?"—that kind of thing. You'll see it in every company in the United States.

The dictionary doesn't describe what IT is, but in any case, Parker Straw didn't have it. He was born with a shyness that did not let him meet people easily. Parker had a harder job than Herman Straw, and he didn't have the confidence of the people. In my opinion, he was only half Herman Straw, just like I'm only half my father.

Herman Straw had IT. He was loved by everybody. They respected him for the way he lived. Even though he had his own driver and carriage, the Company drove him daily to his office in the mill. He'd say, "How do you do?" to everybody. He didn't have to deal with unions. He could go in and say, "Hello, Mary. How is your sick daughter?" Basically, the workers didn't have any grievances under Herman Straw.

At one time, the Amoskeag owned practically everything in town. If the Carpenters didn't own the land, the Amoskeag did. The churches and the YMCA received land from the Amoskeag free. All the parks were given to the town by the Amoskeag. They had sewing classes, cooking schools, gardens. Herman Straw was responsible; he started them all.

The corporation's top engineers and supervisors on the roof of a newly constructed mill, photographed in 1900

I remember when Horace Rivière* said they didn't need those sewing and cooking schools, because they could get all that in the public schools: "We don't need this and that. Put it in the pay envelope instead." That was one of the reasons for the strike. All the things that were done for the employees, they said the employees can do it for themselves. The mothers can teach the daughters to do the sewing and cooking; they don't need the Company to do it for them. These programs were started when they immigrated to this country. For Rivière it was a slogan, and I think the unions used local agents to incite the people: "You can get more if you give up those benefits."

* Horace Rivière came to Manchester in 1918 to organize workers for the U.T.W., and led the strike of 1922.

Originally, the workers did want the cooking school, and the other schools as well. They were not forced to go to them—they loved it! They loved working in the gardens the Company had laid out. They didn't have to do it. They were not told to go there and pull weeds. These plots of land were there, available to them. Some were right near the railroad station.

The cost of wages is a big cost of any product produced. Textile industry wages may run 35 percent of gross income today. The bigger you get, the more nonproductive the labor. The richer you get or the bigger the corporation, the more secretaries you build up. You run into union problems when the manufacturers take on too many nonproductive employees.

Unions are a good thing when management has become too absentee. I think I'm a little more modern than my dad about it. He would go down and talk to the card tenders himself, and it worked then. You can't run a mill that way today. My time is not limited to forty hours a week. I never considered the workers as masses. In 1911, the Company found out from Burns [Detective Agency] that the workers were not dissatisfied. Anyway, Dad heard it from Chief Healey,* you knew it from the Greeks, etc. Dad had a few informers out amongst these people all the time. They knew what was going on. The Catholic church did the same. You have so few Unitarians, you don't even know who they are any more. Anyway, these were all sources. You could tell by going into Varick's store, because a lot of his customers worked in the mills, or their relations did. Dad always had his ear to the ground.

In 1895, Dad worked in the mills and got to know the people around him; and he made a point of knowing all the important people in town: Tom Varick, Arthur Franks, Arthur Moreau, [Norwin] Bean, Arthur Heard (president of the Amoskeag National Bank). Moreau and Varick had stores, as did Franks. Of course, Dad also got to know the Harringtons and Frank P. Carpenter and his brother. As he grew in the Company, he made a point of keeping up close personal relations with all those people. And it was a good thing, because all

---

* Michael J. Healey, chief of police in Manchester, was, more than anyone else, responsible for controlling the picketing during the strike of 1922. Healey was well known in New Hampshire for keeping the IWW out of Manchester.

the leaders of the town knew what was going on in Manchester
—more than Parker Straw knew at the end.

My father was born in South Hadley [Massachusetts], but
his father and mother came from Quebec. In those days, they
ran over the border like everyone else. My father's mother was
married before, and I think she had children by her first husband. My grandfather's business was making brooms out of
broom straw. The Dumaine family all came from France originally. They were Huguenots.

Everyone who knew my father loved him. That's why he
was selected by T. J. Coolidge* and all the men to run the
Amoskeag Company way back in 1904. He was only twenty-
four when he got put in charge of the whole damn thing, so he
must have had something.

My grandfather died when my father was eleven years old,
and my father started working when he was only thirteen. He
used to do whatever he could to help his mother, who had no
source of income except taking in laundry from General Weld's
family and numerous other people around Dedham [Massachu-
setts]. Before that, my father got jobs in retail stores or picking
blueberries. He used to take a blind man to Boston, lead him
around the city, and bring him back home.

One day in 1880, while General Weld, who was one of the
biggest cotton shippers, was being driven home from the train,
his coachman turned and said, "There's Widow Dumaine's boy
running away." The General said, "Whoa!" got out of his
wagon, and spoke to the boy carrying a stick with a bandana
over his shoulder and a toothbrush inside. He said, "Where are
you going?" "I'm going to look for a job. Mother needs more
money." "I think I might be able to help you there," said the
General. So the boy got into the wagon. The driver drove them
back to Dad's mother's house; it was the house next to the one
my wife was brought up in, in Dedham. The General took the
boy in, told his mother what had happened, and said, "Now, I
think I know where I can get the boy a job." Soon thereafter,

---

* Thomas Jefferson Coolidge was the Amoskeag Manufacturing Company's
most prominent treasurer during the late nineteenth century. He served in
this capacity for a total of sixteen years in three different stints between
1876 and 1898. He continued as president of the board of directors until
1911. He was largely responsible for shaping the Amoskeag Company into
the giant it was to become in the twentieth century.

F. C. Dumaine [*right*] working in the mill as a young man learning
the business, ca. 1885

the General went in to see Mr. Coolidge and told him the story;
he knew that Coolidge was looking for an office boy. So
Coolidge called in his office head the name of Lucius Manlius
Sargent and said, "General Weld thinks he knows where you
can get a good boy who's looking for a job." So then Dad's first
job in the Amoskeag was as an office boy.

In those days, the office boy used to have to get in about
daylight and start coal fires—the only heat they had. Of

course, my dad swept out and did everything else that an office boy did in the old days. If someone wanted a pitcher of water, he went to the well and got the water.* He picked up the mail and learned his way around Boston by delivering all these handwritten orders for cotton and wool and dyestuffs and nuts and bolts and pipe and wood—whatever they bought. They bought everything because they manufactured about everything in Manchester. The Company started a machine shop. They tried to buy everything by the carload. They made their own soap. They also had to buy 150,000 tons of coal a year.

How did Dad rise? Hard work, and I suppose he was watching Mr. Coolidge and all the buyers. He could even sample cotton.** He had a hunch as to how cotton markets were made, and he knew when to buy and when not to buy. He had a natural IT about buying. He had hunches. He learned every branch of the operation from Mr. Coolidge, from the management point of view. He went to night school, which taught him some mathematics. It wasn't Harvard, but you learned reading and writing and arithmetic. He used to do it while living in Boston and going home on weekends to Dedham.

He was a natural at finding out what others were doing and how they did it. He was a natural when it came to figuring. He was a natural on the feeling of markets. And Coolidge approved of his integrity, the way he worked, and how he treated his mother. When Coolidge's son died, Coolidge, Sr., left his estate in Dad's hands as executor and trustee to manage the Coolidge trust, which had been formed to provide for the Coolidge children. Dad fought all his life to improve the capital of that trust.

I knew T. Jefferson Coolidge. Everybody called him Grandpa. He was not our grandpa, but he loved being called Grandpa. He was straight as an arrow, six-foot-odd, goatee, mustache. I was pretty young when he died, but I remember when he opened the Coolidge Mill. I was with Dad, and we took Mr. Coolidge up in an elevator to the roof of the mill overlooking the Merrimack River. This mill had a hundred thousand

---

* This is said as an expression of emphasis. He does not mean literally that his father went to a well.

** "Sampling cotton" means grading it according to quality.

T. Jefferson Coolidge, ca. 1890

spindles on the fifth floor to manufacture fine goods. (Some people in the South thought ten thousand spindles was a big mill!) They produced yarns up to a hundred count instead of the usual average coarse count to make denims, ticking, and things of that sort.* The spindles were small, but they were

---

* "Counts of yarn" indicates the thickness of the yarn. The higher the number, the finer the yarn.

high-speed. [That particular spinning room survived until 1975 and was used by the Chicopee Manufacturing Company. It was broken up after the shutdown of the Chicopee.]

Coolidge and Dad were completely different, in my opinion. Coolidge was one of the most respected men you ever met anywhere, and his wife was a most helpful person. Dad was a poor boy who came along and admired his boss so much he wouldn't tear up a one-cent stamp in case it might displease Mr. Coolidge. They had a natural flair, both of them. As Dad grew older, he grew in stature, and Coolidge trusted him more and more. There were a lot of instances where Dad did things for Mr. Coolidge. In the Spanish-American War, Mr. Coolidge came to him one day and said, "The Spanish fleet is off the coast, and here's the key to my box in the Merchants National Bank. You take the securities and hide them. I don't want to know where they are." Dad went down to the street corner, and he asked an Irish policeman friend if he could get off the next day. The fellow said sure. They met in front of the bank in the morning. Dad had a steamer trunk. They filled that trunk full of stocks and bonds. Dad made a list of them and put it in his pocket, got on a train and went to Manchester, New Hampshire, and hired a safe-deposit box in Dad's name. When the war was over—and, of course, we weren't invaded—he brought them back and said to Mr. Coolidge, "Now, you're coming with me." And as he put them back into the box at the Merchants National Bank [Coolidge was director], he made Coolidge count every damn one of them [laughs]. And hell, it was millions of dollars—I don't know, one, two, three million, maybe. This was the beginning of his complete, absolute trust in Dad's integrity.

Dad learned to hate a cheat. Never showed it, like Coolidge. He hated anybody that cheated or stole or was slovenly on the job, even in their attire. Dad believed you got the most for your money when you sold an honest product under an honest label and lived up to the standards of its construction. It was easy to cut out one or two threads, thereby making more money; it was done every day by others. It's easy to take dress goods, and wet them out to stretch them, adding yardage but lightening the weight. Amoskeag was very strict on standards

—color, weight, width, finish—every one of those labels was a standard.

When the Coolidge mill was built to manufacture fine goods, most types were made with combed yarns up as high as a hundred count, such as handkerchief cloth. They turned the print works into a worsted mill. They built a lot of machinery for their own use. They enlarged their water power and converted a coal-burning plant to oil. From 1918 to 1920, they built the present dam, the third to be built at the Manchester site.

Prior to Parker Straw, they had good labor relations. From time to time they had built new tenements, changing them to central heating in Dad's time. He went to work in the mill in 1880. I believe he roomed in one of the tenements. In 1918 I ate at one of the tenement dining rooms. They had better food than you got at the YMCA. Dad also continued the gardens and Christmas parties for the employees. In 1922 the big strike started, and still he continued them. The policy of taking care of the people even during the strike was well done. I got to know Horace Rivière and Frank Gorman pretty well. Samuel Gompers* was Dad's friend. Herman Straw knew most of those employees, especially the foremen and the superintendents, because he worked with them closely. Anybody could walk into his office. This changed with Parker Straw; and then when the recession hit after the First World War, labor was costly compared to the South. The South was running three shifts of eight hours or two shifts of ten hours, and yet New England stayed on a one-shift basis. I don't know when it started, but I think Henry Rauch started operating on two shifts. There was no reason why we should expand. Just run more time.

So many things fed into the decisions that were made. I was there a long time. Dad took me everywhere when I was out of school. He put me to work in the treasurer's office in the mill in 1914.

Parker Straw thought Dad was going to put me in his job. Dad had no intention of ever putting me in the job, but Straw

---

* Samuel Gompers was the founder and president of the American Federation of Labor, with which the United Textile Workers Union was affiliated.

F. C. Dumaine as depicted in a newspaper clipping in 1930

left.* So they sent Henry Rauch up. He knew how to figure, and he got along fine with [Michael] Ahern,** in the employment office. I don't think there was any major change except being competitive. Henry Rauch let a lot of the top fellows go because the Company had had too much overhead—what we call nonproductive overhead. They didn't let the weavers go, they didn't take it out of labor; they took it out where it counted.

Henry Rauch came right out of Bentley College and went into Dad's office, just as Dad went into Mr. Coolidge's office. He had a bull-in-a-china-shop's job to do, and only a few befriended him. He went in there to do a job that had to be done. He had already learned it all at the Hamilton Mill in Lowell. He went to Lowell Textile School nights. I don't know any of the leaders in Manchester who went to Lowell Textile School! The trouble was that Henry Rauch knew too much.

A lot of people in Manchester were very bitter about Henry Rauch. When you let someone go who's been there ten, fifteen, twenty years, and with the Depression coming in. . . . Henry Rauch went up there I think in 1929. Then the crash came. Depression in the textile industry came before the crash of 1929. Mr. Straw wasn't able to be competitive. He thought Dad was pushing him too hard to cut costs. He couldn't let the people go that had been there for years and associated with him and his family. When Henry Rauch went up there, that was his job. How do you keep the mills running and compete with the South? It was just as cold as that.

When I heard that Parker Straw thought I was going to be given the job at the mill, I said, "I'm not any more fit for it than you." I happened to be in the office when he resigned; I was the only one left after a board meeting. He came out; I can see him now. He walked the whole length of the office where I was finishing up the mail. Instead of going out the door, he came over and shook hands and said, "Good luck to you. Congratulations." Then he turned on his heel and walked out. Later I

* Parker Straw may have been asked to resign.

** Michael Ahern was clerk in the Amoskeag's employment office. He was also active in city politics.

Buck Dumaine, 1976

asked Dad, "What'd he resign for?" Dad said, "Well, he wouldn't meet competition, he wouldn't start cutting down his organization." Parker Straw resigned because he couldn't do what had to be done.*

* With Parker Straw's resignation, the three-generation-long tie between the Straw family and the Amoskeag Manufacturing Company was broken. The remarkable continuity in the top management of this company was undoubtedly important in defining its corporate character. The departure of Parker Straw from the Manchester operation had a more profound effect on the Company than is apparent from Buck Dumaine's interview.

▶ Dudley Dumaine

Dudley Dumaine, son of Frederic C. Dumaine, Jr., was born in 1933. He was educated at Brown University, then started work as a trainee with the Worcester Bus Company and the Springfield Street Railway Company, both of which were owned by the Amoskeag Company. After two years in the military, Dudley studied at the Boston University Business School, from 1956–1960. He then returned to the Amoskeag Company as his father's assistant. He is currently chief executive officer of the Amoskeag Company in Boston.

When I was a young boy and I heard this fellow [his grandfather, F. C. Dumaine] was coming to the house, I'd run and hide. I'd run to the woods until he went home. He was very rough appearing to someone like me, eight or nine years old.

One time, when I was sixteen, I decided that I was going to stop in and see the old man, you know, feeling my oats. When I got to the place, I went to the door and the servant said, "What can I do for you?" I said, "I came to see my grandfather." He said, "Do you have an appointment?" I said, "No." He started to close the door, but I ducked underneath his arm. I knew my grandfather lived on the main floor in the back. He was in bed most of the time. He had his stocking hat on; and the story goes that he wouldn't eat much, but he smoked cigars, drank o. j., and had his whiskey because he hated the inflated prices of food.

I'd say he was eighty-three or eighty-four years old. I stood in the open door of his room, and he said, "Who the hell are you?" I knew that he knew who I was just as well as I did, but I told him anyway. Then he asked, "Where do you work?" I said that I went to school. "What are you going to do when you get through school?" I said, "Well, I guess I'll go to college." He said, "If you got IT, you don't need no college; if you ain't got IT, no college in the country is going to help you any." This was probably the only time in my life when I actually spoke to F. C. D., Senior. Despite that, I held him in awe and respect, as did everyone else.

As to my learning the family business, it was strictly what the army called O. J. T. [on-the-job training]. You either reacted to it or you didn't. My guess, from what I've observed, is that Buck [F. C. Dumaine, Jr.] in his generation reacted to it and the others [in the family] didn't.

Buck has always, in my view, fantasized about his dad. Buck would have jumped off the Brooklyn Bridge without any questions asked if my grandfather told him to jump, whether or not it was safe to do so. I can remember, soon after my grandfather died, Buck's decisions were always stated to be what his father would have done. He always came out with those utterances, like, "If my father did it this way, I'm going to do it this way." It became very obvious over the years that his father would not have done things the way Dad thought he would. It took about five years before he stopped making such statements.

I know inside that my grandfather had tremendous loyalty and respect for families who had inherited wealth. Things have changed since his time. I happen to have a certain disdain for that, the way most of my generation who have inherited wealth act.

Grandmother was a Thomas, a direct descendant of Isaiah Thomas, the one who published *The Spy* during the Revolutionary War. His portrait is out in the dining room, as a matter of fact. A very exact copy of the one in The Boston Scottish Rite Masonic Hall. He was the grand master of Masons in Massachusetts, along with Paul Revere and other historically known men of that time. Grandmother was highly connected in that way, and Grandfather was not. When he married her, he

F. C. Dumaine in front of his home in Groton, Massachusetts

was already on the way up. You didn't go up that ladder easily, without a family background, unless you had something over and above what most people had. There's no question, he was a genius in his own way. By the time he died, there were just two or three of his breed left. He controlled manufacturing plants and decision-making positions—but he didn't own what he controlled.

My grandfather was not responsible for the poor labor relations in Manchester. In 1920, when he was about fifty-five years old, the treasurer's office was in Boston; and the manufacturing area, which was in Manchester, was run by local people. William Spencer told me about the time he had to go up and report to the old man in Concord. Most people wouldn't go to the old man to tell him the truth. They would avoid telling him anything. I can well understand that. But Spencer had to tell him about the animosity the people of Manchester felt for him, and the man stood there and cried. Under certain circumstances, when the Company was hard-pressed, he reacted like that. When he got his composure back, he became very hard-nosed. He didn't show his emotions to the outside world—never a smile or frown. He did not express himself facilely, either pleasure or displeasure. In this particular situation, he was a very sensitive guy. There was a social taboo about showing emotions. Executives were literally trained not to show feelings.

I think that F. C. was so much over and above his peers, at all stages, that he really was a one-man show. He never put anything in writing unless he absolutely had to. His letters are full of code words, and his notes and files are the same way. His diary—really it was a notebook of phone conversations, and records of meetings held, but nothing about the meetings was said in them. *He* knew what was said in them. All he needed was a code word. Consequently, a great deal of back-up information on what he did and didn't do is really left to oral history. I wish Nixon had done that.

F. C. made his own opportunities. In his later years, he showed his silence and his strength. He didn't have to have thirty or forty men around him doing studies and creating statistics; he knew the answers. He once said that if he wanted to get answers from someone he didn't know, he would ask him six or seven questions on things he did know before he bothered to ask for information he didn't have. Those who worked with him just waited for the answers to come out of him. He knew what had to be done; he had all the answers.

► *Harold E. Melzar*

Eighty-nine-year-old Harold E. Melzar worked for the Amoskeag Manufacturing Company from 1915–1976. During his employ, he served as F. C. Dumaine's clerk as well as an Amoskeag clerk.

Harold also served as a trustee of the Amoskeag Company between 1956 and 1971, and as a trustee of the Dumaine trust over a forty-year period.

I never worked for anyone else except Mr. Dumaine. From the time I went to work in 1905 till I retired, Mr. Dumaine always considered that I was working for him, as my non-Amoskeag jobs were with Dumaine affiliates. My connection with the Amoskeag was as an office manager and as clerk of the trustees. The first job that I had was to prepare the annual report. I knew nothing about cotton mills, having been, up to that time, in the Old Colony Trust Company. That was my introduction. I prepared the annual report for the year ending in November 1915. I was twenty-seven years old. I would have been called the office manager in any other place, but we never had any titles in Amoskeag.

Mr. Dumaine ran the business. He was the manufacturer, the sales agent, and the mill operator, so to speak, because he knew what each one of these men was supposed to do. He talked to the mill every day, to Mr. H. F. Straw, and then he talked to New York, to Mr. D. W. Jarvis, the selling agent. All the orders and requisitions came through him.

It was the largest cotton mill in the world under one management, one roof; and Mr. Dumaine was the whole operation.
He had a board of directors, very powerful men like George
Wigglesworth, Arthur Parson, Charles F. Adams—men of very
high standards. He called them together occasionally and reported what the company was doing. Mr. Dumaine followed
everything. He remembered everything, too. He had the most
wonderful memory; and if you made a mistake, he'd remind
you of it from time to time. But he was good-natured. If he
didn't like you, he'd just ignore you.

T. Jefferson Coolidge was an aristocrat of aristocrats. He
didn't know the common people. Mr. Coolidge came to the
Company originally as the director; he wasn't a cotton manufacturer like Patrick T. Jackson.° He is supposed to have selected Mr. Dumaine to run the mill. He took Mr. Dumaine
under his wing just the same as you would take anybody and
push them along. When, later, Dumaine was on the board, a lot
of the other fellows [board members] weren't noted especially
for their abilities. Dumaine knew everything. All his information was contained in a little looseleaf booklet, about the size of
your hand: costs of all the cloths, cost of supplies. I don't know
what else he had in it.

I was with him fifty-odd years, and he was just polite. As
far as I know, he would never do a dishonest thing. The only
time I heard he was ever in politics was when they [re]built
the Concord Bridge—the Minuteman Bridge. After it was
done, someone accused him of mishandling funds or something
of that sort, and he got so mad that he never again attempted
any office of any kind.

Mr. Dumaine went to Manchester two or three times a
week. Herman Straw and Mr. Dumaine got along fine, and the
mill ran like a charm. Parker Straw didn't have the ability of
his father. He was nice enough, personally, but he was a long
way from H. F.

There's no question about control. Herman Straw ran the
mill, but he was just a hired man, the agent, like his father,
Ezekiel Straw. But Mr. Dumaine had his finger in everything

° Patrick Tracy Jackson was a partner of Nathan Appleton, and as a member of the Boston Associates, he was one of the founders of Lowell, Massachusetts.

Amoskeag officials at the Coolidge Mill construction site, 1909.
Herman Straw is third from the left, and William Parker Straw is
second from the right.

that went on. He bought the cotton, the coal, and the other
supplies. Nothing anywhere else was as near a one-man operation as this. The agent directed things, kept things running, but
Mr. Dumaine was the motivating spirit. He was the one that
formulated the policies. They built a new block of tenements
up there because Mr. Straw recommended it; but in any event,
Mr. Dumaine had to approve it. The last mill that they built
was the Coolidge Mill, and that cost $4 million, all paid for out
of earnings.

The tenements were like ... I wouldn't call them fringe benefits, but the rent was very cheap. They had a free dental clinic, free nursing, a free recreation department. Everything was free, all fringe benefits. Dumaine wanted it that way. Nobody forced him to do any of these things; you couldn't force him. He did it because he wanted it that way. The Amoskeag Textile Club might well have been Mr. Straw's original idea, but Mr. Dumaine agreed with it and went along with it. I don't think Mr. Dumaine ever got down the line, as far as formulating school dances and things like that. There, Mr. H. F. Straw was the motivating spirit. He was a governor of the state of New Hampshire.* W. P. Straw was a different breed altogether. But H. F. was in a class by himself. Of course, he had his pets up there, his favorites. Up there, people didn't come and go. They stayed on. They never had any reason to be disgruntled; everything was done for them.

Mr. Dumaine did what he thought was right, and that was it. He selected his selling agents in New York. He oversaw the building of the new dam. He was right on the spot when they had the flood, took charge of the operation, even at his time of life. They had a strike up there that lasted nine months; but when they came back, he didn't make any concessions.

During the strike some stayed. He kept the mill open for anybody who wanted to work.** The most people that they had at any one time was seventeen thousand. During the strike, there was a few around just to keep up the premises. Then they commenced to drift back, and no violence. They really had no complaint about wages, when you figure they had all these fringe benefits.

The Amoskeag owned all the houses. They had mansions for all the officers; they even owned Straw's house. They owned a great deal of real estate. As a matter of fact, they were selling lots all the time. They bought a great deal of land way back in the 1840s and '50s.

Mr. Dumaine got along well with the stockholders because they were getting the dividends. For years, at the annual meet-

---

* Actually, it was Herman's father Ezekiel who became governor of New Hampshire.
** Actually, all the mills closed down until June 1922, when the Coolidge Mill was first reopened, and gradually other mills followed.

ing, they served a dinner in Manchester, and everybody came.
They had a thousand people come to that stockholders' meeting, because they gave a free meal. It was held right in one of
the mill buildings.

In 1905, I think, he put through the consolidation of three
mills—the Amoskeag, the Manchester Mills, and the Amory
Manufacturing Company. They all had the same manager and
they all had the same yard, so we just put them together. They
figured out the share value of the stock in Manchester to offer
it to anyone that wanted it, and they all ran as one company
after that.

When times began to go bad, what he did was set up the
mill and give it $5 million worth of capital and all the operat-
ing machinery. The surplus, which I think was $17 million, he
kept in the holding company. He was criticized for not spend-
ing that $17 million surplus until it ran out, but of course that
was silly. He gave the manufacturing operations to the new
company and $5 million of working capital, and said go to it.
Of course, he was also manager, but he couldn't go against the
times. Styles changed, and the machinery at the gingham mill
wasn't adapted to making cloth for these new styles. Finally
they gave up the mills in 1936, but nobody lost any money
when they liquidated. Nobody ever lost a penny on the bonds,
and the stock liquidated for $4.00 and a fraction, and that $17
million surplus is still in Amoskeag.

All his children are living on the income of Mr. Dumaine's
trust; but the Dumaine children never had much to do with the
old man. As a matter of fact, they almost ignored him during
his lifetime. Of course, he had a different way of bringing up a
family. He was a hard man, I suppose. I don't know. I never
had any trouble with him. I know that whenever he made any
pronouncement, he expected to be obeyed; that's all.

► William McElroy

William McElroy's Uncle Sam came to Manchester from Ireland in 1858, and the rest of the family followed later. William's father worked in the Amoskeag spinning room before going into business for himself. William was born in 1890. He went away to college and worked in Pittsfield, Massachusetts, before returning to Manchester and getting a job in the Amoskeag payroll department in 1921. He remained there for three years.

William considered himself an "Amoskeag Man"; and after the shutdown of the mills, he became a director of the Amoskeag Industries, a civic organization founded to attract new businesses to Manchester, which would settle in the abandoned Amoskeag millyard. He remained in that position almost until his death. He also came to be considered one of the principal authorities on the history of the Amoskeag. Among his many civic accomplishments were serving as president of both the Manchester Rotary Club and the Manchester Chamber of Commerce. He died in 1975.

My father came here in 1863, when the Civil War was going full blast. He worked in the spinning department, where he chased the bobbins back and forth as they filled up.* If a family decided to come to Manchester or to anywhere in New England, they would send the oldest member over to get set-

---

* I.e., removed the bobbins as they filled. On some spinning frames, the bobbins would fill in a random order, requiring the spinner to go back and forth to replace them.

tled, to find work and a place where they could live; then he'd send for the rest of the family. In my case, my Uncle Sam came over in 1858, got a job, and sent for the rest of the family. There were two brothers, five or six girls, and the mother. Their father had died. It took several months in those days; and by the time they got here, my Uncle Sam was in the Union Army fighting down South, so they had to start from scratch. My father, who at that time was twelve, had to start working in the mills to keep them together. The older sisters worked there, too, and gradually so did the others.

My father worked in the mill for ten years. Then he decided to go on and do more than that, and he went to business college. He was a self-educated man. Though I went to college, I think that he had a better education than I had because he *had* to do it. My mother worked in the Amoskeag for a while. Her family was English, and they settled in Lawrence [Massachusetts], where she was born. They came up here because her father was in the printing department—printing cotton goods, ginghams, and various fabrics.

Many of the second- or third-generation immigrants didn't want to finish school. Their ambition was "to get a paper," as they called it. That was a slip showing they'd passed the sixth grade or fifth grade or whatever. Then they could go down to the employment department and get a job. The teacher was glad to give them a paper, to get rid of them; but their ambition was to get in the mills. There was a certain prestige in working for the mills at that time. I had many friends who worked in the mills. Some of them went to school with me, through grade school and then to high school.

After I graduated from college, I worked for eleven years in Pittsfield, Massachusetts, at the writing-paper company. The first depression caught me in 1921, after the First World War. When the paper mills closed down, I came home; and after hanging around a few weeks, I went to see Bill Swallow, who was the employment manager of the mills. I said, "I'd like a job, and I don't want to loaf." He said, "What do you want to do?" and I said, "Well, whatever you got." So he gave me a job in the paymaster's office. Of course, I had a little more education than many people that applied there.

I was in the paymaster's office for three years, before and

The counting rooms and the agent's office (in rear), ca. 1900

after the strike. We had eighteen payrolls we put up at the bank every week, all in cash. Most of the people who worked in the mill couldn't talk English, but they knew our coinage. They could tell the difference between a silver dollar and a quarter or whatever they had. Before we arrived at a department, the overseer or the second hand would pass out brass tags to each employee according to his number. They'd file past, and the employee would hand his tag to the overseer or second hand, and he would call out the number; I would look at it at the same time and hand out the envelope. In a room with six or eight hundred looms going, you'd have to listen awfully hard to get the right number.

I would say that when I first worked there, in the twenties, if they got $25.00 or $30.00 a week, they were doing very well. The average employee would have what they called a high pay and a low pay on alternate weeks, because he was paid by so many yards of cloth. He was paid so much a piece. If they stopped the loom as of, say, noon on Friday, that ended the week. There might be a half a piece, seventy-five yards or so, that wouldn't be counted in on that week; it would be counted in on the next. So one week the employee might get $18.00 and the next week $17.50. They called it the big week and the small week. Of course, it varied because one fellow's loom would go faster than the others. When I was there, they each looked after six looms.

With twenty thousand people, there were bound to be some who weren't around on payday. If an employee didn't get his money, he could come in some time later and hand in his brass check or a slip that the overseer had given him and get the pay that was owed to him. There was never a question because they had every payroll sheet marked in the vault. You could look it right up and find the year and the date. If it hadn't been paid, there was a circle around it.

One day I was in the office and a girl came to my window. She handed me a slip, and I looked at the date on it—it was twenty years old! I said, "Would you mind telling me where you've been for the last twenty years?" "Well," she said, "we moved to Nashua, and I meant to bring this up the next time I came to Manchester, but this is the first time I've been up. I wonder if it's any good?" I said, "It's as good as gold. I'll just have to go downstairs and verify it." I called Mr. Caswell, the paymaster, over, and said, "Fred, look at this." H. F. Straw was in his office at that time. "Don't you think you ought to show that to him and find out if it's all right to pay?" So he went in, and H. F. Straw looked at it and said, "My Jesus, where's she been all this time?" I told him what she told me. So he said, "You take this slip and make out two checks. One for the full amount of this slip, and the other for the interest she would have had if she'd had it in the bank." In those days, they were paying 5 percent or 6 percent in the banks, I've forgotten, but that check was bigger than her paycheck.

H. F. Straw said, "Bring her here. I'd like to shake her hand." I handed him the two checks, and H. F. looked at her and said, "Madam, that money was safer for you than if you'd put it in the bank. You certainly earned it, and you're entitled to it," and he gave her the payroll check first. Then he said, "Now, if you'd put that in the bank, it would have earned so much, though I doubt if you would have put it in the bank. But if you had, then here's a check for the interest you would have earned." After she went out of there, he laughed, and of course she wasn't crying either. I think there was something like $17.00 or $18.00 she'd made over all that time, at 6 percent for over twenty years.

But H. F. Straw was always doing things like that. There was something about him that made you feel you should call him "Mister." The workers had more respect for him than they did for Parker Straw. They felt the orders were coming from Boston, and there was nothing Straw could do but carry them out.

▶ *Arthur Morrill*

We first met Arthur Morrill at the Amoskeag exhibit. He arrived on the opening Sunday afternoon, dressed in a dark suit made of Amoskeag worsted, and he brought with him examples of "kiss of death shuttles"* and Amoskeag bobbins. Blocking the traffic flow in the aisles, he gave a demonstration of the spinning process, very much in the style of the guided tours he used to run in the Amoskeag when he was still a messenger boy. We interviewed him first at the exhibit and subsequently at his daughter's home in a small town south of Manchester.

Arthur was born in 1891 in North Weare, New Hampshire, to an old Yankee family. During most of his married life, he lived on a farm on the outskirts of Manchester, where one of his daughters still lives. Despite the fact that he was fired from the Amoskeag, he still thinks of himself as an "Amoskeag Man." He knew the Amoskeag from the vantage point of the sales office and therefore had greater contact with management than most Amoskeag workers. He is very proud of his memory of the Amoskeag and says he remembers enough to write a book himself. Arthur was known in the Amoskeag as the "jovial clerk" and was nicknamed Cappy. The Amoskeag Bulletin *frequently published anecdotes about him.*

---

* These were shuttles used in the nineteenth century which required that the worker suck the cotton thread through the eye of the shuttle, an activity that inevitably led to respiratory disease.

Old man Dumaine himself started to learn the textile business in the same mill—in the same room—as I did! Old man Dumaine, the treasurer of the Amoskeag! I remember when, as treasurer, he used to be around the mills. He used to come up on a Tuesday and talk to the agent. Sometimes you could hear his voice upstairs. After he'd talked business with the management, two or three of them used to take the Company taxi to the cloth room and go over the new samples of cloth that were coming along, and he used to make suggestions. He'd say, "Throw that out. I'm not interested. Throw that thing out. I don't want to put that thing on the market." Then he was always interested to know how the Amoskeag Company was doing on the stock market in New York.

I knew Dumaine personally for years. He used to come up and talk to me every Tuesday. He would come up to the sales department and ask me the composition of different types of yarn. He had a notebook, and he wanted to know what this was and that was. I would tell him, and we'd talk for a while. He was the "boss man," as they called him.

I don't think Dumaine was interested in the workers, but there were some fellows around there that were his pets, you might say, like one foreman over there in the cloth room that really knew his business. He was indispensable. When the Amoskeag used to have sporting events over in the textile field, shooting and such things, Dumaine used to go to them. He was also crazy about English setters. I don't know how many dogs he had, but the old gent used to spend his summer vacations way up in the state of Maine, on the lakes. He was a great trout fisherman.

I met him one time in Boston. He went up to a news agent while he was waiting for his train. I saw this man buy a newspaper, and I said to myself, "Old man Dumaine—I'm going to go up and say hello to him." So I went up, and I said, "Aren't you Mr. Dumaine, that I used to work for up in the Amoskeag?" "You bet your sweet life I am. Hello, Cappy." Jesus, he was tickled to death to see me.

My father was on the Boston and Maine Railroad. He was a brakeman on a freight train between Manchester and Portsmouth for a good many years. He came from North Weare, New Hampshire. My people had been there since just before 1800,

Arthur Morrill as a messenger boy

for about five generations. I think Abraham was the first one in the family in North Weare; he came there from Amesbury, Massachusetts, in the 1760s.

I started working in the Amoskeag in 1906, and I never graduated from high school. I was fourteen. I don't know to this day why I ever quit grammar school and went to work in a stinking cotton mill. I can't figure it out. The money you got wasn't anything, and you had to go to work at seven o'clock in the morning and work till five or six o'clock at night. You had to do it till one o'clock on Saturday [laughs]. That's what you call child labor, all right. Don't you think it wasn't! There were little French kids working there that never saw the inside of a school.

I guess my stepmother had something to do with my quitting school. I don't think my father did. I lost my mother when I was three years old; and if she had lived, I'd never have seen a cotton mill, I'll tell you right now. The last year that I went to grammar school, one day the principal came in and said, "That Arthur Morrill up there in that back seat—if I had money enough, I'd send him to college." So I don't know why I ever stayed in that corporation, but I didn't stay put. I never was what you call a mill operator; I didn't operate a loom or a spinning frame. I always had something to do with the management of the corporation, all the way through. I was official yarn tester, or making up tickets for the warpers or the dressers or the drawing-in girls. The more you knew about the business, the better.

I was with Mike Ahern for about eleven years, right in the same [employment] office. Joe Debski was the Polish interpreter; if a Pole ever came up to the window, Joe went up and talked with him. Joe first worked with me delivering mail in the Amoskeag; we used to deliver mail to each overseer four times a day. We had six or eight or ten messenger boys to do it. All the mail that went to the different offices was handled through the employment department. Joe was a messenger boy. His brother worked in the cloth room. In those days, anybody who worked in the Amoskeag was looked on as someone who couldn't get a job anywhere else.

I was in the sales end of the Amoskeag. That isn't management, but I was a salaried man, and I considered I was part of the main office. After twenty-three years, I was the head of the local sales department. Anything sold in the city of Manchester, I handled it. I had about six people working under me. I used to speak to the agent in the morning, and occasionally I used to have to deliver letters to him.

There wasn't anything up-to-date in that corporation. Today they have a fellow sitting over here and he's general superintendent of transportation, and the fellow over there is general manager of such-and-such, and that fellow's so-and-so. They didn't have any of that in those days. It was an old-time corporation. They had clerks handling cotton, they had clerks bringing in the samples of cotton, and they had clerks keeping track of everything connected with the cotton department. They didn't have any titles; they were just doing clerical jobs or bookkeeping jobs in what was known as the accounting department. All the reports on costs, spinning, weaving, dressing, finishing, would go to the Boston office; and the fifteen or twenty men down there would take care of it. They had a lot of jobs there, too, that didn't have any title. You simply looked after this or you looked after that. One side of the office was purchasing, the other side was sales.

The second year I was up there I sold $1,640,000 worth of by-products that the Company didn't want, including machinery and four-legged horses and wagons and barrels and shavings and all kinds of waste and all kinds of oils and all kinds of wool—everything you can think of, remnants and cloth and whatever.

Amoskeag had a reputation for buying materials about as cheap as anybody. If Amoskeag wanted to buy fifty carloads of cornstarch in a year's time, the purchasing department would put out about fifteen letters to the people who manufactured it. Some of them were up in Maine. They used to make the cornstarch out of potatoes, of course. As far as wool and cotton and coal go, I don't know if that same system was used. But Amoskeag used to buy the stuff at a pretty low price and beat out these people in the textile business down in Lowell and Lawrence. That was the one way they made money.

They also decided to make their own machinery; and they could do that because they had a machine shop that could handle castings, and they had the foundry. We had about sixty or sixty-five men working in the foundry all the time. The machines that the Amoskeag had been spinning cotton on for years and years and years were pretty well worn out, and they started to make their own machinery to replace them.

I was crown prince down at the Amoskeag. We had a textile school. I went down there three nights a week for four years, and I graduated and got a diploma, the whole works. It took in everything from a cotton field out in Kansas somewhere to the finished piece of cloth.

After World War I, I came home and went right back to my job for the Amoskeag. I got this job of taking people around.

Parker Straw, every time he had anybody come into the Amos-keag Savings Bank that wanted to go through the Amoskeag mills—because they were known the world around as the largest [textile] concern in the world—he used to telephone and say, "Get Cappy, I want to see him." So I'd go over, and he'd have a couple of bankers from South Carolina or somewhere else where cotton was grown. One time, they brought some customers in eight Pullman cars, sleepers, over from New York during the night to Manchester, and they backed these Pullman cars clear up into the millyard.

I still resent the way they threw me out of the corporation, and I don't care who knows it. Another fellow was to blame. One day, the efficiency people came over and said, "You fellows have got to work a month, but we're only going to pay you for three weeks." That was all right, but then the first time the payment came around, the efficiency manager's men all got a full month's pay and we got three weeks' pay. There was a fellow who worked in the purchasing department with me, and he went to the purchasing agent and told him the story. He went down and had it out with Meharg, the efficiency manager. I didn't do it; it was the other fellow, but I got thrown out.

When they fired me, they talked to me at about ten o'clock, and I walked out of the place and went to see Mr. Caswell, the paymaster. I told him, "Meharg sent Sammy down and he tells me that I'm through with the corporation." I said, "I've been around here too long to take anything from a runner boy from the Boston office. What's he got to do with me?" Mr. Caswell said, "Cappy, stand right still. You wait just a minute." He went in to see Parker Straw, and Straw said, "You wait for me at noontime, and we'll talk this thing over and find out what's the matter." Well, Straw didn't do anything about it. He said, "I'm liable to get it in two or three weeks, same as you. That's the way it's going around here. You know, they hired this fellow who knows nothing about manufacturing. I don't know what's going on." That was Henry Rauch. I understand that right after I got out of the Amoskeag, they went down to the Lowell Textile School and picked up a young fellow and put him in there in my place. But what did he know? He didn't know anything about the corporation. It wasn't more than six weeks afterwards that Straw himself was fired. I don't know what year it was.

I decided to go to Boston to see Mr. Dumaine. I went down there a couple of days after I was thrown out. I didn't see him, but I talked with some of the boys in the Boston office, and they were pretty mad. Well, I didn't bother enough. I didn't follow the thing through.

Mr. Rauch didn't know any more about textiles than he did about race horses. He was hired to absolutely put that company on the bum. That's the story that we got afterwards. He went to Parker Straw one day and said, "I want you to take all the men, all the overseers who are sixty or seventy years old, and I want you to fire every single one of them. We don't want them any more." They had sixty to seventy-five overseers in the corporation, men who knew their business, and they were old men. Straw said, "I certainly won't do that." So Rauch said, "You're out yourself, then." And he went out. That corporation had been run for years and years by the Straw family—they used to run everything!

I didn't care anything about Parker Straw, though. I had four little girls to take care of. It wasn't a very good deal after I'd been there twenty-three years.

I went to work for the biggest plumbing and heating concern in the world, the Crane Company of Chicago. I fit right into the picture, because I went in there and I said I had sold $1,640,000 worth of stuff in one year. And I thought I could sell something in the state of New Hampshire. They gave me a job in five minutes. I used to go back to the Amoskeag and see the purchasing agent. He used to give me orders.

My wife worked in the Amoskeag a couple of summer vacations. I got her a job in there as a bookkeeper in one of the offices. All my daughters went to college. They didn't go near that place.

► *Part Four* ◄

The
World of Work

Of all the occupations described in this book, there is hardly one which, in assembly-line manner, harnessed workers to machines, forcing them to carry out the same operation repeatedly and without interruption. In some jobs, the pace was more demanding than in others; but generally, a worker's task was more diversified than simply repeating one motion, and it usually involved an understanding of the overall process. In weaving, spinning, carding, and warping, individual workers controlled the machines they were operating. Their pace was not completely determined by the speed of the machines but by the number of machines they had to tend. If weavers were tending five or six looms that were all running well, they could afford to walk around and chat with each other. The water fountain and the washrooms often served as centers for congregating and socializing. Room girls were able to sit and read or to knit and crochet.

Flexibility in work routines encouraged sociability, increased the interdependence among workers, and made their jobs more pleasurable, which was precisely why so many workers remembered the times of the Amoskeag as a golden age. In spite of the difficulties they had experienced, in retrospect their pre-strike work pace in the Amoskeag contrasted favorably with the later years of speedup and loss of flexibility, both in the Amoskeag and in the smaller textile mills in which many worked after the shutdown.

The majority of textile jobs were on the unskilled or semi-

Girl working in spinning room, photographed by Lewis Hine during his visit to the Amoskeag in 1909

skilled level. Many of them were, therefore, interchangeable. For most workers, it was possible to learn such jobs in a relatively short time. A beginner could acquire the rudiments of spinning in about two or three weeks, though it took much longer before such a person could become an expert spinner. Most young girls and boys were first initiated into textile work as spinners. Because of the short learning period, it was possible for management to switch workers from one unskilled or semi-skilled job to another. Furthermore, because their investment in learning was not so great and because they hoped to increase their job opportunities, workers were able to frequently change from one job to another without a setback. If they were laid off or had to leave a job, they could return later to a similar one. The very size of the Amoskeag also gave the workers flexibility. Since there were a number of workrooms dedicated to each operation, a weaver or a spinner who was unsuccessful in one room could try another one. In general, though, most of the job changes which the workers experienced did not represent upward or downward mobility but rather a switch among several similar occupations.

The flexibility in the Amoskeag's work structure should not be taken to mean, however, that the workers had real control over their work lives. Whatever individual choices they exercised were contained within the tightly organized managerial system of the corporation, and they were well aware of the limits. Their ability to short-circuit the hiring route, to switch workrooms or tasks, to be rehired after dismissal, or to socialize during work merely made a twelve-hour day seem more bearable or, at times, even attractive. Very few actually crossed the boundaries of the clearly regulated and controlled factory world, for they knew that once they were blacklisted by the Amoskeag, they would lose their employability virtually anywhere in Manchester and in many other places in New England as well.

The Amoskeag was managed in a centralized fashion. There was a well-defined hierarchy of authority reaching from the agent down to the workers in the different departments. This hierarchy was not alien to the workers' own world, which accented patriarchal family traditions and, for most of them, the ladder of authority within the Catholic church. They understood what was expected of them and accepted the authority of the bosses.

Most of a worker's everyday dealings were with the second hands and the overseer. The second hand was the equivalent of a shift foreman today. He was directly in charge of all technical and personnel-related aspects of the operation; he assured a steady flow of raw materials, supervised the pace and quality of work, handled complaints or disciplinary problems as they arose, and maintained order. Next up the ladder was the overseer. While the second hand was in charge of part or all of only one workroom, the overseer managed and controlled an entire department. He planned the production and supplies for each workroom, hired and fired the help, and handled any complaints or disciplinary problems that were too difficult for the second hand.

The overseers were almost exclusively either native Americans or of English, Scottish, or Irish descent. Within the Amoskeag's policy of paternalism, they were expected to behave like benevolent despots, to provide personal examples to the workers, and to socialize them to industrial habits. Their autonomy in their own department, however, was limited. They were responsible to superintendents, and ultimately to the agent.

The superintendents were in charge of an entire operation, such as weaving, spinning, or dyeing. Being in managerial positions, they usually had less contact with workers than with overseers. From the workers' perspective, then, the second hands and the overseers were the "bosses." It rarely occurred to the workers to complain about either one to a superintendent or to the agent. Even after the union introduced a mechanism for formal grievances, very few workers actually resorted to it.

One of the foremost characteristics of the textile industry is its extensive employment of women. Women made up more than half of the Amoskeag's work force. A good number of the jobs within the textile mill, such as weaving, doffing, spinning, carding, and tying-over, were performed by men and women interchangeably. In most cases, no clear-cut division between male and female work according to specific skills had been established; however, heavier mechanical jobs, as well as all

Overseer and second hands, weave room, Jefferson Mill, ca. 1910

maintenance and machine-repair positions, were restricted to
men, as were the jobs involving the chemical processes of
bleaching and dyeing. Likewise, some semi-skilled jobs, such as
burling, were restricted primarily to young girls. This work
demanded precision, good eyesight, and supple fingers with
smooth skin—characteristics attributed mainly to women.
Loom fixing, the highest-skilled job that one could attain short
of a supervisory position, was exclusively male. The highest
supervisory position a woman could attain in the mill was that
of room girl. The room girl supervised the weaving and was

called upon whenever there was a stoppage in the loom caused by a break in the yarn or warp.

The textile industry thus afforded women special status as breadwinners. Rather than being restricted to housewifery or having to supplement their family incomes through domestic services or menial jobs such as laundry, women, by working in the mills, were able to engage in some of the same jobs as men for the same wages. They gained stature, both in the mills and at home, and enjoyed a sense of accomplishment and pride in their work. But they still had to carry both loads—their jobs in the mills and their domestic obligations.

Textile work was family work. From its introduction in the United States during the late eighteenth and (particularly) the early nineteenth centuries, the textile industry relied heavily upon the labor of women and children. The nineteenth-century tradition of recruiting entire families to work on textiles persisted in the Amoskeag into the twentieth century. Workers often tended to bring in members of their family or ethnic group to fill job openings in their workrooms. Even after the establishment of a centralized employment office, hiring through kin continued. This informal recruitment pattern had significant implications for the structure of work in the Amoskeag. It meant that the more experienced workers could place their own young or newly arrived relatives in the best workrooms, where the work was easier or where the overseers were known to be more lenient.

Most new workers learned their jobs from friends or relatives, and teaching was done rather informally. If a new employee did not know anyone, the "boss" would simply ask a more experienced worker to do the teaching. Friends and relatives would act as translators and would often protect the new arrival from abuse by bosses or fellow workers. Moreover, once one family member was established in a particular department, others would follow. For example, if one family member was a weaver, the others tended to flock to the weave room; if one was a spinner, others were likely to become spinners.

Amoskeag workers were experiencing, therefore, a close integration between the family and the factory. Husbands and wives, or brothers and sisters, often toiled in similar or related occupations. Most important, except for the mechanical departments and the dye houses, workrooms were not segregated by sex. Hence, members of the same family often worked together, carrying their friendships and family ties with them. It is therefore not surprising that many of the workers viewed the factory "like a family."

Child labor, initially one of the most characteristic features of the textile industry, still existed; but the children employed were not as young as those found in the mills in the early nineteenth century, because improvements in the machinery had ended their usefulness. Thus, it was rare to find children younger than twelve in the Amoskeag's workrooms. The New Hampshire child labor law, passed in 1905, established that children from age twelve on could work during school vacations; and by age fourteen, they could start to work full time. Many young workers falsified their age—some with their parents' approval, others without their consent—in order to be able to begin work earlier. Taking on their first full-time job was like an initiation into adulthood. By the time they began work, many of these children had already become socialized to the factory world. Just as a son in a middle-class family knew that he would enter the family business, children in Manchester could normally expect a future in the factory. In any event, there were few alternatives.

Despite its advantages, work in family units also had its built-in weaknesses. Having an entire family group work in the same place rendered all members vulnerable to the changing conditions of the factory. It meant that an entire family would simultaneously feel the effects of wage reductions, layoffs, unemployment, strikes, and the shutdown.

By its very nature, textile work fostered interdependence and sociability. Interdependence among workers in different operations was a particularly important feature. Weavers were dependent on battery hands to feed the full bobbins into their looms and on loom fixers to repair their looms; spinners were dependent on doffers to pick up and deliver bobbins; and burlers were dependent on cloth inspectors to supply them with rolls of cloth to be mended. This was particularly crucial on piece-rate jobs, where the completion of a day's quota was contingent upon the good will and cooperation of fellow workers. It worked both ways: workers could facilitate each other's

work or they could hinder it. A loom fixer could paralyze an
entire section of a weave room by stalling or by refusing to
come to a weaver's assistance; a room girl could leave a weaver
stranded by refusing to disentangle the warp; and a cloth inspector could make a burler's life miserable by steering more of
the defective or dark cloth, which is hard on the eyes, in her
direction. Occasionally intolerant bosses pitted workers against
each other, thus indirectly encouraging them to resort to such
tactics. Other times, to protest the bosses' pressure for
speedup, workers would collectively slow down their production, even if it meant lowering their day's earnings.

Interdependence in the workrooms was especially threat-
ened once the corporation accelerated the pace of work and
increased work loads. Such changes upset the delicate balance
which workers and management had achieved over almost a
century of the Amoskeag's existence. Speedups and the "stretchout" became common features of the Amoskeag's work life,
particularly during the period following the strike of 1922.
Theoretically, the stretchout, as the increase of machines per
worker was called, was part of an effort by the Company to
improve the efficiency of the work process as newer, more
automatic machines replaced the older ones. However, in later
years, as the Company tried to cut costs by reducing its payroll,
there was a substantial increase in work loads without a cor-
responding improvement in the machinery. Workers unable to
keep up with the work load and the speed were unceremoni-
ously asked to leave in accordance with the principle of "survival of the fittest."

In 1927, protesting a whole series of speedups in a significant number of occupations, the workers claimed that a "sci-
entific method of decreasing the wages has been instituted by
increasing the length of the cut." Management responded that
the increase in the work loads could actually serve to offset the
10 percent cut in piece rates because the workers could earn
more "by working harder" to maintain the extra machines.*

In 1924, the box-loom fixers complained that they were
being "driven to death." It was impossible, they said, to keep

* Creamer and Coulter, *Labor and the Shut-Down of the Amoskeag Mills*,
p. 197.

Boys with "broomless sweepers," spinning room, ca. 1920

up their work on account of poor equipment, poor conditions, and poor wages. To add insult to injury, delays in the delivery of supplies and a marked decline in the quality of raw materials further hindered the smooth operation. "Bad work"—poor cotton, rotten wool, and yarn that was constantly breaking—undermined the very standards of high-quality work on which the corporation had prided itself earlier. The workers felt betrayed by the Amoskeag's failure to live up to the standards of excellence which it had preached to its workers and which it had successfully instilled in them.

Weave-room personnel, ca. 1890

► Joseph Debski

Eighty-three-year-old Joseph Debski was the first clerk appointed to the Amoskeag employment office after its establishment in 1911. He identified with management throughout his life.

Joe was born in Poland, but his parents migrated to Manchester in the early 1890s. His brother Tony and their parents all worked at the Amoskeag at different points in their lives. Joseph began his employment there as a bobbin boy at the age of fourteen.

Joe and his wife, Jane, live in a small country cottage in Dumbarton, New Hampshire, where he still audits the town books. He has remained in contact with a number of former Amoskeag men. Jane Debski temporarily worked at the Amoskeag as a bobbin sorter and participated in most of the Company's service programs, particularly the cooking school.

I started to work in the mill in 1910 at age fourteen. I didn't go to any of the places in the Amoskeag mills where my father worked. I went to a separate place, where I thought I'd like it. Of course, I was young and didn't know any of the overseers. I was a bobbin boy from April 1910. Then the next year they opened the Amoskeag employment office, and Mr. William Swallow was put in charge of it. As far as I know, that's the first time I ever heard of any employment agency.

Joseph Debski and Arthur Morrill at their first meeting in thirty years, at the Amoskeag Exhibition in 1975

Two or three years later, McElwain's Shoe Company came down to get the data from us on how we operated and started their own.

I think it was November 11, 1911, when we opened the office. Mr. Swallow had me come in two weeks before and go around with the letter carriers. He introduced me to every overseer in the mills at their locations, because he knew that I would have to do business with them eventually.

In 1911, there were a lot of immigrants, and they couldn't all speak good English, so he had to get assistants to interpret for them. I did the interviewing of all non-English-speaking men, whether they were Greek, French, Polish, or whatever. We had two windows. At one, English-speaking men would talk to Mr. [Mike] Ahern, who was in charge. I would have the other window, with all the various nationalities. On the other side of where we had our two interviewing windows, we had a separate room partitioned off just for women. Mr. Boucher was in charge of the women. The big room was just for men, the women's room was on the other side, and Mr. Swallow had his office right in the middle. The payroll department was in the back.

I was merely an interpreter for two or three months. Then I started in learning to type; and besides doing my interpreting, I started doing office work. I kept the records of the people employed and the people that left the Company. We had a daily report to make out on everybody that was hired that day and everybody that left. If an overseer fired somebody, he'd put a reason down on his final check. There'd be a stub there to say why, and we'd keep that as a matter of record. In the record we had everybody that ever worked in the Amoskeag. We therefore had a running account of just what they could do and what they couldn't do.

When we were interviewing people, the first thing we would ask them was what job they were looking for. Then I'd say, "Where did you work before?" They'd say, "Here." "What's your name?" We'd go to the dead file and get their records. If the record warranted that they were good, we'd hire them. If they weren't so good, I'd say, "I can't hire you today," or "There's nothing for you." In other words, if they're all right—

if they worked in another department and the boss said they were good—I'd give them a job if I had it.

One time there was a fellow whose boss put down on the slip when he got through, "Too light for heavy work and too heavy for light work." That means he's no good for anything! If you looked it up and found that, no matter who he was, you weren't going to hire him. If he was a friend of mine, I'd say, "The only way you can get a job is if you go down and see a boss, and if the boss wants you, have him call me." We didn't always hire him if the boss called up, but sometimes we did.

If a guy didn't get along with his boss, we'd give him a job in some other department, but we wouldn't send him back to him. You'd have to give the guy another job or else you'd run out of help. Maybe that boss couldn't get along with him, but somebody else could. He might be a good worker for one fellow but not for another.

For jobs in lots of places, like in the dye house, where they have to wring cotton, which is very, very tough on your fingers, on your skin, we'd look at their hands; and if they were like ladyfingers, we wouldn't send them on a job like that. Use a little discretion!

If immigrants showed their qualifications on certain jobs, they could advance. A lot of people there, Polish people, Greek people, French people, they advanced very nicely. Some of them went right up to overseer, which was a good setup. Of course, most of them just went in there for a day's pay. They didn't care about advancement.

The spinning room was mostly French, the card rooms were mostly Polish, and the dye house was mostly Scotch. In the worsted dye house, it was mostly Irish. The French people would bring the French into the spinning room, and the Scotchmen would bring their friends into the dye houses. It was the same with the Polish people that worked in the card room. That's the way it worked.

Americans didn't want to learn how to spin or how to weave. They wanted white-collar jobs, mostly. They'd take a good dye-house job, where they could get in amongst themselves, talk and work at the same time. But to learn to weave or spin, they weren't interested in that, except the ones that learned the jobs and got to be loom fixers or second hands and worked up that way. They knew how to do it, but they didn't want to do it. And there were a lot of nice jobs! You have the finishing department and you have the electrical department; you have the telephone exchange, telephone operators: those are all skilled jobs. Machinists were classified. Today you're only a machine operator, but in those days, you had to put in twelve years to classify as a first-class machinist. It was the same with painters. They didn't hire any Tom, Dick, or Harry for a painter. A painter had to go in there and mix his own paint. Those were skilled jobs, and you had to serve an apprenticeship. Spinners had to learn, too, but you only got learners' pay for three weeks; that's about all the time a spinner should take to learn how to spin. Then you'd get spinners' pay.

If you had a job doing a certain thing and you wanted to do something else but they didn't have it in that room, you would give your notice and then go back and try to get a job in one of the other mills at what you'd think you'd like better. They had everything in the manufacture of cotton and wool. They had rayon; they had an electrical shop, machine shop, printing office, boiler rooms, yard help, garage . . . a lot of variety to choose from.

During the day, regardless of who came to the employment-office window, we interviewed them. That's one thing that Mr. Straw was specific about: he wanted us to talk to everybody. But at night, there'd be twenty-five or thirty people there looking for work; and if these three bosses called up and said there's no work, I'd just say, "No work tonight, fellows," and I'd close the windows. One night I was walking home, going up Canal Street, and just as I got above Stark Street, this Polish fellow who had asked earlier for a job came over and hit me. I turned around and punched him in the eye. Some woman hollered, "Look out, he's got a knife." There was a cop there, but he didn't even bother with it. So I went back to the house and called up Mr. Swallow. He said, "You better call up the station." So I talked with the chief's son, who was the deputy chief at that time. He said, "Do you know the fellow, Joe?" I said I did, and I went back to the office and looked up the fellow's name and address. They went to his house, took him in, and booked him. So I went to court, and the fellow pleaded guilty. He had a nice black eye, and the judge gave him twenty-four hours to leave the state—not just the city, the state. Even more, he said, "Go back to Poland where you came from." And I never saw him in Manchester from that day on.

It was up to me whether a person was hired or not. If an overseer requested a particular person for a job, I would check his records, find out if he was qualified and if he had been around in the past looking for employment. I had people there coming in day in, day out, looking for employment. I would consider them before I would the request of an overseer or a second hand, except on special occasions. On certain jobs it wouldn't matter who you'd hire because there were always openings; but when there were no openings, you'd have to take them according to their qualifications, because even after we hired them, the overseer had the final say on whether he'd put them to work or not.

Mr. Swallow had the final say if there was any question on anything. Sometimes we'd hire 150 people a day, but in the burling room, you probably wouldn't hire two girls in one month. Then you might hire six in a week, then not again for three months, while spinners, carders, and weavers were hired every day. Burling was interesting work—all women, clean work.

Lots of times they complained that we hired too many Polish people or too many Greeks or too many French people. The number of employees at the Amoskeag at one time was around fifteen thousand, and we had a chart made up weekly, monthly, then yearly. It showed the percentages of all nationalities. Then if there were any complaints that we were hiring too many French or Irish or Polish or Greek workers, we'd compare them and find out what the variation was, and very seldom would it vary very much. The French people were probably 50 percent; the American people—like the Irish-Americans, Scotch, English—would run probably 20 to 25 percent; the Greek would run 10 percent; the Polish would run 10 percent; Italians we'd classify with "others."

The French were always a majority because it was a Canadian town. Your Canadian people would come to a mill town. They had friends or cousins or neighbors working here, and they'd all write to them, telling them what they're doing and how much they're making. However, we could not directly write to Canada and ask for help up there; that was against the government law. There'd be quite a turnover of French people that would quit for the two weeks' vacation we would have here in the town and in the mills. They would go to Canada. Some would stay there, others would come back. Our turnover would show as large because a lot of them quit, and then when they came back we'd have to rehire them. The Company did not, that I know of, send people out of the country to recruit, but they did it here in different states. We hired very few from out-of-town, mostly local, not Lawrence or Lowell. If we ran short of certain kinds of skilled work, we'd advertise in the Lawrence or Lowell papers. That was only for weavers, special kinds of weavers. We knew their rates in Lowell and Lawrence, and they knew our rates. We usually exchanged rates for various jobs with all the mills in Lowell and Lawrence. Sometimes we'd hire through some employment agency in Boston for special skilled jobs, like wool sorters or special overseers or when we needed somebody to put right on the top.

When I started work in the Amoskeag, the grocery store was important. If you had a friend that was an immigrant and just come into Manchester, you'd get him acquainted with your grocery man because he's got to eat. After a week or two, he'd run up a bill and wouldn't have anything to pay with, so he'd turn around and try to get a job in the Amoskeag. He'd come down to see me or my boss, or somebody like that, and ask if there's anything he could do, anything. They didn't pick their jobs; they'd do anything to get a week's pay.

My father worked at a clothing store here in town. Years ago, when all these immigrants came into town, he would take them in to see some of the overseers he knew personally and intercede for them. He got quite a few of them working. Of course, he was interested in his money, because he was selling them clothes, shoes, boots, wearing apparel, and they used to get it on the cuff.

The Amoskeag had a textile club; anybody over eighteen who worked there could belong to it. It had a reading room, canteen, billiard and pool tables, and card tables; and they

The Amoskeag Textile Club Baseball Team, ca. 1920

used to have dances, probably once a month in the wintertime. They had a golf course with a clubhouse; and in 1927 they took over the Intervale Country Club when they decided to make a Manchester Country Club of eighteen holes.° They had socials there almost every weekend. Then they had the Amoskeag Textile Field, which was a baseball field.

There was a general fund to operate things like a Christmas party for employees' children. They'd take all the equipment out of the garage—it was all bare floor—and prepare it for fifteen to twenty-five hundred children from five to fifteen, free

° The golf course and country club were used primarily by managers and overseers.

The children's gardens, ca. 1920

of charge. They would try to take the hard cases, people who probably couldn't afford a good Christmas party of their own.

The textile club had an annual meeting at the Jolliet Hall up on Beech Street, and there'd be fifteen hundred to two thousand people there. They'd have a big dinner and entertainment. We had committees on bowling, athletics, photography. They used to give prizes out about once a week for the best picture. They had about twenty different committees.

During World War I, they had victory gardens. They used to let people have plots to raise vegetables at three different places in the city, and anybody who worked in the Amoskeag could apply for one. In the Amoskeag employment-office building, they had two trained nurses on duty every morning and a doctor subject to call at any time after that. We had five visiting nurses that used to go to people that were sick and couldn't afford anyone to take care of them. They used to be all over the city. Then we had our own claim department. If somebody got hurt, we took care of them. They didn't have insurance companies at that time. We had a claim adjuster, and it worked out pretty well. Of course, you'd get some suits every once in a while. Lawyers would think they could make more money out of it. Then they'd find out that it would cost them money, so they were better off to settle with the claim agent, because he was pretty liberal. Of course, we had our own lawyers if anybody did bring suit against us.

Amoskeag did all this to keep harmony amongst its employees. The board of directors established the textile club. Ahern and W. P. Straw were in touch with the happenings of the day. They went to Boston every night, so they knew what was going on all the time. The board probably made suggestions, and perhaps Herman Straw made suggestions, but those two fellows had to back them up before anything went through. Mr. Dumaine must have been in on it.

During the strike of 1922, the textile club functioned the most because people didn't have anywhere else to go. They would go play cards, play pool. They didn't draw any lines and say people couldn't come in because of the strike. In fact, while they were on strike, Mr. Straw used to go into the canteen, buy himself a couple of cigars, just walk out, and think nothing of it. The club kept going for quite a while, right up until the mid-thirties. Everything continued after the strike. It was when the mill was shut down that everything was demolished.

The Amoskeag did have a detective agency. They had a watchman at every gate, and they had two detectives walking the yard. Some wore civilian clothes. Some workers knew who they were; some didn't. They also had two policemen to go along with the payrolls, and we had a policeman (we called him a watchman) at the employment office to keep the people in line and keep them orderly. The Amoskeag also had the Manchester Police Department behind them.

Some workers were stealing from the Amoskeag. They would carry it out in their dinner bags or stuff it under their

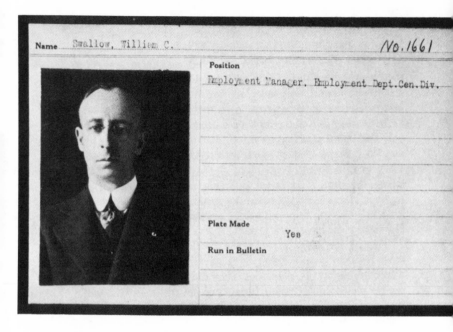

Name	Swallow, William C.	No.1661

Position

Employment Manager, Employment Dept.Cen.Div.

Plate Made
            Yes

Run in Bulletin

William C. Swallow, from the card files of the Amoskeag Textile
Club

arms or under their shirts. They'd take it not only for themselves, but they would send it to Greece, to Poland, or to different places. Someone was caught stealing serge cloth and selling
it to the tailors. All the complaints would come into my office.
They could never get away with it. If it was the first complaint,
Mr. Swallow wouldn't bother with it. But if there was a second
complaint, he'd turn it over to the Manchester Police Department. They'd go to the house, and they'd search through lock-
ers, mattresses, trunks, and they'd find a lot of cloth.

The morning the strike was over, I had a list, a card index
of fifteen or twenty people that I couldn't hire. They were

troublemakers. They'd start things at the picket line, start things amongst the strike committee members. One fellow had turned around and hit one of the superintendents in the face when he was going through the millyard one day. He was on that list. They were *blackballed*, that's all. We knew what was going on. We had informers at every one of those strike meetings, working people, mostly. They'd tell you who's causing all the trouble at the meetings, trying to rile things up. We knew it all the time. I knew two weeks before the strike was over that it was going to be over on a certain day. How do you like that? I knew from the informers at these meetings that they were going to agree on that. The informers were members of the union.

You went to Mr. Swallow to get into the corporation tenements. He had charge of the employment office, the accident department; he had charge of all the outside work in the corporation, and he had charge of the tenements. If you were a conscientious worker and you had worked there faithfully a good many years, and you had a family and didn't ever cause any trouble anywhere, you'd get one, if you waited long enough. Your boss would speak for you or something like that. It wouldn't make any difference if you were skilled or not. What Mr. Swallow'd go by is how many of your family work in the mills, are you a clean-living family, and so on. When you came in to apply, they had a pile that high there of names, what kind of a place they want, how many rooms, how many children they got, all that stuff. If you got one in two years you'd be lucky. But then you could keep it indefinitely.

Mr. Swallow was the fairest man I ever worked for. He ran for the New Hampshire state senate, and he asked me, "Joe, I know you're down as a Democrat, but I'm running for state senate and you're in one of the wards that I'm running in. I'd appreciate it, that's all." So I had everybody in the family—my father and my brothers and my sister and myself—change our registration temporarily until he got in. I did that because I knew the man. I knew he was qualified.

I was the first in my family in the mills. Then I got my brother in, my other brother, my sister, and my wife [laughs]. Of course, there has to be an opening before they can get in. When I got Helen [his wife] in, the boss happened to be in there asking for a girl, and I said, "Well, what about my missus?" He said, "Send her down and let me have a talk with her." So she got the job. But they don't make jobs. There has to be a job open before you can put somebody in there. I don't care if it's your brother, your father, or your sister; it doesn't make any difference. But if there's one job and three people looking, naturally you can give it to your own.

Our quota was fifteen thousand, but after the strike of 1922 they probably brought it down to fourteen thousand. I wasn't there when they started doing that. That was when I got out. Mr. Dumaine sent someone up here from Boston to do away with a lot of the old men. He wanted Mr. Straw to fire them, but Mr. Straw wouldn't. Mr. Straw said, "These fellows showed me my business; they taught me everything." Dumaine said, "Well, if you don't, I'll send somebody up that will." So they sent Mr. Rauch. That was in 1928 or 1929.

I worked there until 1929; then I wanted to make a change. They were trying to economize. I was informed that they were going to cut off one of the older men. I went in and told my boss that I was younger than he was; and if he could arrange it, I'd just as soon be laid off to save him, because he was an older man and he probably wouldn't be able to go out and find work as soon as I could. I was thirty-three, and he was probably fifty.

So I left in February or March of 1929, and that was the end of my connection with the Amoskeag as a working man. I told Mr. Swallow at the time, "You won't be here very long either, Mr. Swallow. Mr. Ahern will take your job over." He said, "I don't think so, Joe." After I left they put Michael Ahern on half-time for about three months. Then Mr. Swallow got his walking papers, and Mr. Ahern took over. Mr. Swallow went right up to the Amoskeag Savings Bank and got himself another job, I suppose through W. P. Straw [who became president of the bank]. Then the Amoskeag closed.

When I started work, I felt I wanted to get in somewhere where I'd be useful to somebody. It seems that everybody wants to be useful, but they don't want to be the underdog. So I was satisfied being in the employment office. When I got into the office, I was more or less contented and I saw a future there. I didn't see this breakdown that was coming.

▶ John Jacobson

Colonel John Jacobson was born in Manchester to Swedish parents in 1898 and died in 1976. He was a self-made man, rising in the Amoskeag from packing hand to assistant superintendent of weaving, and pursuing a successful career as an executive and state official after the mills closed. Most of the people we interviewed remembered him and talked about him with great respect. During the 1920s, Jacobson became a captain in the National Guard and eventually achieved the rank of adjutant general of New Hampshire. He saw active military service in both world wars.

He was interviewed in his office at the Davison Construction Company, where he was vice-president. During his career, he had also served as chairman of the New Hampshire Water Resources Board, president of the Associated General Contractors, and state senator in the New Hampshire legislature.

As far as I know, I'm the last remaining overseer of weaving from the Amoskeag. That's because I happened to be appointed as a young man. In those days, people didn't reach the level of overseer of weaving or superintendent of weaving until they were in their fifties, maybe even in their sixties; but I worked hard at it. I not only worked hard, I went to school nights, to textile schools operated by the Company. And I also took a lot of correspondence courses in textiles, especially textile designing.

My parents came to this country from Sweden but not to

work in the mill. My father came because the streets were paved with gold. He landed in Boston, and within two days he'd run into some bad companions, and they stole all the money he had. He finally ended up in Lynn [Massachusetts] and went to work for the General Electric Company. He became an electrician. He was sent up to Manchester by his company when the streetcars were put in, in 1895; and after the system was operating, they asked him to stay on as a streetcar electrician. In those days, whenever they had a good, stiff snowstorm, they'd have a dozen motors burn out, and they all had to be fixed. So that's what he did most of his life, with the Manchester Traction and Light Company.

I was born in Manchester, but I couldn't speak English until I was seven years old. I went to a Swedish church, and I went to Swedish summer school. There aren't many second-generation Swedes that know the language. I was exposed to the Swedish language all the time because my parents spoke Swedish in the house. But my youngest brother doesn't know it very well. He came along ten years later, and by that time my parents could speak English. The Swedes and the Germans and the Scotch and the English and the Belgians gradually drifted away and became Americans. The French have stayed together better than any of the rest; they still have their French society, and they're still struggling to remain bilingual. Probably at least half of them attend French churches and speak in their native tongue when they're together.

I went to work in 1915 as what they call the runner boy, in the Jefferson Mill, which was the mill with the clock on it. In other words, I ran errands for the weave room. That weave room wove a type of cloth they called ACA Ticking, for which the Amoskeag was famous all over the world. As a matter of fact, it was the only mill in the world that wove that type of cloth. They also wove denims, and to some extent they wove print cloths; but chiefly it was ticking, which ended up as mattresses. So I worked there for maybe a couple of years, and then I became an apprentice loom fixer. After I served my apprenticeship, I became a loom fixer. That was probably five years after I had started in. From there, I was promoted to second hand in the weave room. The second hand might be considered an assistant overseer.

Unidentified overseer, from a photograph by Lewis Hine, 1909

The weave room had about a thousand looms, one overseer, and two second hands. Each second hand was responsible for one half of the room. He would handle all the help and supervise the day-to-day routine. Later I moved from the Jefferson Mill to the Langdon Mill and became the second hand there. That was a mill that was engaged in the weaving of sheeting, quite heavy sheeting. I stayed there for two years, and then I went down to #3 South Mill, which was in the Southern Division of the cotton mill. I became a second hand there; most of the work was the weaving of flannels.

After about a year, I was appointed as overseer for weaving, and I went into the Amory Mill. We wove fancy ginghams and bedspreads, as well as starting in and doing the first weavings on rayon that were ever done in the Amoskeag. We tried to convert the cotton looms into silk looms or rayon looms, which turned out quite successfully. We wove a great amount of rayon taffetas and rayon twirls there.

After being overseer of that room for three years, I was promoted to assistant superintendent of weaving. I was responsible for all of the cotton weaving in the Amoskeag, which was quite extensive: two of the mills on the other side of the river; the present Chicopee Mill [the old Coolidge Mill]; the mill across the street from there, which was known as #11 Mill; and #12 Mill, which is now a shoe factory; plus all the mills on this side of the river. I had a total employment of four thousand people. It was at that time that we first started working double shifts, a day shift as well as a night shift. There was a superintendent of weaving over me, and we would split up the work. Hours of labor didn't mean very much in those days, especially for officials. They worked as many hours as was necessary.

When I first started to work in the mill, I received approximately $16.00 for two weeks' work, fifty-five or fifty-six hours a week. It wasn't considered good pay. It wasn't the kind of pay a man could live on or raise a family on, that's for sure; but it wasn't supposed to be. Actually, it was the pay for a man just starting in as a greenhorn. Then I got to be a loom fixer. At that time, a loom fixer would earn around $30.00 for two weeks. Thousands and thousands of families grew up on wages of $15.00 a week. Of course, in those days, when young boys or girls finished the so-called grammar school and were fourteen years of age, they were eligible to go to work in the mills, and they did. People had large families, and the children went to work as soon as they were fourteen to bring in the funds necessary to maintain the family and keep it going.

When I got to being a second hand, the pay got up to around $175 a month. An overseer's pay would get up to around $250 a month, assistant superintendent about $300 a month. So that's where I was when I left in 1935. It was adequate enough for me to bring up a family with two children.

I lived in the corporation tenements. I'd venture to say that even though they were built around 1912 or 1914, they would rank among the better apartments in the city today. They had six rooms with a basement, a bath, and central heat. They were very well cared for by the Company, which had a department of tenement maintenance who would come out and knock on your door every springtime and ask if maybe there wasn't a room to be painted or a floor to be fixed or something to do. It only cost me $9.25 every month for rent. I could heat it on four or five tons of coke, and coke only cost $4.00 or $5.00 a ton. So you see, we lived differently than we do now.

When I got to be an overseer, I was able to own an automobile. I bought a Ford Coupe for $500, brand new, spic and span. I had a stall for my garage, which cost me a dollar a month. And, of course, in the wintertime we didn't run our cars anyway. We put them up on horses, along about Thanksgiving, and we took them down the day before Easter. The rest of the time it was either Shank's mare or the trolley cars, if you had someplace to go. So everything is relative, and I certainly didn't starve and neither did my children. We ate well and lived comfortably.

We had unions in some of the trades, in those days. We had a loom fixers' union, but it was not a strong union; and probably not much more than 50 percent of the loom fixers belonged to the union. I never joined the union myself. It was not what they called a trade union. It was a horizontal union rather than a vertical union like what we have today, which came in with the CIO. It was considered to be of some value to be a member of a horizontal trade union and have a journeyman's card. Holding that card was primarily evidence that you were a qualified operator in that trade. People were very jealous of the union card in those days. Today, that isn't so. Today, if you get a job, you have to join the union in seven days or you can't hold the job. Your qualification to do the work is of secondary importance. The union card doesn't mean a thing except that you're a member of the union. It doesn't guarantee anything as far as your abilities are concerned. That's where unions have changed.

As for management, the Straws were in control of the mills only so far as Manchester was concerned. I think there was a feeling that the Amoskeag Company was almost their own possession, it was so close. William Parker Straw, who was the last agent of the Straw family, was a fine man. He finally had to quit because of ill feeling between him and Dumaine, and he became president of the Amoskeag Savings Bank. He couldn't take Dumaine any more. As Dumaine got older, he got harder to get along with.

Dumaine had had a couple of boys, and he set them up there. I had one of them [Chris Dumaine] under my wing for a while to teach him something about weaving. Couldn't teach him anything. He wouldn't pay attention. He was not a favorite of the old man. Of course, when he married a Manchester girl, the old man didn't like it. He threw him out of the house, and as far as I know their problems were never settled.

Bucky, who was Frederick Dumaine, Jr., was the fair-haired boy. He was a nice happy-go-lucky kind of a fellow, but he didn't seem to have very much interest in the textile business, as far as learning it was concerned. He got to be quite a big shot, of course, because he had a lot of money behind him. He got to be head of the New York and New Haven Railroad. I guess he got all he could out of that. He's head of the Amoskeag holding company now. I don't know what they hold, but it's pretty good stock.

I know that many overseers and second hands and other people that worked for Amoskeag were intimidated by the Company to vote a certain way on things that the Company was interested in. The Company always had two or three men on the board of aldermen, and two or three men on the city council, when there was one; and they had four, five, or maybe six in the legislature who were employees. Those people were given free time to go up there, and they didn't lose any pay or anything like that, but it was just understood that they would vote the conservative way for whatever the Company was interested in. But I never saw any harassment or anything like that. Of course, where men get together, there's talk; and one maybe is trying to influence somebody else. But you know sometimes a man doesn't have to do very much influencing; he merely lets his help know who he stands for, nothing more, and the help will automatically go for him because they want to please the boss.

Ernest Anderson

Seventy-five-year-old Ernest Anderson was the son of Swedish immigrants who met each other at the old Stark Mill. Anderson himself started at the Amoskeag as a summer worker in 1917 at age fourteen; and when he finished grammar school at sixteen, he became a full-time employee. He worked his way up from loom cleaner to second hand in the spinning room. His five brothers and sisters were mill workers as well.

Even at the time of the interview, Ernest considered himself lucky to be working at the Chicopee Mill, where he had been employed for over thirty-five years. He still has a strong attachment to the Amoskeag millyard and enjoys walking through it.

I was Jacobson's second hand. I can say that all in all I got along well with my bosses, my superintendents. I got along well with whoever I worked for. I can be thankful that the Amoskeag was here. We were eight of us in the family—I had four sisters and a brother—and we all worked there. We made a living at it; we didn't have to go on relief. My mother and father came from Sweden. They started in as weavers, and then my father became a loom fixer. When my mother came here, they were working twelve hours a day in the Stark Mill. At that time, electricity was hardly known, and they worked under gaslight. In the buildings where I grew up, they didn't have modern conveniences at all. They had what they called a shed out in the backyard, an outhouse. You'd look down in the hole and you'd see rats running around. Some people would throw a cat in there; they used to clean them out once a year, with pumps that had to be worked by hand. When we moved to the corporation tenement and they had modern conveniences, I felt just like a millionaire—we didn't have to run outside.

You had to be gifted to come over here and learn how to talk English. My mother had a hard time. If you spoke broken English, it hampered you. You had to be really an exception to get a good job. It was very seldom that you'd see anybody get to be a second hand or a foreman that didn't talk English. He had to be able to talk to the people and make them think that he knew more than they did. You looked up to a boss or somebody like that, even a loom fixer. I remember when I was young, if you saw a loom fixer coming up the street, you tipped your hat to him—you felt he had made something of himself, that he was somebody.

I had to look after over thirteen hundred looms, which was four floors of weaving; Jacobson had the same thing, only he was boss. I never intended to go as high as I did; but before you know it, the boss that I was working for came up to me and asked me to do a job if the second hand was out sick or if he needed any help. I used to do as much as I possibly could. With all the little things that I did, the word must have been passed along in the Company; and when they needed a second hand, they asked me.

It used to be that if your big boss was walking by and saw you sitting down, he'd know your job was running, and he'd be tickled pink. When you're over there struggling and your loom isn't running, well, naturally, your job can't be going very well. But then Mr. Rauch came. He was Dumaine's right-hand man. He'd walk around suspicious-like, with one hand in his coat pocket. He'd go through the room; and if he'd see somebody sitting down or somebody talking to somebody else, he'd keep track of it. He'd tell the boss, "I just walked through this room, and I saw about ten people that weren't even working—get rid of them." So they put the pressure on, all because of that one man, Mr. Rauch. Before you know it, Rauch had cut some twenty-three thousand people down to ten thousand. That's quite a drop. Over ten thousand people—he really ban-

Ernest Anderson, 1977

ished their jobs.[*] But even that didn't pay, because the Amoskeag went out of business.

Sometimes I take a walk through the millyard. A lot of it is
torn down today; but as I look up, I can see those mills, how
they flourished at one time, and I don't feel as old as I am—it's
as if I was just walking through and there was the mill, ready
to go to work again.

---

[*] Actually, these figures are exaggerated.

Joseph Champagne was born in Manchester in 1891, but he was raised by his grandparents in Quebec. He was one of the very few French Canadians who became an overseer in weaving. He started out as a dresser in 1909, was promoted to second hand in 1921, and became an overseer in 1929. In 1936, Joseph worked as a watchman on the emergency crew that had to deal with the damage left by the flood and restore the Amoskeag's operations. He was one of the last people to leave the Amoskeag at the time of the shutdown.

Joseph is widowed and lives with his daughter and son-in-law in a small farmhouse on the outskirts of Manchester. He continues to identify very closely with the Amoskeag.

As a boy, my first job was as a sweeper. I wasn't fourteen yet. After being a band boy, oiler, starter, and sweeper, I worked up to being a second hand in the spinning room. An overseer had kind of taken to me. He said he knew a boss in the dress room—dressing was one of the biggest paying jobs—and he got me a job there. That was in #11 Mill. I got married in 1912; and two years after, I was appointed second hand. Three years later, I was appointed overseer. There weren't many Frenchmen who were overseers in my day. There was me; and a fellow by the name of Blaine, who was a spinner; and Théophile Biron, the father of the guy who built that bridge over

* Fictitious name

the West Side.* I stayed overseer till after the [1936] flood.
Then they shut down the mill, and we all got out.

I always wanted to get bigger money, and I figured I didn't
want to be a bartender, but I wanted to get a job that pays as
much as a bartender. I guess they were getting $18.00 a week
then. There were two jobs that paid the highest wages in Manchester: slashing and loom fixing inside the mill, and bartender
outside the mill. The next good-paying job was the police, but I
didn't have the guts, I guess. In those days, it was pretty tough
in the police.

My grandfather on my mother's side came over here first,
and he went to work for the Blood Machine Shop. My mother
went into weaving; she was a weaver all her life. She died
when she was only seventy-two. I was born in Manchester.
Both my sisters worked in the mills. One was a weaver; and the
other one used to work in the card room, but she was an epi-
leptic and got married pretty young.

My first job in the mill was working for an overseer named
John Cronin. He owned the house where I lived on Cartier
Street. Everybody else that worked for him either lived in his
house or was connected with somebody else that worked for
him. So that's how I came to get a job, and I never went back
to school after. But after I got appointed second hand, I found
out that school was a good thing. I had to go to school—I
couldn't even spell "broom." So I had a private teacher, an
old maid. I'll never forget her, a poor old soul by the name of
Kent. I went for over a year, and that's where I learned how to
write.

As far as my help goes, I have proof of how we got along.
When I moved into this house, which I built, they gave me a
great opening. They used to all get together on Christmas and
buy the overseer something. I had rings given to me. I had two
or three watches given to me. The people used to be like that.
When my oldest boy was born, they gave me a four-ounce gold
cup. It was for the boy, with his name engraved on it. Another
thing: in the years just before the flood, I was working on the
wool, and they had formed a union—a shop union, independent of any of the big unions. I never had any trouble with

* Théophile Biron was the first French-Canadian overseer in the Amoskeag
Company and the first president of the Association Canado-Américaine.

George Brown leaving work in the mills, photographed by Lewis Hine in 1909

them at all. Whatever little grievances they had, they always came like gentlemen, and nobody, I believe, ever started a fight. As an overseer, you were responsible for everything that happened in your department. You hired your help; you fired them. The only thing we didn't have was the clerical work. I had five bookkeepers at one time, but that was controlled by the clerical department in the main office.

The biggest job I had was on the wool. I was a cotton man to begin with, then I was transferred to the wool, and I stayed there until the shutdown. We used to get sheets of paper saying that they wanted a certain style—so many yards of this and so many yards of that. I didn't make the cloth itself—all I made was yarn. I had to prepare it right from the winding up until it was ready for the weaver to put into cloth. I had to see that the fellow that was making the blue and the fellow that was making the white made so many ends of each kind.

When they started increasing the work load, the people began to get disgusted. Then, when we had the flood, they shut down the whole corporation. I don't know for just how long— three or four months, I guess. All the machinery on the first floor got covered with sand and dirt. I was appointed to clean it out, along with a fellow by the name of Oscar Cramm, who got appointed to clean up the Northern Division. I made a channel about twelve inches deep across the mill—it was probably a hundred feet wide, and it was in sections of ten or twelve feet. One would overlap the other, and every four or five sections we had a hose. Of course, all the overseers and second hands were working. They were on salary, and you had to keep them, you had to pay them. Dumaine was left with too many people on his hands. There were over a hundred overseers and probably 250 second hands.

We lined the men up alongside the sluiceway, about five or six feet apart. They shoveled sand into the sluiceway, and then the water from the hose would push it out through the window and back to the middle of the river. After we got it all shoveled out, we washed the machinery as well as we could, but everything got badly rusted. It was an awful job to get the machines back in shape, and a lot of them had to be junked. I think that the mill never would have shut down if it hadn't been for the flood. I think the flood was responsible for the whole thing.

▶ Raymond Dubois*

Fifty-nine-year-old Raymond Dubois is now a high-ranking city official in Manchester, having worked for the city since World War II. He came from a family of mill people who lived in the corporation tenements. While in this respect he resembles many other people who worked in the mills, he is an unusually articulate observer not only of his own family's experiences but of the whole world of the Amoskeag, both inside the mills and in the neighborhoods surrounding them.

I was brought up in the area of the mill. All our people were mill people, and we didn't know anything else but mills. We didn't know anything else existed, really. I suppose if my people had worked for the Public Service Company, I probably would have worked for them, but the only people we knew were mill people. We lived near the mills, we carried dinners for our parents, and we just were accustomed to the mills. It seemed like this was where we would fall in when we got old enough. I went in a few months after I became sixteen.

There was an employment bureau in the mills, and this was run by a Michael Ahern. If you continually presented yourself in front of him, in the morning and at noon and at night, they'd finally get accustomed to seeing you. In other words, you couldn't become discouraged. There was a big line there going in for a job; and when a job popped up, and you happened to

* Fictitious name

be the fellow in the line at the time, why, bingo! you got hired.

I did not enjoy working in the mills. It was hot in the summer, cold in the winter. You had an eight-hour stretch, a half-hour dinner, and you couldn't smoke. There was absolutely no smoking in the mill and in the millyard. The millyard was fenced in and there was a watchman at the gate, so you couldn't run out of the building into the streets even if your particular building was situated near the streets, which mine was. As a matter of fact, I did do that a couple of times, and I almost got fired. So you went eight hours without smoking, and most of the people in those days smoked. Not women, though; just the men.

I didn't like the fact that you were tied to that machine or to your job. It was as though you were in jail for eight hours, and you knew there was just no escaping. Nothing good to look forward to when you go to work but eight hours of work. Fortunately, the people you worked for were in the same predicament, so they would try to get some pleasure out of it with joking; but I didn't like it, and I don't think too many people in there liked it either. It sounds funny, but the only thing I did like was my pay. It was good money at that time.

My job was to wind the spinning frames. When the frames were running, they'd run down; then there's a wheel that you crank, which winds the whole carriage up again. After the bobbins were doffed, we'd rewind the frames so that they'd start a new set of bobbins. Then they'd load them with the filling [unspun cotton]. That was my function.

They used to use older women to put the empty bobbins on because they were cheaper labor. We'd pick off the full ones, and they'd put new ones up there; that's the process. People at the time wouldn't have taken that menial job if they couldn't actually support a family on it. In this room in particular, we had two or three older women who worked for about $12.00 a week. I was getting 38¢ an hour, and that came to $15.58 a week. For a young boy, this was adequate pay. Since I was still living at home, I gave my mother my pay, and I think she gave me $1.50 a week. It was a lot of money at that time.

We considered the overseers far above us, but they didn't abuse us. They were quite good. In the room that I worked in, we were only three men with forty girls; and I was, as I say, a

Carding room, ca. 1890

young boy. All of those girls were like mothers to me; they sort of guided me. Ordinarily in the mills, the balance is perhaps 50-50 in most places. It seemed like the overseers acted a little bit different toward the women than toward us. Not that they treated them better; but I don't think that they were as strict with the women or expected as much from them because the women were as temperamental then as they are now—they haven't changed. So that if they bawled a woman out, she'd probably go into a corner and cry or something, whereas a man would take it.

The other two men I worked with, the second hand and the roving boy, taught me my job. It only took about two or three days to actually learn the job, but it took me about a month to develop the speed that was required to keep up with the production. I was young, fast, and strong, and I found the job to be very, very easy. I was so fast that I had time to spare. Any job that they chose in the mills, they regulated it so that it would keep you going. But at sixteen, you can double the speed of any older person, and I'm naturally fast, so that I had a lot of time to spare. As a matter of fact, I got into some trouble because of that. Of course, if I had been working, I wouldn't have had time to do it. The aisles are narrow between the frames; and if you go down between the frames with a cart to take the bobbins off and there's a girl bent over doffing, you might rap her in the can with the cart, and in turn, she'd poke you or something. You'd end up wrestling in that aisle, and your backside might hit a couple of fillings and knock the bobbins off!

The people that worked in the Amoskeag weren't driven to the peak of their endurance. They kept them busy, but I can't say that they overworked them, as far as trying to extract every bit of production that a person could put out. It didn't seem to me that the people were unhappy. They weren't happy either, but they weren't griping or miserable or tired. They were accustomed to that grind.

The jobs weren't unbearable physically. Nobody kept behind you, pushing for production. For instance, in our spinning room, we doffed once an hour, which meant taking the bobbins off and putting new bobbins on. If you did that each night eight times, it was accepted; if you doffed seven times, somebody goofed. If you doffed nine times, somebody's driving you. They expected eight, so we regulated the speed of the machines. If we found that we were going to get nine doffs a night, we wouldn't start the machines as fast as we would if we were going to get eight. As long as we got eight doffs, the second hand was happy.

The noise in my room wasn't the kind of noise that you get in the weave room. The weave room has a sort of snapping, pounding noise; ours was merely wheels turning and the noise of the bobbins spinning, so that you had sort of a hum. I don't recall being affected by it. But once in a while I went into a weave room to deliver dinner, and I just couldn't stand the noise. I don't know how anybody else could. Gosh almighty, it still exists today. It seemed as though the sides of the building were shaking.

It was amazing, in a sense, that every gate in the mill had a watchman. It was almost regimental. When you came out of that gate, if they were at all suspicious of your taking something out of the mill, they'd search you. So if you wanted to steal a few yards of cloth or a couple of bobbins or roping or things of that nature, you stood a good chance of being searched at the gate. They didn't require a policeman or anything like that; they just stopped you and searched you, and either fired you or had you arrested for stealing. Today things would be far different.

You never saw a butt in the millyard; you never saw anybody light a match. They didn't have very many fires there, for the size of the mill. As a matter of fact, the fire department now has calls down in that area at least fifty times a year, but not then. I don't remember ever seeing the fire department in the mill. They had their own hydrants, of course, private hydrants, but I don't think that they had a fire brigade, unless the maintenance people—they call them millwrights—were trained to put out fires. We workers in the mills were not. You can well imagine that a good fire would wipe out the whole mill.

They had cockroaches three inches long, and they had rats. As a matter of fact, the University of New Hampshire biology classes used to come down and catch the rats in jars and work on them all the time. And the drinking water—I don't know if they took the river water or not, but on every sink in the mill, there was one tap where it was written in several languages: *Do not drink this water.* I assume it had to be river water. But there were taps that you could drink from. I distinctly remember signs in different languages, because it was interesting seeing *Do not drink this water* in Greek and Polish and French. The toilets themselves were not all that clean, but you must bear in mind that when I went in, the mills were going down. It wasn't like maybe sixty or eighty years before, when they were new.

Many whole families worked in the Amoskeag. If they were ambitious to do something else, they could work in a store. The people that work in the stores now, many of their parents worked in the Amoskeag. There weren't any other industries here.

People who went to work at the Amoskeag worked there until they died or until they got too old to work. Some lived in the corporation tenements. To live in them, you had to work in the Amoskeag. A son would move in with the father; and when his father died, the children would take over the tenement. In fact, a fellow told me one day that if he could buy all the real estate here, he would buy those tenements because they would never be empty.

The people in the tenements had excellent living conditions. They all had a good roof over their head—it didn't leak —and they all had toilet facilities, which they thought were all right. They never complained about living conditions, never. And, of course, they had a recreation park that the Amoskeag furnished them, so they didn't have to stay in the house. They had a recreation hall, and they had another place over across the river, with tennis courts.

The corporations were hard to get into. They were always filled right up. You had to know somebody to get into one. Second hands and people like that made it easier than we did. There were some new corporations especially for bosses and their relatives. When I was a young boy, I felt that those that lived in the corporations were better off than we were. They were up one grade higher than us. We lived in a [privately owned] block right across from the new corporations on Hollis Street. We were very crowded. No bathtub, just a toilet and sink. The new corporations were beautiful. In those days they had vines and porches, everything that we didn't have. There were a lot of people and a lot of kids in those houses, though. So the lawns and walkways were mostly always beat up, because the kids played in that area; but it didn't seem to me that the kids were as destructive then as they are today. Not that we were any better than they are today, but I don't think there was so much vandalism then.

People in the street, people that worked in stores, used to go to boardinghouses to eat along with mill workers. They put on family-style meals; you were glad to get a fork in your hand to reach for something. I can remember going to one of the boardinghouses; at 50¢ for a dinner, you could have all you

The lower corporations and the mills, 1968

wanted. They had potatoes, sometimes hash brown, sometimes mashed or boiled; they had meat; and when the blueberries came in, they'd have blueberry pie. It was boardinghouse-style, a long room and a table, just like at a banquet. You would sit in there a little close, and you'd pass the food on down. They were all about the same and all pretty good. There were people that ran boardinghouses for the Amoskeag workers all their lives. You had a half-hour at noon; the bell rang out and in, and if you didn't carry your own lunch, you would go to one of the boardinghouses. Some would have a whole building: some of the family would be working in the Amoskeag, the wife would run the boardinghouse, and they would have rooms up above.

Nationality has played a part in this city since I was old enough to realize what was happening. Up to this date, it hasn't changed much. The French and the Irish always looked down on the Greeks, regarded them as the foreigners, because many of them that came into the mills couldn't speak English. And there was always a continuous banter between the French and the Irish. For many years it was worse than today, because now there's a lot of intermarriage, and people don't joke the same way any more about race and background. They are not as serious about it as they were in those days. If you called a guy a "dirty Irishman" thirty years ago, you had a fight; but now he'll laugh and call you a "dirty foreigner" or something like that.

There were a lot of French who couldn't speak English, and it was aggravating to those around them to have to work with them when they spoke only their own language. And the Greeks—all they talked all day long was Greek. There was a lot of that, because the minute someone arrived from the old country, they went right in the mills. They couldn't speak English, and they sort of had cliques. But you couldn't blame them. What the hell, they tried to work with the people they could understand and who could understand them. I found that out of all the people that I worked with, the nationality that I liked the best was the Greeks, in spite of the fact that many of them couldn't speak English. They seemed to be a jolly people and also considerate and generous.

Parents at that time stressed that you should marry someone of your own nationality. This was very, very strong. If you were a French American and you married an Irishman, it was almost a disgrace. They accepted having ordinary friends, but they always questioned it if you went out with an Irish girl. They discouraged it if they saw that you were getting serious. The French felt that way, and the Irish felt that way. The Greeks and the rest, they would prefer that you marry your own, too. As a matter of fact, that was a byword in those days, "Marry your own." I had a Polish girlfriend once that I was crazy about [laughs].

I think immigrants were kept down, because if there was a choice to promote somebody, it wouldn't be the immigrant. You'd have to be exceptional. They'd have to need them for a job that nobody else would touch. If, for instance, an individual was an exceptional man with his hands, if he was a good mill worker, he might receive better pay but only if they didn't have anybody else that could do it better. If a boss was Irish, he took care of the Irish; if he was French, he'd take care of the French. At that time, the French and the Irish were the stronger faction here in the city, and the Greeks and Polish did the work.

It always appeared to me when I was young that the overseers felt a little superior to the other people. They felt that they were the only true Americans. Of course, we didn't believe that. They couldn't convince us, but they did have that feeling. I think that at that time it was worse than now. You could never reach their level. They were far above us. If we made $1,000 a year wages, rest assured they made five to ten times as much.

Both of my parents were born in the States, and both of my grandfathers were born in the States, so we were far removed from these so-called foreigners who came over and couldn't speak English at all. My mother went to an English-speaking parochial school, so she could speak English better than the average person her age. At that time, it was very, very uncommon for a person's grandparents to have been born in the States. It seems as though everybody's mother or father or grandfather came from somewhere other than here. It was very unusual to see these old men, my grandfathers, walking down the street speaking English fluently. You just didn't get that with the old people. It seemed as though it was a new country, and everyone was coming here. The only ones that spoke English were the younger children.

My mother was one of the few that didn't work in the mills after she was married. She was an exception to the rule. This was the reason why my father worked so hard. I think that most men preferred their wives not to work, but in many cases people wanted to make a better life for themselves. They wanted to move into better neighborhoods. They wanted to buy a home. In those days, in order to buy a home, a man's wife had to work; and most families where the women did work did indeed own a home or property or something, much like today.

I can remember my father working in the mill, seven days a week without a day off, without a vacation. He did that for seven years, without loafing one day. My father worked seven years without loafing one day! Would you believe that something like that could happen? Incidentally, when I say my father worked seven days a week, that included Thanksgiving, Christmas, and New Year's—seven days a week, 365 days a year. That guy had to go to heaven! He worked in the mill on Sundays. It's hard to believe. He worked from six in the morning till six at night, and I carried his dinners in. Then the hours got better; we went to forty hours. That eliminated a lot of this slavery, I'll tell you. He died at the age of fifty-eight. Of course, some people worked as hard as he did, and they lived to be ninety. I can't say the job killed him, but I can't say that it helped him either.

Personally, I think when we work hard, we get into a rut, a routine. I think that if he had taken a day off, he would have felt guilty. It's a terrible thing. He just got into that routine. My father wasn't illiterate, but he was probably only one step above being illiterate. He could read the newspaper, and he could write a little. He didn't have one of the higher-paying jobs, but working so many hours gave him a fair pay, so that eventually we were able to buy a house. I think I was about fourteen years old when they finally bought that house.

We came from Lowell originally; and when we came to Manchester about 1926, he had been out of work and had experienced the fear of his family not being able to have the things that they needed. I think he always had that fear. This is

Children outside the Amoskeag corporation housing, 1909, photographed by Lewis Hine, who recorded the name of Fred Normandin, the child in front

what gave him his drive. While he could make the money, he was making it; while he could get the work, he was working—all because there were times when he wanted to work and he couldn't.

Mills closed in Lowell during the 1920s. Manchester was

doing better than Lowell, so many people were moving up from Lowell to Manchester. He came to look for work, and he found a job here. Our lifestyle in Manchester was the same as in Lowell—just a little above being poor.

We were four children, and we lived in five rooms. We had a boarder, a man that lived in Lowell. He used to come down, work in the mills five days a week, and then go home. He had a family and couldn't get a job in Lowell. He knew my parents, so we boarded him. He had to sleep with my brother. He lived there for many years.

At the dinner table, the father was always respected as the person who was bringing home the bacon, and he was served first—at least in my family and the families of my friends. If I ate at their homes, their fathers were always served first. Respect. Today he's lucky if he can grab the pot, but in those days you'd get your fingers chopped off if you reached first.

My parents didn't socialize very much. We didn't belong to any of the clubs. My father didn't drink, and he didn't have time to go out anyway. And my mother was home a lot. We didn't belong to anything other than our church. I don't even remember my parents going to a picture show. In fact, I don't ever remember my parents going out together anywhere for pleasure.

We went to the Straw School. The Straw School happened to be in the North End,° and the parents of the people that went there were better off than ours. They were more or less higher class than we were. We were not very proud of ourselves because we weren't as well dressed as they were. If we had gone to another school in the same class as our parents, we probably wouldn't have felt that way. The only reason that we got by was that my brother was big and tough, and nobody would push us around. We lived in that area, but we were on the wrong side of the tracks, so to speak. Probably only 20 percent of the people that went to the school were not well-to-do, like ourselves. We were in the minority, but it seems as though our group was the group that nobody bothered because we were stronger, tougher, run-of-the-mill people—far more than the kids that were pampered.

The Church said you would lose your religion if you didn't

° The North End was the wealthy, upper-class section of Manchester.

attend Catholic school, but some of the parents didn't believe that. Being of French descent, I would have had to learn two languages; and my parents felt that if I learned one language, I'd end up better off than going to a school with two languages. There was also the fact that they knew in the back of their minds, though I didn't know it at the time, that our education was going to be very limited. Actually, when we were sixteen years old, it was expected that we would leave school, and as a matter of fact, that was the way it was. I left school at fifteen.

The Church never did much for you other than scare you to death. You thought the priest was the Pope; if he said anything, he was right. If you had a problem, you'd go see the priest, and what he said was right. No one ever questioned him. And this is so wrong. For instance, I have uncles that spell our name Dubos. We spell ours Dubois. When we were baptized in church, they asked your name, and however the priest wrote it is what your name was, because it was on your baptismal paper. He was the educated man; we weren't. He wrote Dubois without an *i*, so I have uncles to this day that spell their name different, because our parents were illiterate.

My mother was the only one in our family that had gone through eight grades of schooling. There were very few people in those days in her age bracket that attained eight years of schooling, so she was better educated than most people around. We always looked up to her because she had as much education as I did, and I was one generation ahead of her. Now, if you see a kid come out of school at fifteen years old, he's only a baby. I thought I was a man at fifteen. Fortunately, there's a lot of work for people that aren't educated, but very few people who are less educated really get anywhere, very few. I'm not very far up the totem pole, but I've done better than I thought I would.

I had been in the service, I went to war, and I saw action. I was in the Marine Corps, and I felt that the service gave me an education. When I quit the Marine Corps, I had a family, and I came home. Fortunately, I didn't get hurt. My outlook after being in the service was that we had a very limited horizon here, in terms of being able to make good lives for ourselves, because of our limited education.

For years my father had chickens; he had a hundred chickens and a garden, and I helped him with that. Most everybody around this area had chickens. Many people had a cow. It was very common to see a guy walking down the street with his cow. One guy in the neighborhood had a bull to serve the cows. It would look kind of foolish today.

The funny part about it was, if you were going to build a chicken coop on your lot, you built it near your neighbor's house. There was no law. You built it on the far side of the lot [laughs]. We built the chicken coop twenty feet from our neighbor's back door. It was the corner of our lot, eighty feet away from the back of our house. This guy couldn't complain that he had a chicken coop twenty feet from his back door. He accepted it. He said, "Jeeze, we're very fortunate that they keep their chicken coop clean" [laughs]. Can you imagine today a chicken coop twenty feet away from your back door? Wouldn't tolerate that any more.

If you had a lot and there was grass on it, it wouldn't be unusual for your neighbor to bring his cow on your lot to eat your grass, if you didn't have a cow. He would just come over with his chain, plunk his pipe in your ground, and the cow would be there all day eating your grass. Next day he'd be looking for somebody else's lot to bring his cow to.

People had more gardens then. They ate more vegetables and greens. I think that the people ate more at that time, but they didn't eat as many fancy foods as they do today, such as cakes and ice cream. In those days, ice cream was a real treat; today, it is common on the table. You couldn't keep it in your icebox, so the only place that you could get ice cream in those days was where they sold it, and you had to eat it immediately. I think there were less sweets and junk foods served then than there are today.

We did have relief. The city did provide for those that were suffering, just as they do today. But it was a stigma, then, to apply for relief. Your neighbors would look down on you if you had to apply for relief.

You didn't seem to complain so much then. You accepted it. You didn't know things could be better. You thought this was what life was all about. You didn't think that there was a Florida where the weather was better, without winters where you froze to death. Of course, our education was very limited.

We didn't know there was another world. We thought the whole world was like what we had. Everybody lived like we lived. I really thought this, probably till I was twenty-one years old. We didn't have cars, we weren't educated, and we didn't know anything that happened outside the little world that we lived in. It's amazing what you can learn after you leave school.

I find that as you get older, if you reminisce about the old days, and you're not looking forward to a better way of life, better things, you're getting ready to die. Many people that I worked with talk about the days gone by, and these fellows are getting on to be fifty to fifty-five years old. They're down, they're practically dead. You get a man sixty-five to seventy years old who is looking forward to something—he's very much alive. I think we always have to improve, have something to look forward to. Even now, I'm looking for a better job. I'm not as satisfied with my job as I should be. Twenty years ago I thought this was out of my scope, but I'm not satisfied now. I think people should do this. That's my feeling about life.

▶ Andrew Desfosses

Andrew Desfosses was in his late fifties when interviewed in 1975. Like his brother and father, he went into the mills as a messenger boy with the intention of getting to know the overseer of the machinists and getting a job in that department, but the shutdown precluded that. Nonetheless, his father and brother were later able to get him a job at Leighton Machine Company, where they worked and where he continues to work today, constructing devices that make arteries for heart transplants.

Looking back, I realize I wasn't interested in school as a kid, which was very foolish. Now I know, of course, that I should have gone. In those days, though, going to high school was quite a thing. I imagine it would be the same thing as somebody graduating from college today. Times have changed. At that time, if you were fourteen years old and you had graduated from grammar school, you could go to work. And, of course, I wanted to feel like the rest of the kids around, have a little bit of money in my pocket.

My parents tried to discourage me as much as possible from going to work, but I couldn't see it. I was bored. I suppose the teachers I had were required to have a B.A., but their methods were not like they are today. A kid goes to school today and finds it a pleasure. I suppose it's so fascinating because there's something new all the time. But in my day it wasn't anything like that. When you got out of grammar school, you could hardly read a paper. In other words, they were babysitters. It gets boring for a kid to sit there day after day, week after week, not learning that much, especially if he has a little ambition.

Of course, the Amoskeag was the biggest industry in the area, and I'd say that the majority of the people at one time or another worked there. I went to work there in 1931 as a messenger boy. The messenger boys were actually mailmen. We worked out of the employment office. We used to take care of all the mail going through the whole Amoskeag Manufacturing Company. The company was divided into four parts: the Northern Division, the Southern Division, the Central Division, and the West Side. We had four routes a day, two in the morning and two in the afternoon. We had all of the mills, and I think we also covered about sixty-three offices every day. If people needed special help, we had to go out and see them, since not everybody had telephones. We were provided bicycles, and we had to go all over the city. That was another part of our duties. At that time we were working fifty-four hours a week for $6.48, and it was all work and no play.

The advantage of being a messenger boy was that if you stayed long enough, you could choose any job you wanted in the Amoskeag Manufacturing Company. Most of the boys wanted to go with the wool sorters, because that's where the money was. But I always liked machinery, so I wanted to go into the machine shop. Being a messenger boy was just like a fellow going to West Point. He knows that at the end of four years he's going to become an officer. A prestige job was almost assured, but it never panned out for me because I didn't stay there long enough.

You got so that you knew anybody and everybody. Of course, at that time there were sixteen or seventeen thousand people working in the Amoskeag. It was really an empire. Just to learn the different mills, the different places, that alone took quite a while. There were only four messenger boys in the whole Amoskeag Manufacturing Company, and two other boys who were like our seniors. Usually they went on special assignments, like going to the bank. They knew a little bit more than we did, as they had been on that job quite a while.

It's unbelievable but that place was so large they had to pay every day of the week. Every Monday the paymaster paid all day long, and then again on Tuesday. All week long it was like that until everyone was paid. In those days they paid in cash, and they used to send us across the roadway to the paymaster's office. We carried trays of pay envelopes. You'd never do that today. They'd hit you over the head with something. Of course, even with all those envelopes, things were so rough and everybody was getting so little money that it didn't add up to much. The paymaster's name was Caswell when I was down there. He had two assistants, and they carried pistols. As far as I remember, they never had to use them.

Besides the textile mills, they had two large machine shops at the Amoskeag. During the Civil War they used to make all the guns for the army. They also had a big foundry, and they used to do all their own casting. They used to build their own spinning frames. I think that they also made some looms, but it wasn't a paying proposition, so they discontinued that. I know that they made what they called the Amoskeag frames—in fact, I worked on them. They were very large frames, about the length of a house. I think there were 288 spindles on each frame. And that's how they prospered.

In its heyday the Amoskeag used to run a million spindles every day. I don't know of any company today that could put out that many spindles, even Burlington Mills, which I'd say is the largest in the world. Where the Notre Dame Bridge is today, to the north of that they had what they called the silk mill. That's all they did in that mill—they wove silk.*

You just name it, and if it was a textile, they manufactured it at the Amoskeag. From cotton to wool to worsted; beautiful material, even expensive silks. At one time, it was about as high a quality of textile that you could buy anywhere in the world. They had a very good name. A lot of craftsmen came out of the Amoskeag. A lot of these old-timers had practically been born in the mill. They started to work in the mills, and they spent their whole lifetime in there.

It's unbelievable how big that place was at one time. Do you realize how many hundreds of thousands of belts there were in the Amoskeag? All those had to be repaired. When I

* This probably refers to the short-lived experiment in rayon, sometimes referred to then as artificial silk. It is unlikely that the Amoskeag ever produced real silk.

worked at the Amory, they had a belt there that was fifty-six inches wide and 240 feet long that was fixed up to run the whole mill, from the water wheel down in the basement up to the fourth floor. That thing broke one time. Do you realize what the weight of a belt like that could be? How many tons? They had to rig up something special to fix that belt. They used to splice them, you know; they had some big heavy clamps, heavy timbers. I think they called them pulley jacks. They'd take the belt and pull it together, splice it, and glue it. Just that process alone would take three days. A belt like that created so much static that you couldn't get within five feet of it. You'd just put a finger out and the electricity would go right up into the belt.

They had all kinds of stuff in the Amoskeag that you probably at that time wouldn't see in other places. For instance, they had two or three boiler rooms to heat up all the mills. I don't know how many carloads of coal they used to burn a day, but it was a tremendous amount. Just one of the boiler rooms over on the West Side had twenty-eight boilers. They used to run the railroad cars right into the boiler room.

They had a strike in 1932, I believe, or in 1933, I'm not sure now. It lasted six weeks; and when I came back, I did not go back to the employment office. They sent me to the Amory Mill. I worked in the spinning room over there for about a year and a half, I think. Finally they closed that mill, and I went to work for my uncle as a filling boy. He was an overseer in #9 Mill in the Central Division, in the weave room. We used to go out to different places and get the yarn. The yarn comes on a spool, you insert that in the batteries, and they feed the yarn to the looms to weave the cloth. I was responsible for 130 looms. I had to take care of all those machines, and the area it covered was so big we had roller skates.

When President Roosevelt came into office, they had the National Recovery Act. They cut our hours from fifty-four hours to forty hours a week and increased the wages. We got $11.00 a week and worked fourteen hours less, so it was quite an improvement. That was still in the middle of the Depression, and when I say Depression, you can't imagine what it was like. There were a thousand people that would have wanted a job like mine. Even for $4.00 a week or $3.00 a week, because

The millyard, 1969

The lower canal

Tower and roof

they would have worked for anything. They were starving. There wasn't any welfare or anything like that. People that are on welfare today are well-off. In those days, if you were on welfare, you didn't have anything for your next meal.

After the mills closed, a group of people from Manchester got together and bought out the Amoskeag Manufacturing Company. They paid maybe $20 million or so. Everything was still very shaky because unemployment was very bad, and you couldn't sell anything anyway. Then slowly but surely they started to get different companies to come in there, small companies. They did very well, and today I understand that those places are going full blast; it's very good. I worked there a whole summer, and then I got laid off. My dad was working for the Leighton Machine Company, so I went there as an apprentice machinist and I've been there ever since.

▶ *Dorothy Moore**

Dorothy Moore, seventy-nine years old at the time of this interview, was an orphan. In 1913, at the age of seventeen, she went to work in the mills to support herself. She was employed in the Amoskeag's office, as was her husband, Harold. Although Harold stayed at the Amoskeag until the shutdown, Dorothy left shortly before their marriage.

Both were very much involved with the Amoskeag's social activities, particularly the Amoskeag Textile Club and the night classes, where Dorothy learned cooking, typing, and Red Cross techniques.

My mother never worked after she married. She had too many children. She had to stay at home. My father, in his early years, was a cabinetmaker for Hayward Whitfield down in Gardner [Massachusetts], and he did some bookkeeping. He had two jobs. Before she married, my mother was a schoolteacher, but that was way back, almost a hundred years ago— 1876. She had eight children, and she died at forty-one.

My mother and all her people from the time of the Revolution centered around Worcester and Sterling [Massachusetts]. My father was born in this country, but his parents came over from Ireland around the time of the potato famine, which was probably in the fifties. His parents met on the boat and were married when they got ashore. So I have quite a mixture in me.

I didn't know my mother. She died when I was three, and

* Fictitious name

the family scattered among relatives. My father didn't stick with us. He died while I was away from Manchester. I was probably nine or ten the last time I saw him. So I grew up without parents. As a result, my husband and I were of entirely different backgrounds. He had a family right up to the time he married. I had sisters and brothers but didn't live with any one of them. We shifted around.

I did live with my older sister for quite a few years and, for a number of years, in other places with other relatives. But they really didn't have room for me. Then I lived in a boardinghouse, and later in a place in Manchester that was like the YWCA for young girls on small incomes.

Just before I married, I was independent. I got an apartment. In that age it was a horrible, dreadful thing to do. No nice girl ever lived in an apartment, no sir! I was actually ostracized by some of my friends' mothers. Living in a boardinghouse would not have been considered bad, but living in an apartment, well, it wasn't being done then. You had more freedom, going in and out, and could have your own friends in. I was quite ahead of my time. Of course, under normal circumstances, I would have still been living with my family.

Where I lived, there were girls with all sorts of jobs. A great many girls came down here to the city to go to business school. I made a lot of friends who were uppertown girls at that time. The building was more or less like a college dorm. I ate my meals there. After all, I was getting only $8.40 a week in the Amoskeag! I had to have a little bit over what I paid for room and board.

I worked in the Amoskeag between 1913 and 1919, six years. I went to the Southern Division packing room on cotton goods in 1913 when I was quite young, sixteen. I had been away, and I couldn't get back into the school system with any degree of order, and I was sick and tired of my family squabbling over me. They thought of sending me to a private school, but they couldn't raise the money, so in a pique I went to work. A man I knew got my job for me at the Amoskeag. I was not intimately acquainted with him; I just knew the man. He had worked for the overseer of the room and knew him on an outside, friendly basis. That was done in those days—if you knew somebody, they would get you a job. You didn't go to the employment office.

I worked mill hours, which were six thirty in the morning till about five thirty at night. It was cold that early in the morning. Once I had my chin frozen going to work. But I had a beautiful time. I did bookkeeping all day long. When I think of all the Amoskeag jobs I had, that one was the most interesting. Men would come with truckloads of cloth, and I would fill out orders. I would assign them in these great big ledgers to China and Asia and India and Japan—places all over the world. It was my prerogative to assign the cloth to wherever I wanted to. I was an imaginative youngster, and I traveled with the cloth. I enjoyed it. It was like a game. And although the hours were long and it was pretty difficult and the pay was small, I was paying my own way. I had the knack of doing office work. It was easy for me. So they made me what you would call a Kelly Girl today. I floated around for a long, long time, simply filling in where a girl was out or on vacation, all over the millyard. Finally, I settled down in #9 Mill, winding. I stayed in that office awhile, particularly because I liked the man I worked for. He was old enough to be my grandfather but had a young son who was rather attractive [laughs].

After about a year, I was approached to go into the office where Harold later came in. That office would receive an order for so many yards or bolts of cloth. That's where I came in. The order would be for a given pattern—a great deal of it was gingham and colored, striped material—and my job was to have somebody call off to me how much of each color had to go to the dye house for the particular order. I would enter it on these great big sheets: so many pounds of blue, so many pounds of red, so many pounds of yellow, all the way across the sheet. Those were the days before they even had adding machines, and when I got it all down, the sheet would be very long. It had to be added up—by me. After the yarn was dyed, it came back to the dressing rooms, where they put it on warps. It had to be laid out in sequence, and from there it was a matter of weaving.

I heard a woman say recently that the Amoskeag was such an awful place. Of course, it could be awful, because the mills themselves were terribly dirty, horribly dirty. But I was there in some of the better days of the mills when they were making a lot of money. It was wartime. Everything was looking up, so they did a lot for their help. For instance, they had a first-aid service, and they employed a doctor. After the mills went out, there was no doctor in town quite like him. Of course, any concern would have a first-aid station, where you could go with minor things, but the Amoskeag doctors would even come into your home. They had nurses who spent all of their time going around to homes where there was sickness.

For their time the Amoskeag did all right, except in the way of money, perhaps. They didn't give much money. Now Jack Howard, my husband's brother-in-law, had a very good job in the mills, but he was brought here because he was a baseball pitcher, just like they bring people to college because they are good players. Exactly! He was the Amoskeag's star pitcher. He had been to Holy Cross, and from Holy Cross he went to the Philadelphia Athletics and threw his arm out. He recovered enough so that he was still a good pitcher, but they didn't want him back again. He used to take care of the dress room in the mill. He'd supply them with the warping tickets. He floated from mill to mill, seeing what they had in process and what was to be taken care of. He had that job until the mill went out.

Still, at the time we worked there, the mill was not really growing. It had reached its peak. They weren't hiring many new people when we went in, other than bringing in a lot of spotters. People like Freddy Meharg and Eddy Dunbar were time [and motion] estimators. The workers called them spotters because they sat themselves down beside a certain person who was doing a certain amount of work and timed them. They do that all the time now in factories, but then it was new. Most of the Amoskeag jobs where I worked had women employees, and it upset them terribly. Those spotters would simply plop themselves down beside the workers and make them nervous, particularly if a girl was tending a spinning frame or even a warping frame, where they would count how many threads she'd have to gather in and tie in. You can understand how she felt if she had never really had anyone stand over her before.

I stayed at the Amoskeag until 1919, when my boss made my life so miserable that I thought it was either get fired or get

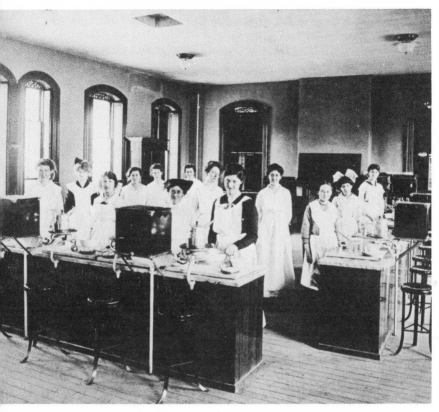

The Amoskeag Domestic Science School Cooking Class, ca. 1915

a new job, which I did—outside the mills. I was a little bit of an introvert, and my boss made my life miserable by teasing me and holding up my work, because he thought he had to be a little faster than I. When I gave my notice, though, they wanted to keep me, and they were even going to raise my salary. But I got a very nice position on Elm Street with a commercial firm, which was what I wanted. It was a tire company.

My ambition, which I finally achieved, was to get out of the mills. I started at the wrong end, because I didn't have a great amount of education, so that at first I was grateful for a mill job. I had to work my way up. But the desire of any young woman who was doing office work was to get onto Elm Street and out of those awful, dirty mills.

▶ *Ora Pelletier*

*Aurore (Ora) Anger Pelletier was born in Manchester in
1906 to French Canadian parents. Her father was born in Manchester and her mother was born in Quebec and brought to
Manchester as a child. Ora's father was a fireman, and her mother
spent most of her time rearing her eight children, all of whom
worked at the Amoskeag, often in the same room. For instance,
Henry and Robella, Ora and Robella, and Yvonne and Lucille
overlapped in the spinning room at different times, and Ora and
Irene both worked in the dress department at the same time.
Later, some of them worked together in the smaller mills that
opened after the Amoskeag had shut down.*

*Lucille Bourque, Ora's older sister, also lives in Man-
chester, as do most of the Anger siblings. However, because of
earlier family quarrels, they rarely meet. Ora and her husband,
Arthur, had two children, one of whom died in infancy. The
Pelletiers now live in Florida with their daughter, Pauline.*

I never cared for school. I'd rather work than go to
school. They used to take us during the school vacation if we
were fourteen or fifteen. Then at sixteen you'd start steady
work. We all expected to work in the mill.

My mother didn't even know when I went for a job. It was
just my sister Bella who knew. I used to go to see her at the
mill, and she taught me the work. My first pay was $4.85 for a
whole week. I thought it was great to go to work to earn some
money—when you got big, you went to work.

Bella was the one who was pushing me to go to work. She said, "Don't tell Mom because she wouldn't let you go," so I didn't. We were a big family. My parents didn't believe in education like they do now. So I quit school at sixteen; I started working full-time just before the strike.

When I was working at the mill with the other kids during school vacation, I liked to go around and ask questions. Three of us girls from the same school were working together, and I was always game for anything. We had an hour for dinner; and when you're a kid, you can't sit down for an hour. We were a nosy bunch, so I said, "What do you say we go and inspect the mill?" They said, "Where?" "The whole mill. We'll start at the bottom and keep going up." So we went over the mill from top to bottom to find out just how they made the cotton. The raw cotton was like a big pile of dust to us. They'd put it in the machines, and when it came out, it was in a big roll. They took that to the card room, and from there they put it in another kind of machine, and it would come out looking just like big pieces of cotton. Then they put it on a spool; but when they put it on the spool, it would get smaller. From there, they put it on a smaller spool, which they sent to the spinner. You could still pull it just like cotton. After they sent it to the spinner, it would come out like a thread. It wasn't cotton any more, it was thread. From there, they'd send it to the winder to be wound on a spool. The winder would send it to the warper, and the warper would put it on a big beam. And on that beam, they'd send it to the slasher, who'd put it through a big machine to starch it. Then they'd send it to the combers, and they passed each of those threads through a sort of comb. They'd send the combed threads to the weaver, and the weaver would put them on these machines, looms that were going up and down; and when it would come out, it would be material.

Nobody was allowed to smoke in the mill. If they wanted to smoke, they had to go outside of the gate. Those who were doffing (my brother doffed for the spinners) used to get out if they were done. Nobody said anything. My brother was always leaving to eat. Around ten or ten thirty, he used to run up the hill to a baker's shop and get about half a dozen jelly dough-nuts.

We had what they call a sink room in the mill. In a corner

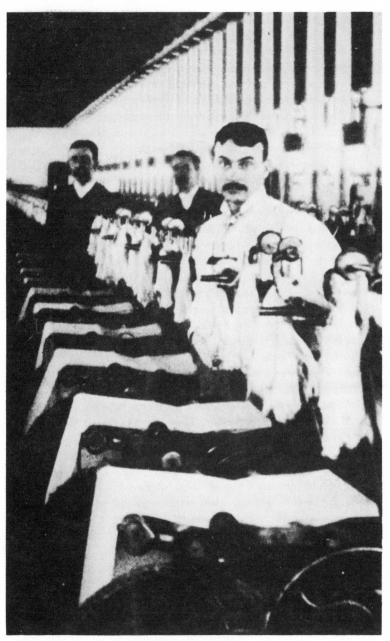

Weavers, ca. 1880

was a great big, long sink. It always had a little water in it, and there was a steam pipe going into that water, so it was boiling hot. We'd bring soup, cans of corn, cans of tomatoes, and heat them in there for our meal. The Greek, Mary, used to bring eggs and put them in when she came in at seven o'clock in the morning, so she'd have hard-boiled eggs for dinner. And we'd swap lunch and everything. Those who were living closer used to go home. My sister Irene and I, we lived on Orange Street, so all we had to do was go up the hill for dinner.

Our boss was married, but he had a girlfriend. He'd skip out with her about five minutes ahead of time, so there wouldn't be too many people ahead of him, and he'd get home quicker. With all those people going down those stairs, from the top floor where we worked, you'd lose about five to ten minutes before you could get downstairs, go across the yard and out the fence, and climb the Bridge Street hill to Orange Street. So when I noticed he was skipping, I started to follow him. He said, "Where are you going?" I said, "I'm going home." He said, "You can't go now." I said, "If it's all right for you, it's all right for me, too." So he said, "Uh, don't tell anybody else." I was with Irene. The guy at the gate would open it only when he heard the whistle and the bells, so we used to jump over the fence. Those fences were high—they had them all around the Amoskeag. Irene jumped over, and so did the boss and his girlfriend. When it came to my turn, I got hooked. My dress caught on one of those spikes. They were there on the other side of the fence, watching me and laughing like fools. Finally somebody came and pulled me up. It was easy, because I weighed only eighty-two pounds, even when I got married. But I had to take my dress off to get unhooked. Nobody wore pants at the time, except those who went tobogganing. They used to have knickers, but they didn't wear them to work.

It was a good thing we were working in the cellar, because a guy named Leo Jacob could have killed himself one day. He was always after me to go out with him, and I didn't want to. He was jealous because I was going out with someone else. I got mad at him because he had played tricks on me, and I wanted to get even. I knew he was afraid of rats and mice. He'd see a little mouse in a truck and run like hell. One noon, I went over to have lunch with my brother Henry at the roundhouse. He was working for the Boston and Maine Railroad. I took one of my friends with me. We were talking together on the way back to work when all of a sudden he pointed to the edge of the canal, and there was a dead rat, about that big [indicates length]. I said, "You got a bag or something? I'm going to bring it to Leo Jacob." Henry said, "Wait a minute." He got a newspaper, grabbed the dead rat, wrapped it up, and I put it under my arm. The girl that was with me was laughing her head off. When I came into the mill, Leo was sitting on the window sill waiting for the whistle to start work. I went up to him and said, "Leo, your friend told me to give this to you." (One of his friends always came in at the same time as me.) Leo didn't believe me; he thought it was a trick. Finally I said, "I don't have time to stand here, Leo. You either keep it or I'll take it." So he grabbed it and opened up the bundle; and when he saw the rat, he fell out the window [laughs]. The other girl told everybody in the mill about it, and one of the old women got mad at me. She started to pull my curls and said, "Do you know that you could have got him killed?" Then I realized what I had done. I told him I was sorry, but he was so mad at me that he didn't speak to me for nine years.

When we played jokes at work, the bosses weren't supposed to see what was going on. They'd ignore us or look the other way. What could they say? We were waiting for the frame to stop so we could do the work. They couldn't send us home. It wasn't like today, when one job is done and you are expected to go and do another.

In the mill, people stayed among themselves to talk about whatever they had to talk about. Married people would be friendly, friendly enough to come and sit with us sometimes during the noon hour. Other times they'd stay in their corner and talk about their families and stuff like that. But we kids didn't have any troubles. We'd sit in our little corner and we'd have our dinner together. Then we'd play games and we'd dance. One of us played the harmonica. She'd play and we'd dance, we'd sing. We used to raise hell. If we had a chance to play a dirty trick on somebody, we'd look around and think of something. Nobody would know the difference [laughs].

When I started working in the mill in summer vacation, the boss's son was working there, too. The boss treated us the same

way he treated his son. You'd think we were all his kids. If we
did anything that he didn't like, he'd come over and let us
know, as if he was our father—and we were afraid of him just
as if he *was* our father. But he was not mean to us, ever. As
long as you did your work and tried your best, he'd never say
anything. Not to me, anyway.

When my work was going well, you could hear me singing
all the way down to the other end of the room, even with all
that noise. In school I was in the church choir; we usually
learned all church songs, and everybody would laugh when
they heard me sing them. When my work was going badly,
everybody in the room knew because they wouldn't hear me
sing. They'd come over and look at me. Sometimes I cried.

Bella had got me a job working with her at the Langden
Mill spinning, and Henry was working there, too, in the room
upstairs. He was warping. I really hated spinning because you
have to run around so much. When the work went bad, the
ends kept breaking and I couldn't keep up with it because
there were too many broken ends. The bobbins would run out
and the unspun cotton would get wound around the rollers.
When I had a hard time, I'd just sit there and cry. Sometimes
when it was too dry in the room, that would make the ends
break. It wasn't the Amoskeag's [management's] fault. It was
the machines' fault, I guess. It was the way the spinning frame
was made. You can't keep on going when there are about fifteen bobbins running out at the same time. You can't tie the
fifteen all at once. You've got to tie and change one after the
other.

I didn't want to be like Bella and stay on spinning the rest
of my life, so I quit. I decided that there were enough other
kinds of jobs in the mill that you didn't have to do one that you
didn't like. You could leave a job in the morning and have
another one in the afternoon, so I got out of there and worked
on wool in #2 Mill. They put me on doffing at first. I was the
one who had to take care of the frame that was in the twisting
room. I had to stop the frames, start them, make sure they
didn't run over, and watch the girls. There were twenty-five
girls there working as doffers.

Later on I used to like warping because we were doing
samples for striped dish towels. I was the only one on that kind

of work. With stripes, you had to know how to place the spool so that the line would come out just so. You ran big warps; and you had to be careful to make sure that the edges were even, because if they weren't, the thread would break when it got to the slashing machine, and the boss would come over and let you know about it. You had to make a perfect beam. Then it was sent to the girls who ran it through the comb, and then they'd bring the comb and the warp to the weavers. The weavers would have bobbins on the side if they were going to make checkered cloth. The warp came down one way, and you had to have the bobbins going the other way. If I had the color scheme for the threads wrong, then it would be wrong when the weavers got it on the other end. That's why I liked my job; I knew I had a responsibility. The boss would give me a chart of the colors, and I had to learn how to read it. The chart tells you just where each thread goes in the front of the warp or in back of the warp. At the edge of the warp was the stripe, which went along each side of the towel. I had to arrange the different colors at the end of the warp, but all the rest was white. When there was enough yarn on the warp, we'd stop it and cut it. The man would come over to take that warp off and put another on, and the girls would tie over. They'd put the little spools in, and then we'd pull the threads up and start the new warp.

When I went to work at #3 Mill as a warper, I looked at my pay after the first month: I was getting the same pay as a tie-over girl. So I told my boss, "I'm not tying over any more; I'm warping. You have new girls who came in after me, and you're paying them more." He said, "Yes, but they were hired as warpers and you were hired as a tie-over girl." So I looked at him and said, "How can I get the pay of the others, then?" "Well, you can't unless you change your card at the main office." So I left my machine, got my coat from my cupboard, and started walking out. He said, "Where are you going?" "I'm leaving. I do my work when half the time the other girls let their work stop to talk. Well, I don't let my work stop. I keep running like a fool all day. When you can pay me the price you're paying them, then I'll come back." I got my release papers from the mill office. Then I went over to Mr. Boucher at the employment office and told him why I quit. He said, "How would you like to go back and get paid for warping? I've got a note here that says he needs warpers." I said, "I know he does; he needs three more." He said, "Yeah, now it's four." So Mr. Boucher called my boss up, and he agreed to pay me warpers' wages. I went right back.

The only place we could go to complain about things like that was the main office. They always listened; and if they thought you were in the right, they'd help you out. I suppose there were a lot of us that were underpaid. I don't know if others complained because I never asked. When I first worked there, we didn't have a union. After a time, they started one. I don't think it made much difference. I had to pay my union dues like everyone else; but when I had a complaint, I'd go to the office and tell the boss. I wouldn't bother with the union. If you talked to the union, they'd come over and look; then they'd turn around and ask the boss and do what the boss said. What good was that?

After the strike I worked for a while in the mill, but I was sick of the mills. I had a lot of reasons to quit. We were working in the cellar. If anybody asked us, "Where are you working?" we'd say, "We're working in #2 with the rats!" [laughs]. Actually, I never saw any rats except the one I brought in myself. The workroom was pretty clean because the sweeper would go around two or three times a day, and then the mopper would come every other day. I kept it clean around my work because if the dust from the wool got into your machine, your work would bunch and make a break. If you kept the machine clean, though, the work would run well because there was no dust or anything to spoil the yarn. I left, though, because I didn't like that dungeon [laughs].

After I quit the Amoskeag dungeon, I went and tried the shoe shop, but I couldn't take it on account of the cement glue and the ether. Nobody I knew ever thought of going to the shoe shop to work. They started me putting cement on the crepe soles, but the doctor said, "You're allergic to cement and ether. You can't work on this." So the boss gave me another job in the same room, at the other end, where I couldn't smell the cement.

When I began work in the shoe shop, there were about five or six girls; they came over and started to size me up from head to foot. One of them looked at me and said, "Well! I see we got another mill rat." I turned around and looked at her, and I said, "Who, me?" She said, "Don't you come from the mills?" I said, "Yes, I do." She said, "Well, *you're* the mill rat!" I said, "I'll tell you something. I'd just as soon be a mill rat as a shoe-shop skunk." If I was a rat, they were skunks, because I didn't like the smell of their shoe shop. They never bothered me after that.

I liked working in the mill better, so I went back to the Amoskeag as a warper. I got Irene a job as a tie-over girl, and then she went on warping, too. We were even making silkwear [rayon], so I wasn't on wool there. I was working during the second shift. They were working on some black stuff. I don't know what kind of stuff it was. There were so many black frames and so many maroon; and on the other side of the room, where the black dust wouldn't fly, they had the white. Those who worked on the black got a cent more in their pay. When we got out of there, we'd look like real Negroes, we were so black.

When the Amoskeag closed up, I went to work for the J. P. Stevens Mill. I saw that they needed some more reelers, so I talked to Bella, because she was cleaning at the movie at the time, and they were going to close that, too. If you had gray hair, they didn't want you. You were too old for the job. That was already starting. So Bella had tried to get in at Stevens and she couldn't. It took me a whole month before I could get her in. And boy, was she glad that she went in, because she stayed in until she was sixty-five.

We sisters were always working with one another. We used to exchange our lunches. At that time, I used to bake my own bread, and I'd make soup. I'd bring soup, and I'd give half to Bella; and then I'd change sandwiches with her, because she wasn't making the bread. We'd take turns making doughnuts, and we'd bring doughnuts to the mill.

One morning when I was working, I had a brand-new dress on and I said to myself, "God, it's hot! It's so hot in there with the steam to keep the wool humid, I don't think I'm going to wear any slip today. Nobody will know, because the dress is so heavy." So I didn't wear any slip. We weren't supposed to open the windows because they wanted the steam to stay in the room, but the one who had worked on my frame the previous

Unidentified young girl leaving the mill, photographed by Lewis Hine in 1909

night had left the window open. I went to close it. I had already started my frame; and when I came back, I stopped near the frame to put my lunch bag there. My dress was flared, and the bottom got caught in between the gears and started to roll around. I tried to pull it but I couldn't. The frame was still going. I tried to reach the handle and I couldn't. Bella and I were working back to back. I said, "Bella! Help me!" My dress kept going in, and the reel was getting me in the back. When she saw that she came over and grabbed me in her arms to pull me. I said, "Bella, don't pull me! You're choking me! Try to stop the frame." And she started to cry. "Oh, my God! What am I going to do?" One of the inspectors looked over and told another girl, "This is the first time I've seen Bella and Ora fighting. What in the world are they fighting about? It can't be Bella, because Bella is so quiet, but Bella is on top of Ora!" Then they looked closer and saw she was trying to help me. They stopped the machine and went over to get the boss.

Nobody could get me out of it. I was twisted all around the gears. Those gears should have been covered but they weren't. The boss took his knife and cut my dress off. I was shaking like a leaf. I sat down on a box. Boy, was I shaking! He was laughing, because I told Bella, "See! The first time I don't wear a slip, and look what happens!" And he said, "Oh, look at that! Doesn't she have a cute, little, pink fanny?" He laughed at me and told the shipper to take me home. I said, "I can't go home like this! I've got no coat, no sweater, no nothing! All the back of my dress is gone. I can't go home like this!" One of the night girls had forgotten her raincoat in there, so they brought me the coat. And shaking like I was, I went home, changed, and went back to work the same day. The boss told me, "I know you'll be shaky the rest of the day, so take your time." But I couldn't take my time. I ran all my life. How could I take my time?

▶ Lucille Bourque

Lucille Anger Bourque, Ora Pelletier's sister, was sixty-five years old when we first met her. Only months earlier she had finally retired from the mills, where she had spent the whole of her working life. Her husband, Ernest, had also been a mill worker.

Lucille took pride in her work and enjoyed explaining to us the different stages of textile production. Despite her strict upbringing, she is an open and outgoing woman.

If I was to start over again, if it was like the Amoskeag, I wouldn't mind it. The money was better than working in the store. Today, salesgirls make pretty good money, but years ago they didn't make so much. My sister Ora worked at the five and ten, and she didn't make a thing. I was making more money than she was. I was single, and I was taking in $10.00 a week, clear.

At first, I didn't want to go to work. I was only sixteen when my mother sent me down to the mill. I wanted to continue with high school, but she wouldn't send me. She'd say, "You don't need an education. You're going to get married and wash diapers." I thought if I didn't find a job, maybe she'd let me go back to school. So in the morning, I'd leave and walk uptown the minute the stores were open. I'd go from one store to another, just looking. Then at noontime, I'd come home. I did that for three or four days. My mother asked, "Did you find a job?" and I said I hadn't. I didn't go to the employment office either. I was afraid I'd get a job, and I didn't want one. When my sister Flora came home for dinner, my mother said, "Why don't you take her with you?" Flora brought me to the employment office, and they sent me to the rayon plant.

I thought, "If I do enough bad work, they'll kick me out." I saw a man coming, and I figured he must be some big shot, so I got my scissors and made like I was cutting a skein of yarn. I saw him looking dazed. "Stop her! What is she doing?" I thought, "Oh boy! I'm going to get fired. I'm glad." But my boss showed the man some trucks loaded with yarn where the skeins were bad. After he left, my boss said, "We cover for you, you cover for us. It must've been a bad skein." We got a lot of bad skeins because they were dyed different colors. "Maybe there was too much dye," he said. "Some of them get so thick they keep breaking. They're impossible to run. But don't ever do that when Kluckholm is around. Don't ever do anything like that! Jesus!" He covered up for me, but my skein wasn't bad. I just wanted to get fired!

When the work was slack on spooling, instead of laying us off, they sent me to work downstairs. I had to take some bobbins (they were cardboard) and stick them one over the other, and then count them. One day I was playing hide-and-seek with another girl. There was a great big barrel where they used to dye and change, and the other girl was hiding inside the barrel. The boss came down, and I was sitting there counting up to twenty-five or something. I looked up, and there he was. "Are you alone down here?" he said. "No." "Well, you're not supposed to be alone. Anything could happen." You had to have a couple of girls to defend yourself. Nothing ever happened, but just in case. They used to take precautions. I wasn't going to tell him she was hiding in the barrel. I didn't know where she was anyway, so I said, "She must have gone to the ladies' room or gone for a drink or something." He said, "All right," and walked out. Just as he went by that barrel, she started to lift the lid; but she saw something moving, so she put the lid down and kept quiet. After he left, I was still looking around. "Where the hell are you?" I called out. Then she came out of the barrel.

It was easy to learn your work. The boss would ask a girl, "Do you want to teach her how to do that?" He wouldn't force her. The girl who taught me was my nicest friend. She explained everything to me, every angle, anything that would help make it easier. Now they have somebody hired to teach you, but they just give you the fundamentals, and that's it.

We'd have an hour for dinner. Some would crochet, and some would sit down and tell stories. We'd have a lot of fun. You knew everybody's name, and everybody talked to you. Everybody was friendly. One day the boss said to us, "When you don't have anything to do, why don't you go in front and learn?" So I went up to the front of the room where Ora was learning to be a warp tender. I said, "What do we do?" She showed me. Then one of the ends broke. At first, I couldn't see it. She said, "See that little crack, where there's a little space? Well, that end is broken. Just take the broken end and bring it to the front and tie it." I said, "Oh, I know how to do that."

I went back and sat with the women, and the boss said to me, "Hey, weren't you supposed to go learn when you had a chance?" I said, "I know how." "Well, then, there's a little baby warp there. I'll put you on that. It's already tied. Just pull your ends and start it. If you have any trouble, ask Ora." Anyway, I pulled all my ends—there were quite a few broken ones. When Ora came over, I said, "I'm all ready to start it. Check and see." When you're used to it, you can tell by just looking if the ends are crooked or crossed. "No crossed ends!" she said.

I stayed on the warp, and it paid more money. If you wanted a job that paid more, you had to grab the chance. When somebody quit and you said you wanted that job, then they gave it to you. If you wanted to, you could work your way up. That's what I did. Warper, weaver, and slasher were the best-paying jobs in the mill.

In the warping room and in the weaving room, they used to have what they called floor ladies. Today they call them smash piecers. If a warp had too many broken ends, the floor ladies would come and fix them. That was their job. They would go from one end of the room to the other. There were probably four or five of them for a hundred looms. At the Amoskeag, if the weavers needed help, they'd put up a stick of wood that they called a flag. One end was red and the other end was blue. Red was for the loom fixer, and blue meant that they wanted one of the floor ladies. If the smash was big, there would be two of them: one would go in the back and one would go in the front.

At the Amoskeag, they always wanted to hurry to get a warp started. There would be a whole bunch of us, I think about seven or eight girls. We'd get into the warp, put the spools in the truck, and tie the ends. The warp tender would pull those ends and start a warp. Sometimes there were no warps out, so we'd just sit down together. In those days, if there was no work, you could sit on the window sill and look outside. Nobody ever bothered you if your work was done. The bosses weren't like they are today; they wouldn't push you. They wouldn't say anything mean or shout at you for nothing. If there was a warp out, we'd all run in and help the girl who was on it. The minute the job was done, we'd all take a seat. Nobody was on piecework in that room.

It will never be like the Amoskeag again. The good old days weren't so good because they were harder. But in a way, I think it was better then because things were cheaper and they were made better than they are today. We didn't make so much money, but what we had went further. They wanted the work to be good. Today, it's nothing but shit.

Yvonne Dionne, seventy-one at the time she was interviewed, was one of sixteen children in a French-Canadian family. Yvonne first went into the spinning department when she was fifteen, in 1920, but she hated the dirt and smell of the mills. When work there was slack, she would work in the local shoe factories; but she did not work at all after the Amoskeag shutdown, devoting her time instead to raising her six children.

Although she and her husband had spent most of their married life on a farm, after all the children left home, they moved to a city apartment. They had just celebrated their fiftieth wedding anniversary at the time of the interview.

I always enjoyed the work at the Amoskeag when I was there, though if I could have done without, I would have stayed home. But when everything is hard to get, and you want to have a few extra things, you have to help out the family. We were brought up in a large family—my father was a weaver and a loom fixer—and as soon as one girl was old enough, she went to work. That was the way. The oldest one started, and the rest of the family had to follow suit. We didn't feel bad about not going to school because nobody could afford to. Our parents were too poor. None of us even finished grammar school. I think I got through the eighth grade.

It did bother me at one time when I was at Sacred Heart School, because I had good marks. As soon as somebody got sick, I was supposed to go and help out; schooling came next.

One day, Alice, my sister-in-law, took sick, and Mom told me that I had to go help my aunt, Mrs. Girard. "She's very tired, and she's old and very sick," she said, "so you leave school and go and help her for a few days." That was during the middle of June. We were just going to have our graduation, and they used to have a prize for not missing school. I had gone to mass every morning the whole year, and I had my good conduct and everything. It was all *Très Bien.*

The nun called up my mother and said, "Where's Claudia?" (My name was Claudia at the time.) My mother said, "She's helping another family that needed help." "Have her come back right away," the nun said. "She has a surprise, a gift coming to her. If she's not here by the afternoon, she loses it." So my mother called me right up. When I got into class, the sister told me, "You almost missed it." I got a nice big book. On it was a leaf, which had a banner inside that read: *Prix d'honneur.* That means honor prize. I managed to get good grades when I was there, but that was the end of my education. It would have been a wonderful thing to be able to speak English, to meet with people.

I used to ask my mother, "Why is it always me?" The nuns were very lenient with me at that time because they knew the family needed help. My mother used to say, "Why don't you come back right after school?" I had to do my share of the cleaning up, sweep the floors and clean the blackboards. I had to be in the choir even though I had no voice at all. So my mother had a talk with the sister superior: "I wish you could send her home right after school because I need her."

My mother said she always had "one in the crib and one in the oven," so it was pretty rough on her. When I was little, she worked in the Amoskeag. She'd leave one of my sisters, who was twelve or thirteen, in charge of us; but my sister wouldn't stay in the house. She'd go outside to be with her friends. One day, I tried to reach the kettle to take it off the stove, and I dropped it and burned myself and one of the babies. My mother never went back to the mills after that.

I hated working in the mill. It was terrible in the spinning room. It was so warm in there, and the smell! During the vacations they used to hire schoolchildren to take apart rollers on the spinning machine and clean them. They were full of grease, and my hands would get all greasy. And the roaches around there! They had closets to put our clothes in, and we'd have to shake out our clothes to make sure there weren't any roaches to take home with us. Every part of the Amoskeag mills in those days was loaded with roaches, great big ones. They had washerwomen, old people washing the floors, but the roaches came from underneath the pipes. You'd see them in the ladies' room and the men's room.

My mother said—this was in 1921—if I wanted to work in the weave room, this woman that lived down the street would teach me. So I learned how to weave from her, and for that she got $3.00 extra in her pay every week.

The first time they put me on my own set of looms, she didn't tell me that I had to oil it. The looms have to be oiled all the time. You have to dust underneath. The first thing I knew, it was smoking. I got after the loom fixer: "What's the matter? There's a fire underneath my loom." "When was the last time you oiled it?" I said, "When do we oil it?" "Didn't she tell you?"

The woman had taught me about the pattern, all right, but she hadn't told me how to take care of the looms. A friend of our family, Mr. Valois, the barber, was a loom fixer at that time. I said, "Look, Mr. Valois, I don't know anything about it." I was only sixteen then. He said, "When you're sixteen, you're very irresponsible. You don't hear all those things."

I stayed on that job for maybe another three or four months, but I got disgusted. I was always the last one to have a good set of looms. Being the last one on the job, you're the first one out. My mother got after me to go in with my brother and sister on wool. She said, "Did you try in the woolen department? Maybe you'll do better. Then you won't have all kinds of patterns. All you'll have to do is make sure your loom is oiled." She knew something about weaving, you see.

They didn't have batteries in those days, they just had handlooms. I started with two looms. Then they gave me four more. They put on the batteries in 1924, the year that I was married, and made me a battery hand. My work was to fill up the batteries with yarn, while more experienced help, older help, ran the looms. They had twelve looms to run. The batteries made the loom run automatically. In an automatic loom the bobbin falls into the shuttle, then the shuttle goes back and forth, back and forth; and when there were just a few yards of yarn left, the shuttle would fall [out of the loom] by itself. You had to watch the machine and stop it before the end of the yarn in the shuttle. Otherwise you had a "mis-pick." That means that it will be damaged cloth. You had to tear out the part that didn't fit and start over again. It wasn't easy. It all depended on who your loom fixer was. If you happened to have a good one, the looms kept going and you earned money.

We all had a hard time with the wool. We made those pants with purple stripes. The hard part of it was to find where the stripe belonged in the cloth, because you can be off by one thread. That was our job as room girl. In order to check the cloth, we would pass a black filling beneath it* to see if there was any mis-pick or any wrong draw. The errors have to be corrected because your name is on that piece of cloth. Then they take it to the supervisor to put under a heavy glass, to make sure that everything is started right. If it's wrong, they come and stop the loom and say, "Do it over again." They had to be strict, because if you had a roll of material with one thread missing, it's like you had a pencil mark right through it—though someone that didn't know anything about cloth wouldn't see it. It had to be repaired, and in the cloth room they had women called burlers that did that.

I worked for a few weeks on burling in 1932. I probably would have advanced if I had stayed there longer. It's a very good-paying job. You could learn to mend the cloth, repair the damage. I know a mender is paid probably $15.00 or $20.00 an hour. If you have a burn on a piece of cloth, they can repair it, stitch by stitch. I never did that in the burling room. All I did was to pull out any little threads, any lumps or defects in the thread. Sometimes, for instance, a hair would fall in between the threads.

If the mill was slack, I'd go to the shoe shop. I always had a job waiting for me there. I liked the shoe shop a lot better because there wasn't so much pressure. I liked stitching, and I liked the smell a lot better. In the mill it smells like an old goat. Of course, after a while you get accustomed to it. But the noise

* This means that she held a filling bobbin with black yarn on it under the warp to see any gaps.

Quilling room, ca. 1910

in the weave room—you'd come out of there and it would take you a while to hear what the others were saying. The noise just about blocked your ears. When you get through with the mills, you're hard of hearing [laughs].

I learned how to dance in #4 Mill, with the girls, not with men. At that time I didn't start work until eight o'clock in the morning because I was only sixteen. Those that were over sixteen started to work at seven o'clock. At noontime, the frames were stopped for an hour. We'd sit in the alley and eat our lunch; and if there was a good singer, she would sing and we would dance along the aisle.

▶ Cora Pellerin

Cora Pellerin was born in 1900, one of sixteen children in her family. She is still a vigorous woman, mending clothes for her eight grandchildren. She started work in 1912 at the age of eleven and remained at the Amoskeag until the shutdown. During her career there, she worked as a spinner, spooler, weaver, and room girl.

In 1931 she married Jules Pellerin after a long period of courtship, neither wanting to marry while each was supporting an aging mother. Jules died while their two daughters were still infants. During his prolonged illness and after his death, Cora continued to work as a weaver. After the shutdown of the Amoskeag, she worked first at the J. P. Stevens Mill in Tilton, New Hampshire; later at the Waumbec Mill, after it opened in one of the empty Amoskeag mills; and subsequently at the Chicopee Mill. During her late sixties and early seventies, she worked for the Habitant Soup Company, also located in one of the old Amoskeag mills.

Today Cora Pellerin resides in one of the former Amoskeag tenements now renovated as FHA-assisted housing for the elderly. We first met her at the Amoskeag exhibit, where she recognized the door from the corporation tenement (by then demolished for urban renewal) in which she had lived. She knew it by the doorknob, which she had chosen herself as a replacement for a broken one.

When I talk about my work in the mill, to my daughters especially, they think it's a story; and when I say something about living on a farm, to them it's a story. They don't believe it's true that we were that backward.

I came from Canada in 1911. I started working in 1912 when I was eleven. My brother-in-law, Bert Molloy, was overseer; and my other boss was John Jacobson.

I started my first job in the spinning room, and my last job was in weaving at the Chicopee Mill. My last job in the Amoskeag was in 1935; that's when it closed down. I was one of the last ones to come out.

My father and two of my brothers worked in the mills. My father used to help in the dress room, setting the beam up for the drawing-in girls. We were thirteen in my family: eleven children and my mother and father. My mother had sixteen children, but five of them died as babies.

When I was eleven, my father had a birth certificate made for me in the name of my sister Cora, who died as a baby, because you couldn't go in to work unless you were fourteen. I worked in the old Amoskeag as Cora, but I was naturalized in 1936 as Valeda. Now I stick to Valeda because of my Social Security, but everyone knows me by the name of Cora. Even my daughters didn't know until they were older that that's not my real name.

My father didn't want to sell his farm in Canada. He cut the first tree when he was thirteen years old in the forest where he made that farm. He was a farmer, and that was his life. He came to the States because my mother was brought up here, and she talked my father into bringing the whole family together to Manchester.

People were doing that in Canada. When they had three or four children that could work, they would come out for a few years to make money, and then they'd go back to the farm. It took my father a long time to decide. They came and stayed for three years; and when they went back in 1914, I was thirteen and working here, so I begged my mother to leave me. My mother said, "If I can find a good boardinghouse, I'll let you stay." So she found a family-style boardinghouse that would take me, my sister, and my brother. My sister was eighteen and my brother was sixteen. The woman who kept the boardinghouse said to my mother, "As long as they mind me, you don't have to worry. If they don't mind me, I'll write you and let you know." So my mother went back to Canada and we stayed here, but I'm the only one in my family who has always lived in Manchester.

If I wanted to go back on the farm, I'd have had to go work in private houses in Montreal and Quebec, take care of the house, wash clothes, help with the food, and whatever there is to be done. Housemaid. My mother didn't want that because we were brought up in the States, and she knew that if her girls were going to go wrong, they were going to do it away from home also. So she said, "At least if they work in the mills, they work a certain hour, they get paid, they do what they want." But she wanted us to stay with a woman that she could depend on. And it was a family life for us in the boardinghouse. The woman I boarded with had six children.

When I was a little girl, I liked it on the farm in Canada. But I didn't miss it, because for me it was paradise here in Manchester. Everything we had on the farm was for a purpose. When we used to go to school, we'd stop and pick up some berries. We'd bring strawberries or raspberries or blueberries or maple syrup to the village, and the ones that didn't have any farms would give us sugar or some food. We'd exchange that instead of money. I didn't want to live that way, not after I got my pay every other week. Live on a farm, raise eight, ten kids —oh no! Have to have your baby in the house, only one doctor for three parishes. And in the winter, the snow was so high it would come all the way up to the windows. We had a sled. I remember we sat on the floor of the sled and they put a big fur rug on top of us; that's how we went to church. Otherwise we'd freeze to death [laughs].

I never missed Canada. My life is more American. I worked in Canada during the strike of 1922, in Three Rivers [Trois Rivières], but I never would go back there to live. It was paradise here because you got your money, and you did whatever you wanted to with it. I liked to go to a movie. Nowadays, it's modern in Canada. When my mother went back in 1914, they had a telephone, but before they had none of that. It was murder.

When I first started in the Amoskeag, I worked in the spinning room in the Amory Mill. We all worked together. The spinning room was for young girls. We used to dance in the

Cora Pellerin, 1977

aisles. We'd go in the hallways, and one would watch for
the boss while the other one took care of our work. We danced,
and a Greek boy played the harmonica [laughs]. We thought
the weave room was for married women and old maids.

We had a good time in the spinning room. After we got our
pay, every time we had something new, we'd stay out to show
off our new clothes. In those days it wasn't like today. We'd get
dressed for the holidays. It was a must—you had to have something new. At Easter we'd have something like a new coat, new
shoes, new hat; and we'd stay out the week after we got our
pay. They used to come on Thursday at two o'clock to give us
our pay. We'd take turns. We didn't all stay out the same day. I
would stay out one Thursday, then the following week my
girlfriend, and then the following week it was another one's
turn [laughs]. I never would wear the clothes from the mill in
the house. We changed in the mill. I made my own smock to
wear there. It had to have pockets to put the scissors and roving in.

When I was seventeen, I got my own room. I lived there for
four years, and then I got an apartment all by myself. I had
nice furniture because a furniture store furnished the apartment. I used to pay $5.00 per week for everything. In the
corporations it was much cheaper, but you couldn't get an apartment in the corporations if you weren't married. It was family
housing.

Not too many women were living alone in their own apartments. I was a wildcat [laughs]. Some mothers of my girl-
friends, after they knew that I was in an apartment, they didn't
want their daughters to chum around with me any more. In
those days, if you lived alone in a room, they were afraid their
daughters would get the idea.

I had my own home, I had everything. I cooked my own
food. I didn't have to go to the boardinghouse and eat what
they had. I learned how to make pie and bake my own beans,
and I liked that. My boyfriend, who became my husband, came
to see me. He was welcome any time he wanted to come. He
was fifteen years older than I.

In 1918, I started to weave. I had a very good teacher. She
was the niece of the woman who ran the boardinghouse where
I lived. The woman said, "If she's going to make a weaver out

of you, it won't take long." I was a little bit afraid of her. They give you two weeks to learn. So the first day of the second week I started two looms, then three, and by noontime I had four looms going, and I kept them going all day. She said, "Hey, start another one and I'll keep a watch on it." We had six looms for a full set. So I started another one. By that second week I had all my six looms going.

My work was handlooms—four-shuttle, four-color.° Some weavers weave all their lives and never get the hang of it. Some women especially, they just weave because they have to earn money; they never apply themselves to it. They were house-keepers. I preferred to weave because it paid better. In weaving, you were on piecework; you were paid so much a pick. You had a clock with numbers to count the picks, and every day the second hand took the numbers on the clock. In the old Amoskeag, we only had one shift, so nobody got in your looms. You had your work, and that was it. But after the strike, they had two shifts, and then they had three shifts.

If you happened to have a good weaver on the third shift, it was more pleasant to work when you came in in the morning. If you had a weaver that didn't care or was sleeping on the job, you could lose an hour before you got your loom in shape to work. But you didn't stand for that. Sometimes a weaver would be sick—it's tough on the third shift—but if it happened a lot with the same weaver, then I'd report it to the second hand or the overseer, because if you had a good shift, you'd make better money all around. The boss on that shift would give him a warning; and if he didn't change his bad habits, then they'd let him go. It's like the cliché: "Either you fit or you don't." If you did your own work, nobody would bother you.

Your loom fixer could make it hard on you. When you had a loom break down, he could make believe he was busy. You

---

° "Two shuttles" were two-shuttle looms making cloth with two colors in the weft. Four-shuttle looms made cloth with four colors in the weft (the color of the warp was already on the beam and was controlled by the harnesses). Mary Cunion's Aunt Susan was brought to America by the Amoskeag in 1868 to work on the first four-shuttle, or four-box, loom. The term "handloom" refers to the fact that these were machines that did not have batteries to feed full bobbins into the shuttles automatically. The loom had to be stopped, the shuttles removed, and the bobbins replaced every few minutes, all by hand—thus the term "handloom." A weaver could manage only a few looms of this type at a time.

didn't know if he was busy or not, but you couldn't leave your loom until it was started. He'd come when he was good and ready, so you lost all that time. Your clock was running. You'd tell the boss, but what could he do? He wasn't going to fire a good loom fixer.

Some of the fixers or bosses were rough, but they were reported. They gave them two warnings; the second time they fired them, and they went on the blacklist in the office. I remember plenty that were fired, especially the men when they were drinking on the weekend.

If you needed the help of the room girl, you put a stick up. In the old days, when we didn't have sticks, we used to go after the room girl and tell her we had a smash. They'd go to each in turns if they were honest. But they could give you a hard time, too. Sometimes they'd jump over you, and you'd lose an hour. All the time your loom is stuck, you don't make money.

In the old days we used to get fined. If we had some bad cloth coming back, we had to pay, but later they passed a law that they couldn't fine us any more. Even if you're a good weaver, sometimes it happens, you can't help it. Sometimes even a fixer himself makes a smash when he fixes a loom. Some weren't mechanics—it was pitiful when you didn't have the mechanic in you.

Before the strike, the union wasn't too strong. There were a lot of people that didn't believe in it. The stewards asked you to join the union. They'd come after you with a paper to sign your name and pay your dues; and if you wanted to go in, all right. If you didn't, well, you didn't have to. But there was a catch. If you had a second hand or a boss that was for the union, he wouldn't declare himself because he didn't have to, so you would have no way of knowing it. If you didn't like the union, he could make it hard for you. On the other hand, if you liked the union and he didn't like it, he could also make it hard for you.

When the union people came to Manchester, it was up to us to vote whether we wanted them in or not. Dumaine himself said in a meeting that "the grass will grow on Elm Street before the union will come into my mill. I'll close it down." He said, "I've always been fair to my help, and I don't need the union. They have a union in Massachusetts, and they don't do what I do for my help." It was true in a way. It was on his account that we had all the benefits the Amoskeag gave us. Nobody else would do that, but the newer generation wanted more money, and they wanted someone to represent them.

We needed the union even though Parker Straw was a good man; it was old Dumaine who pushed him. Straw was only the agent; Dumaine owned the mill. Parker Straw did a lot of things to save us. He waited until the last minute to do what Dumaine wanted him to do. My brother-in-law, Bert Molloy, was an overseer; he began as a filling boy and worked himself up. Bert told me that sometimes they'd have a meeting with all the overseers and all the superintendents, and they'd tell them Mr. Dumaine wanted to do this and Mr. Dumaine wanted to do that. And Straw would say, "Let it go for a while." Sometimes he'd say, "Well, we'll try it; try it and see how it goes." Then the old man put his foot down, and he gave us more work and a cut in pay, so we went on strike.

Some went back to Canada during the strike and never came back, but the younger generation found work here and there. In Lowell and Lawrence there were good woolen mills [where the strike was settled sooner], but my brother and sister went nine months without working!

I hadn't gone to Canada to see my mother for seven years, so I went to stay with her on the farm for a couple of months. One day I went to a wedding, and I met a girl from Three Rivers who worked as a waitress in a restaurant. She said they needed a waitress. I had never been a waitress, but I didn't want to scab while the strike was going on, so I went to work in the restaurant. I worked there nine months, and was I lonesome in Canada! I had my steady boyfriend here [in the States], so I couldn't go out with anyone. It was hard, because after a boy went out with a girl for six months or a year, they got married or else the family got after them to make them separate. But I didn't want to come back until it said in the paper that the strike was all over.

When we went on strike in 1922, we wanted eight hours a day, forty hours a week, but Dumaine didn't want to give it to us. The president of the union wanted to make a name for himself. He thought Dumaine was going to give in. He never thought Dumaine would actually close the doors, so we're the ones that lost out. Anyway, it turned out the state law was forty-eight hours a week,° so there was nothing we could do about it. But in those days, with the education I had—and a lot of them were like me—how could I know the law in Concord? I didn't read English, and the French paper didn't tell us anything about it. The *Manchester Union Leader* was for Dumaine, and so was the French paper. It was run by French people that had come from Canada. They were educated people, and they thought the working people were low-class. They put things so you could take them both ways. I never bought the French paper after that. Sometimes they told the truth, but we couldn't believe it. We thought they were trying to put something over on us.

If we didn't think we could get the forty hours,°° we wouldn't have gone out on strike—in February, mind you, in winter. I believe that there were a few that wouldn't come out, but they couldn't stay there all alone. Dumaine was mad, but he always did what he wanted. I don't blame him; if I had owned the Amoskeag, I wouldn't have been too happy either. I didn't own the Amoskeag, but I wasn't too happy about working in Three Rivers for $7.00 a week besides the tip. I was so glad when my boyfriend wrote to me on the farm and told me it was all done, and everybody was going back to work. I gave my notice and came back the week of Thanksgiving. That was the best Thanksgiving that I ever had.

In those days I didn't believe too much in unions. I was afraid of them, because in Massachusetts they had a lot of trouble. It seemed that nobody won in the end, only that the people are out and they lost their wages. I didn't get into the union until after the strike of 1922. A couple of years before the Amoskeag closed down, they announced they'd be giving us a 5 percent wage cut. We had a meeting at the union hall, and everybody voted against the cut. Then two or three weeks after, a notice went up that, effective the next day, there would be a 5 percent cut. I didn't pay my dues after that.

° She is confusing the later campaigns for the forty-hour week with the effort during the strike of 1922 to return to forty-eight hours from fifty-four hours a week. She is also confused about the forty-eight-hour law, which was not enacted in New Hampshire until well after the strike of 1922.

°° Actually, forty-eight hours.

In 1926 I went in as head weaver and sample weaver for nine years, until 1935, when the Amoskeag closed down. A head weaver was like a luxury, an overexpense on the payroll; so I worked as a head weaver, but on the payroll I was marked as a spare fixer. A spare fixer was a man's job. It was the superintendent himself that suggested it to my boss. My boss had said to him, "What am I going to do? I need somebody to teach the people." There were a lot that were like me; they didn't have any education, but that doesn't mean that they can't learn things. We showed the weavers how to weave on the dobby looms; they had never had any looms of that kind before.

My husband, Jules Pellerin, was a loom fixer. I met him when my brother was in France, during the war. We had a ball for the soldiers, and that's where I met him. We both were working in the mill, but I didn't know he was working there. I thought he was a rich guy. A week later, I saw him at the gate. I almost fainted [laughs]. I knew him for ten or eleven years before we got married, because I would never get married while my mother was living. No! I wanted to take care of her when she got old and sick. My husband had a sister who was an old maid, and I didn't want to go and live there. He was also still taking care of his mother. She was eighty-two years old when she died. I didn't want him to break up his house on account of me. I was satisfied the way I was. I had plenty of time to raise a family.

I was an old maid at thirty, but I was happy to be an old maid. My friends were all married with four or five kids. Some of them were divorced. I didn't want that. My mother had sixteen children, and I was right in the middle, so I learned in a hurry. I made good money, I dressed up well, I went dancing —I was having a good time. Nobody was telling me what to do and when to go to bed. I didn't want to switch with my friend who had five or six children and a husband that came in drunk every weekend. Nothing doing!

In those days, it was the woman who stayed in the house; she was a housewife. You were a wreck for a man, that's what you were. A wreck for a man! You were supposed to do what your husband told you to do. I didn't like that. My mother always said, "Leave her alone. She can take care of herself." Now my daughter says that.

When my husband was fifty-four, he began to have a heart condition. The doctor said, "You'd be better off if you placed your children in a boarding school." So I sent my girls to the Villa Augustina. I had never been to a school with the nuns. It was hard for me to put them in there. It is a big, big building, and it seemed that it was just like a jail. That's the way I felt inside. I used to go and see them every Wednesday night, and they'd come home every Saturday. They'd have supper with me and leave every Sunday afternoon at four o'clock. If they didn't come, it was because they'd been bad and were being punished. I used to cry on my way home. I wiped my eyes before seeing my husband because if he'd notice it, he'd take the girls out.

My husband died twenty-nine years ago last October. Twenty-nine years, that's a long time. I began to work at eleven; and when I retired I was seventy-two, so I've done my share. But I was happy in the Amoskeag. I loved my work; it was my life. I'm not idle yet. I still mend for my two girls. I have some mending hanging here and there all the time. My grandson Michael came in with a big pile today to mend. Sometimes, though, I don't go as fast as I used to.

▶ *Anna Schmidt**

Seventy-nine-year-old Anna Schmidt was the daughter of a German couple whose marriage in Manchester had been pre-arranged. She grew up in the old German sector of Manchester and still lives next door to her father's house, now owned by another relative. Her father was an alderman in the city of Manchester, and Anna herself remembers canvassing votes from women after the ratification of the Nineteenth Amendment. Her grandfather was a blacksmith, and it was in his shop that she had her burling needle specially wrought, because she did not approve of the unrefined quality of the needles supplied by the Amoskeag. When she was nineteen, Anna married and moved for a short time to Lowell, where she gave birth to a daughter.

After her husband's death in an accident, Anna worked at the Amoskeag until the strike of 1922. She then tried getting started in the real-estate business but was unable to maintain a steady income. Her second husband, whom she married in the 1920s, did not have a steady income either. During the thirties she opened a beauty shop, which she ran until very recently. Her salon became a meeting place for former burlers and other Amoskeag workers.

Today Anna lives in her own home, next door to her daughter and son-in-law. Their lives are very much rooted in the German community of Manchester.

* Fictitious name

You had to be taught burling for about a week before you could go on your own. I was taught by a relative. First I went on burling, and then I went on mending and burling. In burling, you picked the knots out of the wool in the cloth. You had to overlap them. In mending, if there was a thread out, you had to put that thread in just the way it should be. You had to follow the pattern. A knot would pull all the threads, and you had to take the thread and fill in that hole so it wouldn't show after the dyeing. A slug was a coarse thread, and the percher would put a mark on it, just a line so you wouldn't miss it. I enjoyed that work. They were strict. You couldn't leave your frame when the dinner bell rang, and things like that. We used to have tea at our frames. We had a steam pipe, and you'd put a can with tea in it there to heat. It was terrible. It tasted like the steam [laughs].

We didn't get much money at first. We got $14.15 every two weeks. That's sixty hours a week—imagine! You got 14¢ an hour if you made bonus. If you didn't, you'd lose that extra 4¢ and get only 10¢. You'd get a piece of cloth, and it would say one hour or two hours or ten hours on it, and you had to get it done in that time to get the bonus. At the end of the day, you'd add up all your coupons, and I was always way ahead. The boss used to say, "I wish I could catch you losing." I was kind of active. I was only a kid—I started when I was just fourteen —but I made good in there.

I didn't work in the burling room during the strike. I was working in a real-estate business then. They were out nine months. When they went back, we were paid every week. We made more money by that time, too. We went up to around $20.00 or $25.00 a week. But this was mending—it was almost a business.

Mr. Berman, the second hand, showed no favoritism, absolutely none. He didn't care who you were, but he was very easygoing. He was the right man for Mr. Berglund, the boss, because if he was told to do something, he would do it. I got along very well with Mr. Berglund. I didn't know anybody that didn't like him. He was your godfather; he took care of you.

Mending was hard. They were fussy at the Amoskeag. When I worked in Lawrence after that, they weren't so fussy. I was so fussy there that the boss in Lawrence said to me, "You

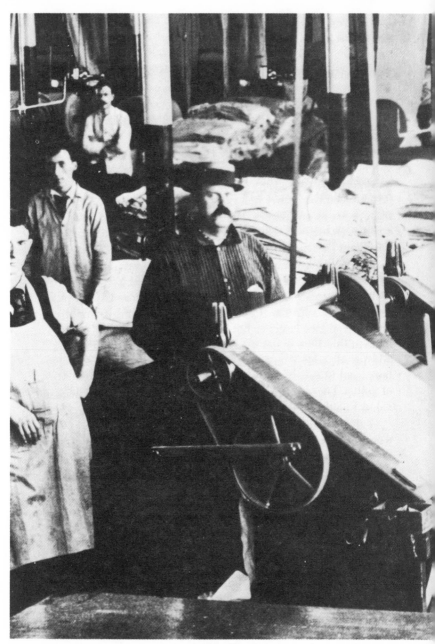

Burling room, ca. 1910

better get your work done faster than that." I said, "In Manchester we were taught to take the knots, unloop them, and warp them over. But you don't do that here; you just pull them out." In Lawrence it was altogether different; you pulled your cloth over a perch, as they called it. But oh, I was disappointed down there. I was really disappointed. They talked so awful to their bosses. We respected ours. We never talked back. That one time when the boss said I had to work faster, I told him I couldn't do it right. He said, "Do it the way they do it here." This other girl turned around and said, "Tell him to go to hell." "Oh, he's a boss," I said, and she replied, "I don't care what he is." Imagine, we'd never do that in the Amoskeag! When Roberts [the superintendent of the burling room] came in, you could hear a pin drop. Once, we didn't know he was coming. The girl on the other side of the burling room was getting married, and we cut up our bonus slips into confetti and threw them all, just past his face. The floor lady was called on the carpet, and she wasn't even there.

I got so homesick in Lawrence; I wanted to go back to work in the Amoskeag. Mr. Berglund was a wonderful boss. He had just been boss three or four weeks when I got in there. Everybody enjoyed it. You'll never find anybody who will say they didn't have a good time in there. After all those years—it's been fifty years—we're still friends, the whole gang of us. Where we were it was nice and clean. We had good scrub ladies; they scrubbed every week. I loved that work, everybody did.

I did have one little argument once with one of the floor ladies. Everybody got only so much black cloth because it was hard to mend. That day my eyes were getting watery, and the cloth inspector gave me my third black roll. She was English, and I guess she didn't like the Germans, I don't know. Anyway, I said I couldn't do it because of my eyes. Finally, I thought it was time for me to complain, so I went to the boss, and he said, "Don't you take that roll, that isn't right. Those girls over there haven't even had one." He didn't say anything else. He just put me upstairs on mending. In those days, the bosses had a lot of power.

There's still plenty of work right now if you want to do it; and these kids, instead of going to college, if they took a job for

$25.00 a week, just to work their way up, they'd be better off. All of those big shots were paperboys; they never went to college. I think nine tenths of all this trouble is the parents. In the old days, you had to go to work. They went to work at twelve. When you were twelve, you could go to work in the summer. Today they wouldn't let all those kids in the spinning room on account of the machinery; but young as we were, we used to get mad because all the Catholics had been there ahead of us and had got all the jobs.

I used to carry dinner pails into the mill when I was a kid. We got a nickel a day, a quarter a week. I had to go from the North Main Street School to West Street, wait for the dinner pails, and run all the way up to #11, then all the way to 142 Second Street, pick up a basket, and take it to the blacksmith shop. After that I ran all the way home and got back to school. I'm seventy-six and I'm living. I think of the running around we did, but I don't think it hurt anybody. I think people are dying younger now because they are not doing so much.

For a while, we went to a German school. I don't know if it did me any good. But my parents didn't speak much German at home. They only spoke German when they didn't want me to know what they were saying. We still cook German food, though. People love German food [laughs].

We were really six in our family, but my sister died at eleven months, and then there were four boys and myself. My father owned twenty-two tenements and a cottage; and he didn't care how many kids you had, he just took them. The rents on some were only $8.00 a month. My brother was a filling boy. I think he was a runner boy first like my husband, and then he got to be a filling boy. My grandfather worked in #11, weaving. He was seventy-two, and he never wore glasses.

I went to live in Lawrence when I was eighteen because I got married and my husband was from Lawrence. After my little girl was born, we decided to come back to Manchester and live with my mother. My husband died the second day after we returned to Manchester. He and another man were working on the roof of the shoe shop. They grabbed hold of a wire, didn't know it was alive, and were electrocuted on the spot.

My husband knew he was going to die, but I didn't believe

him. He used to cry all the time. One night in Lawrence, I was in bed nursing my baby, and he had fallen asleep on the divan in the kitchen. Suddenly, I heard a terrible bump. I got up, and he was shouting and crying, saying over and over again he was going to die. He kissed me and the baby, and said we must go back to Manchester. He had told me to buy myself a beautiful coat. I ordered one in an orange color, and when they sent me a black one by mistake, he said, "Keep it. You'll wear it to my funeral," and I did. I wore it to his funeral. There was no compensation in those days. The shoe shop told me right out that they weren't liable. The other man who was killed had five children, and his family got nothing. Nothing.

► Thomas Smith,
and Lewis and Virginia Erskine

The dye house in the Amoskeag was something of a Scottish institution because of Andrew Mungall, an expert dyer who came to Manchester in 1881 and introduced the "long-chain system," a system by which entire warps of cotton yarn, rather than the raw cotton itself, were dyed. After his death in 1902 his brother ran the dye house. Thomas Smith started his career in the dye house in 1907 as a protégé of Mr. Mungall. He gradually worked up to overseer and later assistant superintendent of dyeing.

Born in Glasgow in 1890, Tommy was four years old when his parents migrated to Manchester. His father worked as a weaver and then as loom fixer in the Amoskeag; his mother also worked as a weaver. They were part of an extensive network of friends and relatives, all of whom had moved from Glasgow to Manchester in order to work in the dye houses and weave rooms.

Lewis Erskine's parents and Virginia Martinson Erskine's mother and maternal grandparents came from Glasgow as part of the same migration. Lewis was born in Manchester in 1917. His father was a cloth inspector and finisher in the Amoskeag. Lewis's wife, Virginia, was born in Manchester in 1916. The Scottish (maternal) side of her family was firmly established in the dye house where her Uncle John Carlin was superintendent. Her father's family, the Martinsons, had come from Sweden and had worked in the shoe factories of Manchester. Both Lewis and Virginia worked briefly at the Amoskeag but were forced to stop because of the shutdown. Afterwards,

Lewis became an industrial engineer in the shoe industry,
where he still works; and Virginia worked at a variety of textile
jobs in Manchester. She is now working as a secretary.

Over the years, the Erskine and Smith families, although
not directly related, lived in the same neighborhoods and as-
sisted each other. When Tommy's wife died, leaving him with
a twelve-year-old daughter, Virginia's mother took in the
daughter and helped raise her until Tommy remarried. The
close ties between the families have continued to the present
day. Tommy, widowed for a second time, now lives with his
married daughter, who is in her sixties, and still works as a
clerk and delivery man in a Manchester drugstore. At eighty-
seven, he is indefatigable. He reads extensively, travels around
Maine and New Hampshire, is witty and lively, and carries the
Amoskeag memory as part of his identity. He often visits the
Erskines and meets as well with other Scots in the Presbyterian
church and at clan gatherings.

VIRGINIA: My mother told me that the reason her
mother and father came to this country around 1880 was because of the three Mungall brothers. They were brought over
here from Scotland by the Amoskeag to start a fancy dye
house. That was probably in the 1870s. They had had a dye
house in Glasgow, Scotland, so they sent back to Glasgow for
people that they knew could do the work. Then those people
hired their relatives and friends, and that's how the different
mills came to have certain ethnic groups in certain areas. In
the dye houses, it was Scottish people.

TOMMY: Of course, they had the best jobs. Later on, the
influx was predominantly Polish and Greek. Still later on, the
Amoskeag went up and induced hundreds of Canadians to
come down here and work. A lot of them couldn't talk any
English at all. They gave them rentals, guaranteed their children who were of age a job, that sort of thing.

In Scotland and England, they had advertised in the newspapers and put out fliers about the wonderful opportunities for
weavers, spinners, and dyers in this country. The advertise-

The blue-dye-house workers. Tommy Smith is second row, third from the right.

ments they put up were like circus posters: *Wonderful conditions at Amoskeag, in Manchester, New Hampshire.* They showed a man just coming out of the millyard with a wallet in his hand full of money, and he was going up to the bank. A lot of people never even saw a bank in those days. Things like that induced people to leave.

My mother brought me over here in 1894, when I was four years old. When my parents came here, the people over there who were hiring their help paid part of their passage and guaranteed them a house to live in. In Scotland my father had been a foreman in a bicycle factory, but when he came over here, he worked in the dye house. Then he became a loom fixer in the weaving room. My family was very poor in Scotland. My mother was a weaver, and the whole family worked in the mill at various times.

VIRGINIA: My father worked in the dye house, and my mother was a weaver. My Uncle Johnnie Carlin was superintendent in the dye house. He was Tommy's overseer. My aunt also worked as a clerk in the dye-house office, and practically all of my mother's family worked there. Their father had come over to work in the dye house; and when their children grew up, they went to work there. My father was Swedish, but he went to work there after he married my mother by virtue of her family connections.

LEWIS: My father worked in the Amoskeag, and my mother came to this country from Glasgow to work as a weaver. She'd lived in a boardinghouse in Glasgow, and the woman who ran it also had a boardinghouse here in Manchester, so my mother stayed there. My dad went to the same boardinghouse when he came to this country, and they met there. In Glasgow, my father lived just a few blocks from where my mother lived, but they never knew each other there. Strange thing!

I'd say to my father, "How about going back to Scotland, Dad?" "No, they never gave me anything." They hired out kids back there as soon as they were old enough to go to work. They'd be out in the fields, with mud up to their knees. He said, "No, I don't want to go back there."

Over across in Scotland, though, they had a means of taking care of families. I can remember my dad telling me how they lost their family support when their father died. They were a large family, farming outside Belfast, in Ulster; and I'm quite sure the Church helped them. At least in Scotland, and I presume throughout most of Europe, the churches were supported by the government. When people came over here, because of the separation of Church and State, they couldn't go to their churches for aid. That's one of the reasons why the Scottish clans started in this country—to keep people together, to give them support when they were down and when they were sick, to give them hospitalization.

TOMMY: I can remember my mother and father telling me that in Scotland, when my sister and I were born, the government helped families. After a child was born, they got two weeks of recreation at a resort on the Clyde River. We in the United States were the last big nation in the world to help people with Social Security and that sort of thing. They were all ahead of us.

Here children were a very great asset, especially in some nationalities. They could go to work when they were thirteen or fourteen years of age. I know there were a lot of immigrant people in Manchester—Greeks, Poles, and Irish—that had two or three tenement houses in their families. The father worked, and the mother worked as long as she could, and two or three children grew up and went to work. They all pooled their money, and they developed a pretty good economy. But my father never should have had five children, really. It was too much for his economy to stand. The pay was so small, and we were subject to terrible insecurity. Every time the market went bad, the mills closed down, maybe for three weeks, maybe for six weeks. Still, the doctor and the grocery man had to be paid once a week with the few dollars that you could scrape together.

LEWIS: I remember when we were kids, the boardinghouses used to hire boys to bring the workers in the mill their lunch pails. The first section of the pail was a main dish, the second section was potatoes, then dessert and pie. The coffee was on top. You know how boys are, we would sling them around and occasionally they would get mixed up, and you'd end up with the bottom of the lunch pail loaded with coffee. If the fellows we were delivering it to asked what happened, we'd say, "We fell down" [laughs]. The most I ever had was six pails. We used to sell magazines like the *Saturday Evening Post* and the *Ladies' Home Journal* with the lunches for a nickel.

TOMMY: Each of the mills had its own bell tower; and when the signal came over the electric wire, the bell ringers would jump onto the ropes. I used to watch them to see how high they could jump. They'd pull the rope down with all their weight. The ropes went up through all the floors to the bell tower, and all the bells would ring.

When the bells rang, it was time to go home. The people flocked out of the mills. All the gates on Canal Street would be opened, and the people would come across the bridge. That was something to see. Picture the people coming out of the main gate on Stark Street! They'd be hustling and joking—nine thousand people trying to get out of those gates to get home as quickly as possible. It was fascinating to see! When people heard the bells, they were ready to fly.

I started my first job while I was in high school, during the 1910 summer vacation. Afterwards, about 1912, I went to work full-time in the dye houses where they dye cotton: some piece goods, some yard goods, and then raw cotton. I stayed there until the mill shut down.

In raw dyeing, which was the biggest part of our job, we had kettles that held twelve hundred pounds of raw cotton. First they carded this cotton—it was a tough job—and then they blew it over in pipes across the river to the dye houses. where we collected it in big wooden crates. We had four men on each kettle, and they'd load about six hundred pounds of the raw cotton in and tramp it down. Then we'd put a heavy, perforated cover on it and flow water through it to make it more absorbent and make room for the other six hundred pounds.

We'd make up our dye batch in fifty-gallon barrels. The different chemicals would be fed into the batch by a man with a dipper. After the bath had been prepared with the different chemicals that were necessary for dyeing, those chemicals and dyes went into a tank that was connected to a pump, which circulated the liquid through cheesecloth and into the kettle. We had a prescribed running time, say an hour or an hour and a half. Then we'd put hooks down the sides of the kettle and pull up samples of the cotton. We'd wash them and dry them to make sure we were getting the shade we wanted.

That was the process with shades that had already been proven a great many times. New shades were made exactly the same way but in small kettles that held a hundred pounds. We would dye a hundred pounds and fool around with it, adding

The lower canal, 1968

one thing or another until we got the required shade. Then we'd transfer that formula into the big machines. Many weeks we dyed and bleached 750,000 pounds of cotton in our raw-stock dye house.

After we dyed the cotton, the men would put it into boxes. Owing to the discrepancy in density between the bottom and the top layers in the kettle, it was hard to get a uniform shade. So we'd put the center portions in four boxes and mix the top and bottom portions in eight other boxes. After that, the filled boxes went up to the third floor to the hot-air dryers to be blown dry and bagged, a hundred pounds to a bag. The bags were shipped out to the different card rooms, and they did the carding, spinning, and eventually the weaving.°

We did chain dyeing. We dyed indigo [for use in shirting] as single-chain dyeing. We dyed warps. After we dyed warps, they were ready to go right to the frames for weaving. They had an average of four hundred ends on a perforated beam, which was put in the machine, just like the operation of raw stock. The pumps would circulate the dyes to the perforated beams and dye them that way.

We had all types of dyes, of course: fast ones that could stand sunlight, and others that were very fugitive and couldn't stand much sunlight. I worked in the period when so-called vat colors, or fast colors, came in. We had to develop them with high-sulphide soda. The Germans had them first. We progressed from crude efforts to almost perfect ones.

In the fancy dye house, the biggest one, we had two hundred men working. All the manual labor there was by men. They had catwalks around those big kettles where they dyed the raw stock, and they frequently threw people into the kettles. Say somebody had a birthday. A group of his friends would get together, grab him, rush him over there, and throw him into the kettle—only when it was cold and empty of cotton, of course. The kettles were on a platform, and pipes ran underneath them.

We had a couple of cloth dye houses where we dyed piece goods, and we had a bleachery. It was a tightly controlled operation and had to be watched all the time. I had 250 people

---

° The cotton had to be carded again after it was dyed, in preparation for spinning.

working under me, and I had contact with most all of them. The cloth dye houses had mostly Polish and Irish, whereas the dirtier jobs were done by Greeks and some Polish and French. In the dye houses, there weren't too many French, while in other parts of the manufacturing company there were a lot of French.

When they made mistakes, we'd have to go to work. If it was a blue component, then we could re-dye it and overcome the blue thing. Eventually, if it was too bad, we'd dye it black. If you have a lot of blacks that are re-dyes, it's a better job than a straight black. Most of the colors had to be light blue and washproof, too, to be wearable.

We developed ten new dyeing techniques during my time. New things were coming along all the time in those days. Remember, we weren't many years away from the very basic things of dyeing skeins with vegetable dyes. The coal-tar dye-stuffs were just beginning to come in from Germany.

I finally ended up being assistant superintendent of cotton dyeing and bleaching, but I started at the bottom and worked my way up. When I worked school vacations, I got $10.50 every two weeks. I remember we thought if you could live long enough to get $10.00 a day, you'd be a millionaire. When I graduated from high school, I was very ambitious and wanted to get someplace, so I went to school in Boston for a couple of years. Northeastern University was running classes in the YMCA on Huntington Avenue, and I took chemistry, mathematics, and physics. I worked at the mill while I went to school. I would take a train to Boston at twenty minutes past four in the afternoon, come back on the paper train at two o'clock in the morning, and then go to work the next day. At that time I was a general errand boy, twenty-two years old, and married.

When I got through in 1936, I was getting $75.00 per week. Relatively speaking, that was good pay. The highest-paid men who worked for me down in the mills, the fellows who ran the pumps and the kettles, were getting $18.60 a week for sixty hours.

I've noticed the change in the pay ratios today. If a man works as a foreman in a factory now, and the highest-paid man working for him happens to work a few hours overtime, he gets the same pay as the foreman. In the old days, the man at the top got much more money than he really deserved, compared to his workers. Of course, I guess that has changed everywhere.

The only innovation that happened in my time at Amoskeag was the rayon transfer. The rest was all status quo, the same kind of weaving and the same kind of dyeing. The only new things we did were little personal tricks. In fast dyeing, for instance, you would take a roll of cloth and dye it at accelerated speed, but that was limited to certain dyes and certain types of cloth. Today, the machines are a little more perfect, but the process and the theory of it are still the same. There's no way of doing it any differently. Rayon was the biggest new thing because they dyed it right there in the solution while it was being made.

In weaving, the only thing they could do was speed up the load on the weaver. Instead of six looms, they'd give a weaver ten, if they could get away with it. They tried it several times, but it never worked. I remember one time, the superintendent of the Northern Division boasted that he had the weavers doing ten. And I remember W. P. Straw coming in and saying, "I don't want to hear any more bragging about the weavers running ten looms in the Amory Mill. I want you to put it back to eight. I've gone through there two or three times, and their stuff is not normal." They had ten looms, but they didn't have time to get around all ten. If they had six they could keep them all running, so it was kind of silly. If a thread broke, the loom would stop, and they often had two more stopped with ten looms than when they ran six or eight.

Spinning is a little different. Spinning is run by the individual spindle; and if one went down, you could get away with running it like that for a little bit; it wouldn't stop the frame.

Amoskeag had its own union, and it worked pretty well until the strike [of 1933]. Then the whole thing fell apart. When the workers had a grievance, their committee would meet with ours and we'd thrash it out. Some of those grievances came when the management put weavers up to ten looms or when they added another spinning frame. That sort of thing usually died right down because management lost production. Finally, to settle things, they got time-study groups in there.

You couldn't do time study in the dye house because a lot of the work was manual labor. Take this kettle in the dye house that was eight feet in diameter and eight feet deep, with twelve hundred pounds of cotton in it, all to be dyed with bleach. You had this massive cover that held the pressure down. If you raised the cover and threw a knife or a fingernail clipper in there, it would bounce out because the cotton was hard as a rock. It was also very cold after it had been dyed, bleached, and rinsed off completely. Those men had to go in there with their fingers and claw it up. It would come out in thick sheets, and they had to throw it into boxes. They tried doing many things, like coiling a rope in it while you were loading it, and then pulling that rope out, but none of them worked. It took five men to do that job, and they just had to claw it out as best they could with their hands. The new men would develop calluses on the ends of their fingers. Then they'd have to stay out a couple of days until they cleared up.

So, you see, there wasn't often anything you could gain on labor because the machines ran 90 percent of the time. The only thing you could work on was getting the machines to run 95 percent of the time. It's altogether different from something like weaving, which requires the ability and the desire to work.

The dye-house workers were more or less in control of their jobs. They were skilled in the operations and in handling their machines. But their skills had to do with making formulas or knowing when a thing was right. The drug man filled out a formula for each machine, and the machine operator had to go by a time schedule. So many minutes for this, raise the temperature 10° for ten minutes more, and so on. Some batches went to a boil, and some dyed at 120° Fahrenheit. Then, when the dyeing process was completed according to schedule, they'd take samples out. They'd bring them into the office, where they tested them. If the samples were right, they'd empty the kettle and start rinsing with cold water or an oxidizing agent, whatever we needed for that particular shade.

It's a funny thing about our dye houses and bleach house: the bulk of the people in there were older. There were very few young people. The younger people didn't go into that type of work too much because it was heavy work. It required a man, and he had to be physically pretty well set up. The hardest job I had in the mills was when I was fourteen and took a job for the summer. It was a job I'll never forget, cleaning out the picker machines. They didn't have vacuum cleaning like they have today. All the cotton seeds that came out of the cotton would drop down under the pickers, and we would have to go under there and get all those seeds. We'd have a wad of cotton in our mouth to filter out the dust and keep us from choking. It would be so hot, and we'd get that cotton seed on our skin, and it would hit you something terrible.

VIRGINIA: Those were the good old days, when there was no pollution [laughs]. When I was a teenager, I lived in a corporation tenement on Canal Street, and the trains used to go right by, many trains every day. You could smell the carbon monoxide more than you can from automobiles now. But it wasn't just the trains; there were a lot of smokestacks, too. Most of the Amoskeag ran on coal-fed boilers. So there was a lot of smoke and pollution, but we didn't think of it as pollution. It was a livelihood.

TOMMY: In those days, it was an advantage to live in that area because you were close to your work, close to the main street, so you didn't need a ride. People didn't have cars, so it was a nice place to live, other than the pollution [laughs]. We used to think we were a little better than the people down in the lower part of the corporation. They were the ones that were living down below the tracks. I can never remember any other home, so my family must have lived there when I was just an infant. We stayed there until the forties, I guess.

VIRGINIA: Of course, there were a lot more people that needed housing than there were houses. When the French Canadians came, there probably wasn't much [corporation] housing available, so they congregated on' the West Side of Manchester, where mostly French was spoken.

TOMMY: The city was set up that way, by different ethnic groups. Polish people would go to a Polish area.

VIRGINIA: Even little ethnic groups had their own areas. My father was Swedish, and the Swedes lived in a little part of the city by Bridge Street that they called Janesville, which was like a little town.

There was a group of people in the mill from Scotland who built the Presbyterian church here in the 1890s on land owned by the Amoskeag. Previously, there had been a German Presbyterian church in town but no others. When the Scots moved in, they wanted their own Presbyterian church, so they built it.

TOMMY: When the mills closed down for two weeks' vacation, most all of our Scotchmen went to Wells Beach. They all belonged to the Scottish Clan McKenzie; the auxiliary, which was called the Heatherbell Lodge; and the Presbyterian church.

We had a wonderful time, especially where mostly Scottish people worked, like in the dye houses. They were more or less clannish, even at their work. They were together at home, on vacations, at church, everywhere.

LEWIS: Like a big, happy family.

TOMMY: Yes, indeed. It didn't give us power; it just made life easier. If you wanted power or a better job, you had to study or work for it. But the usual thing was to associate with your own people and friends.

VIRGINIA: When you work twelve hours a day, you have to find pleasure in work. There's nowhere else to find it. You can't look forward to going home or going out in the evening. I remember my father and my aunt talking about the good time they had in the dye house, laughing a lot in the office.

Things didn't start to tighten up there until around the time I went to high school. It was the Depression, and times were getting hard. My father couldn't find too much work, and he wasn't well at the time. We lived up on Union Street and North Street, about a mile from where he worked. He worked from six o'clock in the morning to six o'clock at night, because they had a twelve-hour day. He'd have to get up at four thirty to get

Tommy Smith, 1977

there; and when he got there, the foreman would say, "No work today." So he'd come home, and the next day he'd walk down there again. I remember how discouraged he used to get.

TOMMY: I worked closely with the carding department, filling the orders that came through every week. We had to break the orders down so the dye house would not overdye and yet do enough to take care of them. There were three dye houses in the cotton end: one that dyed raw stock, one that dyed cloth—two different processes—and one that dyed yarn. I was in charge of everything at the cotton end, where we had maybe 350 men. The best jobs in the dye houses were running the shifts. A lot of old men stayed in the good jobs all their lives. They didn't have to get through at sixty-five. There were no pensions in those days, so they just kept the old guys on, that's all.

There was a lot of paternalism there. Look at old man Spence; he was second hand of the dye house. He was lame, he couldn't walk around or do anything, but they kept him there for many years. I was the one who did his job. He just stayed in the office and took life easy. Management knew, sure. Of course, the man that was superintendent then was his good friend, he had worked with him all his life, so he was trying to help me and also help the old man. It worked out all right. There was no unemployment compensation and no insurance, but in those days anyone that wanted to work could work.

Before they had an employment bureau, people would go in and see the overseer for a job. Then a couple of overseers down in the mill got caught taking bribes. It was right after they built the employment office. With an outfit like that, it was hard to do something out of the ordinary. The employment office didn't have to let the overseer pick his own people if they didn't want to, but in most cases they did. Ahern, in the employment office, was an extrovert Irishman, inclined to be a politician as well. He was a good fellow. He knew everybody around the city. The Amoskeag was a continuation of the old feudal system, where the lord of the country, or whoever it was, took care of hundreds of people that worked for him or were connected with him. The attitude was there.

VIRGINIA: It was in the whole mill, the paternalistic attitude. This is why they took care of their own people. The Greeks helped the Greeks, the Scots the Scots, and the French helped the French.

TOMMY: As far as the dye house was concerned, it was run by Scotchmen all my life. That's my solution right there. The Scotchman that was in authority would hire a Scotchman over a Frenchman. This is still quite common. You even see it in the education line, where a graduate of Dartmouth, if he's in charge of a large company, will have a lot of Dartmouth grads working for him.

Ethnic groups really did control a great percentage of the jobs—like, if I wanted to or could use a man, and a Scotsman was in need of a job, I would call Mr. Swallow up and tell him I was sending Mr. So-and-so in to see him and to please send him down to the dye house, that I had a job for him.

I remember Archie Smith, the boxer. He had kidney trouble, couldn't walk straight or anything, and Mr. Ahern was friendly with him. He needed a job, and Mr. Ahern called me up in the dye house and asked if I could give this man a job, which I did do. I took care of them, and they took care of me.

The different nationalities are very clannish among their own, even to this day. Look at the so-called social clubs. They're Ukrainian or they're German or they're French, and they tend to stay that way. I think that's the way people are. I was treasurer of the Clan McKenzie in Manchester.

I also belonged to the Amoskeag Textile Club. It was a good move to open up sociability among the workers and give them an outlet, a way to meet each other more often; but the bulk of the membership was really the more important men in the Company. The others didn't go into it too much, even at the end. They'd walk around with their neighbors, even go visit relatives and friends on the West Side after supper, and walk home.

I had a real good life. I worked hard at it and was ambitious and got a lot of satisfaction out of it. One time, when the mills were slack, I thought of being a pharmacist. I talked to a fellow I knew that had a drugstore here; but before anything

An exhibit in the mill of one day's product

developed, the mills started up again, so that was my profession. A doctor probably sometimes gets sick of taking appendixes out, but he has to do it. It was the same with me.

Being an Amoskeag man was our life, our mode of living, our ultimate thing. I figured I'd be there until I died, somehow or other. I think anybody would say that; the great majority would say that.

▶ *Part Five* ◀

Families

▶ *Ora Pelletier*

(SEE ALSO PAGE 181.)

My mother was working in the Amoskeag when she was ten years old. My father worked in the Blood Shop [Manchester Locomotive works] at the Amoskeag when he was nine years old. When they closed the mill, he went into the fire department, and he stayed on until he died. He was sixty-six when he died. My mother was fifty-eight when she died.

My mother didn't work at the Amoskeag more than a year or two. She got sick, and then her mother started a boardinghouse, so she stayed at home to help her. After she got married, she was too busy having children. If she hadn't had so many, maybe she would have had a chance to go to work. She tried to keep the house clean and cook for the whole bunch. She even used to make her own bread.

I guess we were in the middle class, like we are today, because we never starved. We always had plenty to eat. That's something my father would look out for. "Eat first. Pay the bills and eat." That's what he used to say. But we never had any money to spend, no allowance or anything. When we worked, we all gave our pay at home, except one of my sisters. She gave it at the beginning. Then, when she thought she wanted to get married, she'd give $7.00 and keep the rest. At the time, it was a pretty good price to pay $7.00 a week for room and board, and have the washing and ironing and everything else done, too. They gave the rest of us who worked $2.00 a week. We never thought of asking for any more, but on that $2.00 we had to pay our mass on Sunday, and if we needed stockings or other little things, like powder or rouge, but no lipstick! My father

The parents of Ora Pelletier, Edmund and Florida Anger

wouldn't let us use lipstick, not even on the day I got married. He told me if I put on lipstick, he wasn't coming to my wedding.

My mother would make all our clothes, except for coats or a Sunday dress. She even used to make our stockings. My aunt had a big family, and they were all working. She used to give my mother big bags of stockings that were ripped at the foot or something. My mother would cut the foot off and make a new one. She used to make us house slippers from old men's coats.

I was six years old when I started to go to school. Some of the kids would bring bars of chocolate, others an orange; they'd bring something good. I suppose they were richer than a big family like ours. My father used to buy a bag of candy and a bag of peanuts every payday, and he'd divide it up. He'd put it on the table and count it to make the shares even. And that's all we'd have until the next payday. If we asked for something, my mother would say, "Well, we're too poor. We can't afford to buy that." We grew up that way, so we would say nothing.

I suppose that was in my mind—that we were poor—because Ma kept saying it. At school one day, the sister said, "All the little children that are poor, you stay in your seats. I want to talk to you. The others can go home." There were a lot that walked out, but my mother said I was poor, so I stayed. The nun looked at me and said, "What are you doing here?" I said, "You said all the poor kids. I'm poor." She said, "You're not that poor." I said, "Yes, my mother told me." She thought it was funny because she knew the family very well. So she said, "Well, all right, come on," and took us upstairs.

I was surprised when I got there because it was the room where they used to have the plays, but now there were five or six sewing machines, a big long table, and a lot of clothes. The nun who was holding me by the hand took me to one of the women and said, "This little girl says she's poor." They took a look at me, the way I was dressed, and they all started to laugh. I felt embarrassed. One of them said, "You're poor? You need something to wear? What would you like?" So I started to think, and I said, "A coat." I had seen a grey tweed one there, and I thought it looked nice. She brought me to the table and tried it on. It fit me, so she said I could have it. I looked at the coat, and I said, "There's no buttons on it." "Oh," she said, "you want some buttons, too?" So she brought me to the big long table. "Choose the buttons that you want." There were some nice big buttons in plastic, blue and black. They were shining. I said, "I'll take those." "Well," she said, "she has style," and started to laugh.

When I got home and my mother saw that coat, was she ever mad at me! She told me that we weren't that poor to go and beg. She started calling me a beggar. I said, "Yes, that's why they were laughing at me. Because I was a beggar," and she said, "The way you were dressed, that's why they were laughing at you." At that time it was the style to wear little aprons on top of our dresses, and I had on a nice starched little apron with ruffles around it. I didn't look like a poor little girl with that starched apron. So I brought the coat back. The nun said, "You can keep it," and I said, "No, my mother doesn't want me to." I put it down and ran out.

My brothers and sisters and I would go down to the mill together. We'd work together all day and come back home together. We were never separated when we were living at home. My father was always working. He had a day off just every ten days. My mother was alone, and she had to watch over us, so she kept us close to home. We all had our little jobs to do. Two of us would get together to wash the floor, or one would wash the dishes and the other would wipe, or one would sweep and the other would dust. We'd help our mother.

I remember during the strike my oldest sister had just got married, and my father and mother told her, "Come back home with your husband." We had to pile up four in the bed instead of two so they could have a bed to themselves. Jeanette, Lucille, Irene, and I were in the same bed. One time, Lucille wanted Jeanette to give her the end of the bed, but Jeanette didn't want to. So Lucille got mad. She got out of the bed. We thought she was going to the bathroom. Instead she went under the bed and tied Jeanette's two braids to one of the posts, and when Jeanette went to turn around, her hair was caught there. The next night, after Lucille was in bed, Jeanette stuck some gum in her hair. In the morning, my mother had to cut off half of that hair!

We were so many at home, we didn't need any entertainment. We had our own. My mother would tell me to watch the others, to keep them quiet and keep them around so she wouldn't have to run after them. I used to put on a show for them. I'd put an old long dress on and get up there and sing. I'd sing opera. I had curls then, and I'd put my curls under my nose, change my shoes, and I would be Charlie Chaplin. I used to make them laugh.

All the neighbors would come upstairs, and my mother would push the table and the carpets back, and they'd dance. Almost every night there was a party at the house. But my mother wouldn't let us go out dancing. I went twice with my oldest sister after she was married. She asked my mother if she could take me with her, and my mother let me go, but that was it. She didn't want us to go anyplace. She'd say, "You can enjoy yourself just as well over here as you can outside." Of course, she was alone with so many daughters, and she was worried that something would happen to us. That's why she did her best to try and keep us home.

My mother never explained anything to me about the facts of life. When I started to work, I was fifteen, and a guy who used to go to school with me was there working in the same room. I never paid any real attention to him. I'd say, "Hi, Wallace," and we'd talk as little kids talk. When he had time off, he'd come over, and we'd talk about school. What else could we talk about? That's all we knew. He never made any advances or tried to make any dates. One day I was right at the end of the frame, and I suppose one of the older guys must have said something to him, because he came over and started speaking to me. All of a sudden, he kissed me on the cheek. I turned around, and SLAP! I slapped his face, and he went flying. He started to cry. At the other end, they were laughing like hell.

For two weeks I couldn't eat, I couldn't sleep—I thought I was pregnant. My mother always said, "Don't ever let a boy touch you." He had touched me; he kissed me. I was too afraid to tell anybody. My mother didn't know what was the matter with me. I'd bring my lunch to work, but I couldn't eat, so I'd bring it back home. I'd just pick at my food and leave it there. I had heard from one of the girls that if a girl was pregnant, she wouldn't menstruate; so after two weeks, when I saw I was menstruating, I knew I wasn't pregnant [laughs]! So I started to eat like a horse.

I had to find out by myself what married life was, and it was a shock [laughs]! My husband was just as dumb as I was because he had been alone. His mother died when he was only ten, and his father never said anything to him.

My mother didn't even tell me when you were supposed to start menstruating. I didn't even know what was happening to me. And I wouldn't tell her either. It was my brother that found out and told my mother. I was going to take my bath, and he wanted to go to the bathroom. So I had to leave my clothes there and put a bathrobe on. When he came downstairs, he said to my mother, "She dirties all her pants, and she leaves them like that. She won't even change." I started to cry, and I told my mother it wasn't true. I started to tell her what it was, and she was trying to tell me with her eyes to shut up. My brother was seventeen years old, but he was dumb himself. I kept trying to defend myself, so finally she called me into the kitchen. She told me to keep my mouth shut. "Why?" I said. "I'm not lying, I'm telling the truth." She said, "I know, but don't say anything." She said now I was going to be a big girl, and I started to cry. I didn't want to be a big girl. So she said, "You're going to feel like that all the time now." Well, I thought I was going to feel like that for the rest of my life. So I said to myself, "When I have children, they're not going to be this dumb. I'm going to try to help them a little bit." When my daughter started to grow, I could see it in the way she was acting. I said, "I think I better start to tell her before it's too late." I told her one day, and I believe it was a week after that that she started. So at least she wasn't as dumb as I was.

I remember the girls in the mill saying that one of the girls was going to have a baby. I couldn't believe it. They said, "Yes, it's true." She was always sitting with us, so I asked her if it was true. She said, "Yes," and she started to cry because nobody would talk to her. She said, "It isn't my fault." She told me she had been raped in the woods.

When I was sixteen, going around looking for any job I could get, I used to go to St. George's Church. I went to church one time, and I happened to see Arthur [the man she later married]. Then I saw him again at the Salvation Army. One day he was in front of the bowling alley with my brother Henry's chum when I happened to go by, and after that he started to say hello to me on the street. On Ash Wednesday, we went to church, and he stood near me. When we went to receive the ashes, he held me with his finger so that I had to wait for him to receive before I could get out. He held my finger until we got out of the church. I said to him, "I don't even know your name. What do you want?" He said to me, "Can I take you home?" I said, "No, I don't even know you." He said, "That's all right," so I let him walk up to the house with me. He told me his name was Arthur Pelletier, and I said I didn't believe him. When we got near the house, I asked him if he wanted to come up. I knew my mother was at the window. He said, "No," but he kept on talking. I said, "Look, either come up or get out, because my mother's looking out the window, and I'm not going to wait for her to say, 'Come up,' in front of everybody." He said, "Can I see you again on Sunday?" My sister Jeanette was with me, and he said he'd bring a friend with him. But it turned out Jeanette didn't like his friend. She wanted Arthur. My mother saw that Jeanette was in love with him, and he was paying as much attention to her as to me. So my mother told him, "Look, you choose which one you want. You can't have both." I told Jeanette she could have him, but he told my mother he wanted me. Then my mother told Jeanette to look for her own and leave him alone.

When we were ready to get married, I said to Arthur, "If you like me the way I am, good. If you don't, there's the door." Sometimes I got mad at him—I had a temper—so I said, "I don't want you saying after we're married, 'Now you're coming out with your true colors.' " He knew what he was marrying.

He was my first steady boyfriend, and I was his first steady girlfriend. He had gone out with another girl before, and I had gone out with somebody before, but it was just one or two times, and that's it. I would stay home. I didn't want anybody. The fellows would ask to go out with me, and I'd say no. My mother didn't want me to have boyfriends because she thought I was too young, and they didn't know how old I was with my curls. I was afraid of them.

► Mary Flanders

Mary Flanders, seventy-five years old, is the daughter of Josephine Perkins and William Parker Straw, who was the agent of the Amoskeag from 1919 through 1929. Mary was born and raised in Manchester and was sent to finishing school in Florence, Italy. Subsequently while she was in school in Connecticut, in the midst of the strike of 1922, her younger sister died of a fever. The strikers called off the picketing for one day and sent the Straw family a wreath of white roses. The loss of the child cast a lasting shadow on the family, since it resulted in a continuing state of depression for Mary's mother.

Mary married Robert Flanders, a physician, in 1925, and she continued to live in Manchester until her husband's death. She presently lives in Bermuda during the winter and New Hampshire during the summer.

At home I was taught to cook and to sew. Before I went out to play, I had to hem a dish towel or something, and it had to be done properly. Although we did have help in the house, my mother felt that I should know how to do things, and I had to do them right. I had to keep my room in order, and I had to shine my shoes every night. There was one maid. She came every morning and knocked on my parents' door. Then she'd braid my hair. I had long braids.

My parents did the child-rearing since we didn't have a nurse or a governess. My mother was a disciplinarian, so she did the training. Daddy got home around five thirty, and we'd

Mary Straw Flanders, 1976

see him for about an hour before we went to bed. Weekends, we all went together to my grandparents [the Herman Straws] for Sunday dinner. It was quite a formal affair. We started with some kind of soup, then a great big roast beef. My grandfather always did the carving. That was a great treat. He always stood up to carve. I don't know if people do that today or not. We always loved to go up there. Of course, we'd get excellent ice cream, homemade ice cream. They had servants; I think there were two waitresses. One would be a chambermaid during the day, but she would help at dinner if there were extra people, and one was a cook. In those days it was very easy to get servants. Lots of them came over from Ireland. We had a lot of Irish, and they came up very green—we used to call them green.

We were with my grandfather a lot. Sundays, during the summertime, we'd all go off somewhere in the car for Sunday dinner. Sometimes we'd go to the Derryfield Club for dinner and have nice thick steaks we didn't have at home. I think Mr. Holmes was the man that ran it; they were the only colored family in Manchester at that time. The club members were mostly the Amoskeag overseers or superintendents.

I was the first girl in the family for some time. My grandmother used to love to buy clothes for me because she'd always bought boys' clothes. I had one best dress, for going to dancing school—a beautiful dress of Liberty silk made in England. I also had a dress with two colored sashes to make it look different. One was coral-colored, and I wore coral-colored stockings and a coral bow with it. And then the next week it'd be yellow instead of coral. I only dressed up when I went to dancing school. The rest of the time I wore Amoskeag ginghams. We had a seamstress come to the house; I think Dad brought her home. My dresses had pearl buttons on them; but if you put them in the wash, all the shine would come off. I used to have those little things to hold the buttons on so I could take them off before the dress was washed.

I suppose as a child somebody else's things always look grander than yours, and I'd always worn gingham, so I looked forward to wearing something else besides Amoskeag gingham. When they started making rayon during the war, I got a lot of

The Parker Straws, while living in the corporation agent's house near the mills, ca. 1920

rayon dresses, and that was much nicer because they had a sort of silky thread in them.

The house that we were in on Pleasant Street was a terrific house. I loved that house. I think of it often. I even dream about it every once in a while. It was the Amoskeag agent's house. It had an old stable, and there was a tennis court out in back. But I don't think mother wanted the house on Elm Street. She probably would have enjoyed moving to the North End. Most of her friends were in the North End. I never heard her say that by living near the millyard she was living in an inferior location, but she might have thought that. I'm sure that's why she wanted me, or us, to go to school up the other way.

I went to the Straw School. The school was about a mile from home. We'd walk home, but we were taken to school in the Amoskeag taxi. If we had roller skates, sometimes we'd roller skate down. I can just see us going up and down those curbstones. We also had what you call a little scooter. You'd put one foot on it and push with the other foot—and wear your shoes out, of course. But you'd get home much quicker that way.

The prime reason we went to the Straw School, even though we were in the Franklin school district, was because it had such good teachers. But I'm sure they also were good at the Franklin Street School, which was for children from Spruce Street and all the . . . you know, children from not really educated families, I might say. Margaret Manning [Vandermeer] and Margaret Woodbury* both went to the Straw School because their mothers felt that they should go there, even though they were in the Webster school district. Of course, for that you had to get a permit from the superintendent's office. There were also mill workers' children in the Straw School because the tenements around, down on Elm Street, were in the Straw school district. Most people, though, came from upper . . . well, I wouldn't call them that. Just nice families.

My parents didn't let me play in the corporation playground, which was way down near the station. I guess they thought I had plenty to do up where I lived. But they never objected to the children from around there coming to our yard. Never. My mother didn't think there was anything wrong with the other children, but she thought that the playground was meant for those who didn't have as many opportunities or the yard that I had. We had everything right there. We had the baseball grounds, and we had the skating rink in the wintertime. The only thing we didn't have was slides.

Once in a while I disobeyed but not very often. One time I went to the Amoskeag playground, and I ripped my dress. My

---

* Margaret Manning was the granddaughter of Charles Manning, Chief Engineer in the Amoskeag. Her family was related by marriage to the Carpenters, a wealthy Manchester family mentioned in other interviews. Margaret Woodbury's mother was one of the founders of the Thimble Club mentioned later in the interview.

friend's mother stitched it up for me so my mother wouldn't know. She was a seamstress and her husband was a mill worker. They lived way down on Pleasant Street but not in one of those nice houses like the superintendents' were. It was two or three flights up and had one of those little porches. They had a great big stove in the kitchen, like I guess everybody had in those days, and they sort of sat around the kitchen table. They did have a parlor, but I don't think it was used very often.

I was brought up very strictly. I was chaperoned and all that kind of thing. My mother gave a tea for me when I came back from finishing school in Florence and had all her friends come. I suppose that was sort of a coming out but not the way they did it in Boston and in the big cities. No one comes out in Manchester. When I was fourteen or fifteen, there was a boy I liked, but I knew that I'd probably never be allowed to marry him. I was old enough to know better. I couldn't see any reason why I wouldn't be happy, but as you grow older you see these things. His father was an overseer in the Amoskeag, but he never amounted to anything. I thought he was nice, though. He used to carry my books and do things for me, but we never had a date or anything like that. I suppose you could call it a crush. Maybe because I wasn't allowed to see him or associate with him, I think that's why. I went to a dance with Arthur Perkins, whose father was Judge Perkins. I was taken there, met him there, picked up at nine thirty, and taken home. That was when I was a sophomore in high school. I was allowed out, though, for Halloween night. That was great. I would put on my brother's clothes and go out with the rest of the gang. We'd go around and jump over trash cans in the tenement areas, put chalk on people's windows, and ring their doorbells and run. It was just tricks, thinking we were being devils.

I remember very vividly when my sister died during the strike of 1922. I was in school in Connecticut. I came home, and my brother was to meet me at the station. My Uncle Ellis came to meet me instead. He told me on the way home that my sister was dead. She was so much younger than my brother and me, and she was the pet of the family. It was just terrible. The striking workers sent their condolences and stopped the picketing for that day.

I don't think my father did much business at home, but I'm

The Thimble Club in 1920, a club of the wives and daughters of prominent local men, including top Amoskeag managers.

sure he discussed everything with my mother. My mother was a really intelligent person, and she had a lot of good ideas. She came from New Hampshire, and she grew up on a large farm. I used to love to go down there as a child and milk the cows.

My grandfather was very intelligent and I'm sure a very good agent of the mills, but I think he didn't have much outside his family and his own home. After a meal he would always go right to his library and read. He was a great reader.

My mother was a member of the Thimble Club in Manchester, like my grandmother. They used to meet at different houses. They kept it pretty small, only about seventeen or eighteen. They made layettes for babies, and they put out a cookbook. I used to help give out the gifts to the children at the Amoskeag Christmas party. Some of the wives of the workers helped, too. I think they gave them all one piece of wearing apparel, and the rest of the gifts were things they wouldn't ordinarily get, toys of some sort. People had helped my father organize it, but I'm sure it was his idea. I think at that time the whole country became more conscious of doing things for their workers.

I thought Dad's resignation from the Amoskeag was voluntary. There may have been pressure, but I don't think he was ever asked. I think that he just didn't want to go along with Mr. Dumaine's ideas, whatever they were. Mr. Dumaine didn't want to give the workers what Dad felt they deserved. Henry Rauch was a much younger man, and it was a big job for him. He went there from the American Thread Company. He sent me a great big box of thread, all colors of thread. So we were always on good terms with the Rauches.

The Lacasse family was well known in Manchester because despite the family's size and extreme poverty, three of the sons became priests, and all of the children, except the two oldest daughters, received at least a high school education.

Maria Poitras Lacasse, now eighty-six, was born in St. Clothilde, a small village in Quebec. She lost her father at a young age and moved with her mother to Trois Rivières, where her mother worked as a cleaning woman in a convent. When she was sixteen, Maria migrated to Manchester, where she lived in a boardinghouse and worked at the Amoskeag. She married Alexis Lacasse in 1910 and had twelve children; her last one was less than a year old before her husband's death. Alexis was a second hand in the weave room, and Maria worked off and on as a weaver.

Following Alexis' death in 1935, the family was destitute. Their poverty was intensified because the two oldest sons had left home to study for the priesthood in a seminary in Trois Rivières. At that point, the major burden of the family's support fell on Maria and on her two oldest daughters, Alice and Laurette. Somehow the family pulled through the Depression.

Today, Monsigneur Lorenzo Lacasse, sixty-four, officiates at the Sacred Heart parish in Concord, New Hampshire. The oldest son, Aimé, sixty-five, who had served all his life as a White Father (missionary) in the Congo, has now returned to the States. A third son is also a priest and serves as a missionary in the Philippines. Yet another son was ordained for the priest-

hood but left the priesthood and is now a social worker for the Council on Aging in Concord. Of the daughters, one is a nun and teaches at the University of Alberta. The other five daughters are all married.

Alice worked in the Amoskeag until the shutdown. She then worked on WPA projects until her marriage to Marcel Olivier. She returned to work as a nurse's aide after her children had grown up. She finally settled accounts with the past by enrolling in high school, from which she was graduated in 1976.

ALICE: The mills were our home. They were our whole life, and we were very happy there. We had a wonderful father and mother. There was twelve of us. We were quite a family.

My parents worked in the mill. They were immigrants from Canada. They were married in 1910, and I was born in 1915. After my parents got married, my mother just worked periodically, for two or three months at a time, when things would get too hard and my father didn't have any money. My father didn't really want her to work. That was a big issue because she always wanted to go in and earn a little money. But the minute she said she wanted to work, there would be a big fight. He'd say, "No, you're not going to work. You're going to stay home." And that's why she did other things. She'd make clothes for him, take in boarders, rent rooms. She used to rent one or two rooms for $12.00 a week to people who worked in the mills. Sometimes she'd also work little stretches at night, from six to nine, because we lived right in front of the mills. When there were big orders, the mills were always looking for people to work. But my father didn't want to keep the children. That was women's work; his work was outside.

We were always very proud to think of the large family that we were. My parents were always able to manage somehow with hand-me-downs—even our shoes were hand-me-downs—and my mother made our clothes. People then wore old clothes. My mother would rip them out and make them over. We were never on relief. Not once. We always lived very modestly, but we never went around for help. We never would have thought of it. We worked.

In those days, people depended on the priest to solve a lot

of their problems, because they were uneducated. They never went to school; my father and mother went to school for about a year. Today, people are educated, and they don't have to have anybody solve their problems. Plus, the Church says you have freedom of conscience. What you do is just between you and God. So it's far more liberal now than it used to be. I remember when I was a little girl, I was petrified when I thought about getting married. All the priests talked about was having children, having children; you don't hear that now. They used to preach that you had to do what God wanted, and that's what God wanted you to do, to have children. You could do nothing to prevent it.

When the French Canadians first came to Manchester, having many children was the only way they could survive. That was one reason why they had such large families. My mother had twelve kids, and she tells us she was always either pregnant or nursing. The only way that they had to prevent having children was nursing. Even today they say that if you nurse, you aren't apt to become pregnant. We're all two years apart, almost in a neat order, which shows the trend of her thought: she nursed them until they were about fourteen months old, then the minute she stopped, she'd get pregnant again. My father was not the type of person who would stop having sex, and he was too moral to go with another woman. He wasn't that kind of man either. His upbringing wasn't like that. So I guess they were left no choice.

My brother Marcel was called César because he was born by Caesarean. The Church had to give permission to the doctor for the mother to have this operation, and it took three days. Oh, God! It's horrible to think of this now. She was in labor and hemorrhaging all the time. That was the only time she had a Caesarean, but she had seven more children after that. They used to take her to Grasmere Hospital because we were very poor, and they didn't treat her very well. Each time we thought she would die.

MARIA: The doctor said they almost lost me and the baby, too. I asked the doctor how long it would take before I got repaired, and he said, "Two or three years." I said, "You better

talk to my husband." The doctor talked to him. My husband
went and talked to the priest. First he went to the parish priest,
which was St. Augustine's. He wanted to use something so that
I wouldn't get pregnant. The priest said that he wouldn't give
him absolution if he did that. So he went to St. George's. The
priest there told him that he needn't worry. He said, "Did your
wife ever say 'no' to you?" My husband said, "No." The priest
said, "Your wife is always ready, she never says 'no' to you?"
and my husband said, "No." So the priest said, "You do just the
same thing you always do, and nothing will happen to your
wife," and the priest proved true. I had seven children after
that. My husband died before me. He was forty-four when he
died, and I'm still alive.

ALICE: I had a Caesarean with my fourth child, and I didn't
have any more after that. I'm sure they tied my tubes or something, but I was such a Catholic they wouldn't tell me. My
parents still had that very strong Canadian-Catholic tradition.
If my husband had made the decision not to have any more
children, I would have gone along with him, but I would never
have made that decision myself. It was in my marriage all the
way through: that you have to have children and do nothing. I
don't see it so much in my daughter. But in my mother's time,
and even my own, most of the French people were not rebel-
lious in any way. They were not given to revolution. They had
lived very poor lives, even at home in Quebec. They were people with a deep, simple, religious faith.

My father died in 1935, just a few months before the big
crash, before the Company went bankrupt. He was a second
hand in the spinning room, and he never made more than
$22.00 a week. From Friday till Tuesday, when he was paid in
a paper envelope that he would bring home, there wasn't
money in the house, except for a penny for each child to put in
the collection basket on Sunday morning and 15¢ for my father
and mother for the church. The only thing that enabled us to
live was that we had a corporation tenement. We lived at 313
Canal Street, on the corner of Middle and Canal. There were
nine rooms there, four stories. There were two large rooms on
the first floor; the living room, kitchen, two large rooms, and a

bathroom on the second floor; two large rooms on the third floor; and two attic rooms upstairs.

We had a big stove in the kitchen and three grills in the ceiling, so in the winter a little bit of heat went up to the second floor but hardly any at all reached the third and fourth floors. My mother had a whole set of those old-fashioned irons with the detachable handles. We'd all undress downstairs, and we'd each get one of those hot irons that had been heated in the kitchen stove, wrapped in a towel. We'd run upstairs with the towel, stick that under the covers, two or three of us in each bed, and put our sheet on that.

In the summer, every weekend, my father would go to a farm and cut wood for a man; and for his payment, this man used to give him wood. That way he'd earn all our wood for the winter.

LORENZO: My parents were such self-sufficient, industrious people! It amazes me how they ever did it, with twelve children. My mother used to feed people from the mills at lunchtime. We'd always have two or three; and with the money she'd get, she could buy food. So I don't ever remember going hungry in my house. We used to walk to the bakery to get day-old bread. We'd slice it up and come home with it, ten loaves of bread.

We were just as poor as you can imagine. When my father brought his pay home, he'd lay his envelope on the corner of the table, to the last penny. My mother handled it. For a few extra cents, he sold chocolate bars in the mills. All the employees had a little cupboard there, and he kept a whole display of candy in his. Whatever little money he made was for his expenses, for a glass of beer once in a while. During Prohibition, my mother made beer at home. I remember them making the beer—they'd buy three cans of malt syrup and mix it with water.

In the summer, we went picking blueberries. We would leave early on Saturday morning. We would walk from Middle Street down Canal Street, across Bridge Street Bridge, all the way across Kelly Falls Bridge to Shirley Hill, and we would pick blueberries all day. One of us would take the tramway home with the pails, two or three twenty-pound pails filled with blueberries. The tramway cost 10¢, so the others would

The Lacasse children in front of their corporation house opposite the mills

walk back home. We must have walked twenty-five miles during the day. This was my father's recreation. He had no other recreation. His recreation was with us.

LORENZO: My father always had a piece of land across the Amoskeag Bridge, where he made a garden. It was Amoskeag land. We had an old bicycle. My brother Aimé would ride the handlebars, and I would sit on the back. My father would have a hoe and whatever else he needed, and he'd pedal this bicycle all the way from Middle Street.

MARIA: During the strike, the union didn't give us much money, but they gave us food. My husband didn't want to go to the union store, so I said, "I'll go. Maybe they'll give us a little something." The woman in the store said to me, "If you can carry a twenty-four pound bag of food, I'll give it to you because you have a large family." So the woman filled the bag, and I carried it from the corner of Chestnut and Bridge down to Canal [which is almost one mile].

LORENZO: I know there was resentment against the union movements that were beginning at that time. In the Amoskeag, the people were submissive. They didn't like the idea of unions, though actually they were necessary in a way. It could be said that our parents are people who didn't know any better. They were satisfied with the little that they had. The Amoskeag certainly took advantage of the people who worked in the mills. But it is true that they provided a tenement at $9.00 a month. Whenever we needed dental attention, we simply walked to Dr. LeClair, the dentist, and he'd fix our teeth for nothing.

MARIA: It was the men who didn't want to go back during the strike, because there were pickets. They were afraid they were going to get killed. There was another woman on the block who said, "How about us women going to work? If we go to work, they're not going to attack us because we're women." So I decided I was going to go back because fall was coming, and we didn't have any money. We didn't know how we were going to live. That's what the strike was all about: they didn't give the workers enough money. But I knew they were not going to win; so when that woman asked me, I had the children kept, and I went in to work. I told my husband to stay home; I was afraid he would be hurt by the pickets.

After the strike, my husband did not get his job back. He was a trained hand, but they put him back to runner boy. His pay went down, and we had to pay back all the summer rent [which was in arrears because of the strike]. So I kept on working. I was earning more than he was at that time, and besides, I liked to work. I liked to meet the people.

But I'd had a baby during the summer, so I didn't want to work all day Saturday. I said to the boss, "You're a married man, so I'm going to tell you—I had a baby, and I'm nursing it." He said they had a big order to fill, so I said I'd stay until four.

My husband never stopped me going to work when we needed the money. I had to make all the clothes, even the pants for the little boys. I used to sell sandwiches to the girls in the mill if they didn't bring their lunch. My husband was just across the street, and he used to whistle from the millyard and tell me how many sandwiches he wanted.

My husband always wanted his meal hot, so I would send him something hot in a pail. My boy Lionel would run over there to bring lunch to his father, with his paper, every morning. And you know your father [she is addressing her daughters], the way he talked to the kids; he'd say a lot of things and the children believed him. Lionel believed he was a magician.

ALICE: On top of #3 Mill, where Papa worked, there's a cupola, and in the cupola was a room that he set aside. It was like a storage room, and he had told us kids that he'd retreat there to eat his dinner and read his paper because it was quiet. Lionel would bring his dinner there and wait until he got through eating to bring the dishes back. One day, my father was reading his paper, and Lionel didn't want to wait for him, so he just brought home one dish. He put it on the sink and told Mama, "I locked the door. Papa's going to do his trick." You see, Papa had told us that any time anybody locked the door to that room, he could get out, because he was a magician. So Lionel locked Father in the tower.

MARIA: He tried to get out by the window up on the roof, but they saw him down at the employment office, and he got caught. The office called Mr. Cramm, my husband's boss. They said, "What's happened in your mill? There's a man on the roof." So Mr. Cramm went up, unlocked the door, and looked around the room, but he didn't find him there. My husband had broken the window and gone out over the roof. Mr. Cramm really laughed when he found out what happened.

Mr. Cramm was a very good boss. Once, around Christmas, he asked my husband if we had a Christmas tree. My husband said, "We don't have too much money, and my wife doesn't want to buy one. She'd rather keep the money to give some little thing to the kids." So Mr. Cramm sent over a big Christmas tree.

Sometimes, when it was very hard times or if there was less work, my husband would have to send a man home. It was part of his job as second hand. So the man would give him a tip, maybe 25¢, in order to be kept on.

ALICE: In our culture, the oldest children always went to work. Our family was most unusual because the oldest sons went into the priesthood. My mother had read in the paper that an association in the city, which my father belonged to, called Association Canado-Américaine, was going to give scholarships to boys of large families if they passed tests. So my mother went and put in the names of the two oldest boys. The boys were very smart, and my brother Aimé got the scholarship. There was only one scholarship given per family, but the two brothers, Aimé and Lorenzo, had never been separated. Lorenzo wanted to go, too, so my mother went back and told them it would be impossible to separate the boys. In the end, they came up with some professional people in the city to provide the money, and they sent both of them to school.

In those days, it was unheard of to go to public school if you were a Catholic. You went to Catholic school. There was one Catholic school in the city, but it was an Irish-Catholic school; and in those days there was a lot of friction between

The Lacasse family upon the occasion of the ordination of Aimé Lacasse. Lorenzo (left), Maria (center), and Aimé (right) are seated in the first row. Laurette and Alice are second and third from left in the second row.

the Irish and the French. So a lot of boys were sent to school in Canada.

Eventually, my two brothers became priests, which was the highlight of the family, since we had been so very poor. What made it terribly sad was that my father died before Lorenzo was ordained. Now Lorenzo is a diocesan priest, for the diocese of Manchester, and he's a monseigneur. Monseigneur Lorenzo Lacasse. He has a parish in Concord. Aimé has spent forty years as a missionary with the White Fathers in Africa. He returned last year at age sixty-six, and he's more African than American now.

When the boys started to go to school, they were too young

to work. Then they started to like school, and my father and mother didn't want them to leave, because they wanted them out of the mill. By the time I was twelve years old, my father desperately needed money. He couldn't support the family by himself. Jackman's boardinghouse was right next door, and they offered my parents to give me a job, which was really illegal in a sense, because I was so young. I worked in the kitchen, and I got $3.00 a week, which I gave to my mother, plus my board. That was a big help to my family, because I was a twelve-year-old, and I had a good appetite. In those days, $3.00 was enormous. Why, at the boardinghouse, they used to serve a meal for 35¢!

I worked an hour at noon and three hours at night, four hours a day. I worked six days a week. That wasn't very good pay when you think about it. I did much better when I went to work in the mill. We were all very healthy, and everybody was expected to work. Everybody did something, but work was never an issue in the family. If you wanted a child to get a job, you didn't feel it was imposing on him or anything like that. We were a very compact family, very united; and if the decision was made, that's the way it was done.

When I graduated from grammar school at fourteen, in 1930, I got a job in the mill. I was actually scared of the mills. As a child, I used to go and visit my father in the spinning room. You can't hear yourself talk in there, the noise is so loud. He worked there all his life, the poor man. No wonder he died at forty-four. So I was petrified when I found out I was going to work in the mills, because I had never seen any other place but the spinning room. My mother came with me to the office to get a job. We spoke to the man, and she told him that she preferred that I didn't work in one of the places where men and women were working together. She wanted me to go where there were only girls. So I got into the cloth room, where it was nice and quiet. It was all finished cloth. It was delightful, really. I was so happy there. I guess it was the relief of not having to go to those horrible mills that I hated so. When I would go to visit my father, I would almost cry.

When I started working on cotton, it was all young girls that worked in there, fourteen, fifteen, sixteen years old. So it was rather pleasant, and it wasn't dangerous. My parents were very concerned about the morals of their daughter, so my mother was absolutely delighted that I wasn't exposed to men. And to tell you the truth, I was, too, because I was kind of a shy girl, and I had never been out. I was only fourteen years old then. My family was very strict. The moral code was there, and you followed it.

But the amazing thing about the family, and I'm proud of it, is that all the other children went to high school. In fact, most of them are college graduates. Marcel was the next boy after Laurette, and he would have been available to work, but he also went to a priests' seminary. He wanted to be like the others. So after my father died, I became the sole supporter of the family. Laurette and I are the only ones who didn't go to high school.

LAURETTE: We found out later, as we were growing up and we started realizing we never had this or we never had that, that we must have been poor. But as we were growing, I never felt poor. We never felt that we were any less than other people, but I always had the feeling that other people thought they were better than the people that worked in the mills. Even living in the corporations was considered inferior. When you'd meet people and you'd say you lived in a corporation, you had a feeling of being a poor relative or something on that order.

I remember how, about twenty-five past five, we'd begin to see the workers in the mills getting up out of their chairs and getting ready to go. The whistle blew at five thirty. The gates would open, and the people would stream out of there. We'd all get to the window and watch the people go by. A lot of them would wave; they would know us. Some would just run— the younger ones, I suppose. The older ones would look tired when they came out.

When I was at school, I worked at the boardinghouse next door in the summertime. I waited on tables at noontime. I'd help clean up, bring the food from the table, wash the dishes. They'd have boxes of berries in the morning, and we'd sit on the porch and hull the strawberries. They were good cooks; they'd make their own stuff. But what I remember is the smell of those potatoes! Mr. Blanchard, the owner, had a big black

Workers leaving the mills, photographed by Lewis Hine in 1909. Most workers changed from their work clothes before leaving work.

stove; and on the back of the stove, he'd have the potatoes that were left over from noontime. He'd slice them and fry them, home fries, and they'd be on the back of that stove from about one o'clock until about five o'clock, when suppertime came. There were never any left over.

I felt bad when I couldn't go to school. I cried; boy, did I cry! I wanted to go to school so bad. All they had at St. Augustine's was a commercial course for two years, after grammar school. The sisters who taught at St. Augustine's had a boarding school in Goffstown, Villa Augustina, which was also a high school. They would give a scholarship to the one who came out first at St. Augustine's. The one who won that year didn't want to go, and then it was offered to the second one. I was the third one. It was offered to me, but there was no way I could go. I had to go to work.

At home I would get into trouble all the time because I had books sitting all over, and I would read. Saturdays I would spend what time I had at the library. I read all the books in the library at that time. My father was forever taking the books away from me because he said it wasn't good for me to be reading them. I liked to read, and I was doing really well in school. I liked school.

LORENZO: My mother was a hard woman. She hardly went to school at all herself, but she had it in her mind that her kids would go to school. She got the idea on her own. She often says now that she would have loved to go to school.

As we grew up, as we got a little bit older, we became more aware of the situation at home. My brother and I knew that the men who worked with my father in the mills would say to him, "You're nuts. Here you have your two oldest boys. Why don't you keep them home and get them to work? They'd help you support your family." Of course, we were not privy to the exchanges between our mother and father, but Mother always said, "As long as I have life, they're going to stay in school." We used to write home, "If you want us to come back and go to work, just say it." But she would say, "No, you'll stay there."

They put us on the train to the seminary in Trois Rivières in September 1925. I was eleven years old and my brother was thirteen. We had gotten a list from the school of things that we were supposed to get—so many pairs of socks, so many pairs of underwear, so many this and so many that. My mother spent the summer begging for those things. She actually went begging to city hall to get these clothes. To put us on the train, she had to beg and borrow the twenty-five bucks that it cost then to go by train from here to Montreal, and then from Montreal to Trois Rivières.

We were in the seminary six years. When we got a little bit older, we worked in the summer. For four summers in a row, I worked as a messenger boy at the Amoskeag. One time, I was a roving boy at the Jefferson Mill. I covered the whole top floor, the whole spinning room. You did whatever you could by hook and by crook to earn a few cents, a few pennies.

It really is a providential thing. You look back, and you can't explain it from a purely material point of view. When I tell some of my friends, priests, classmates, what our situation was, they just can't believe it. They say, "How could you go to school?"

MARIA: When I put their names in at the Association Canado-Américaine, my husband was so mad. He said, "When they graduate from the eighth grade, they can go to work." I said, "No! They're not going to go to work! I told you that when I got married." I tried so much to go to school, but I never could. I had three years of school, that's all I had. I was eleven years old when my mother got married again, and she wanted me to work, so I had to go.

ALICE: In our family, the girls had to work to support the boys. It wasn't the custom ordinarily; it just happened that in our family, two boys were first, and they wanted to go to school. My mother was determined that somebody was going to get an education. My sister Rita wanted to be a nun, too. They all wanted to be nuns and priests in our family; don't ask me why.

I was really the pillar of the family. The only thing I ever did was work. I don't see one other thing that my parents could have done, being the kind of people they were, to make it any different for me. They never used me. It was the times and, of course, the need. But I always resented that they said that the boys had to be educated. Maybe I shouldn't have. Among the French Canadians especially, the big thing was the boys have to be educated but the girls don't. They never stressed education for girls.

As I grew older, it became more evident that I always had to do physical work. Of course, I could see the others, so I started to think about how my parents didn't make much of an effort to send me to school. Whether they could have done it is another story. When I look back, they probably couldn't. My mother always had babies. How could they have done it? But I always felt cheated that I never got to school. That's why I'm going to school now.

My brothers and sisters are all very well educated, but they have never held it against me. In fact, they admire me to have done what I have done without an education, but it has always held me back. I probably would have been able to study to be a nurse's aide, for instance, if I had had a high school education. The experiences that I've had are worth more than what a lot of people have in education, but they don't consider that, and sometimes I think that is not right either.

LORENZO: When my father died, my brother Aimé was away. He had joined this religious society of the White Fathers, and their training was in Algiers, so he had left in September. I was in my third year of theology. I had come home for Christmas as usual, for ten days. I remember they took me to the station, all the family—kids, brothers, sisters, and Father and Mother. My father had a cold, a bad cold, but otherwise, I didn't think there was anything unusual. The first letter I got was toward the middle of January. He had been taken to the hospital. He worked until a Friday night, and he was bleeding, and my mother prevailed on him to go to the hospital. He was the kind of man who just couldn't stop working. Remember, there was no kind of insurance, no security of any kind. Had he lived, he would have ended up at sixty without a penny. There was no pension or plan of any kind with the Amoskeag.

ALICE: When my father died, there was nothing. He had $1,000 of insurance. They buried him, they bought a washing machine, and that was the end of it.

LORENZO: My father was a very affectionate man. My mother is cold. My mother doesn't express herself outwardly. She keeps everything inside. She's very hard. I don't recall her even shedding a tear when my father died. Here was a woman left alone with not a penny in the world, with twelve kids on her hands. The youngest one was six months old. She didn't even shed a tear. I asked her, "How could you do that?" "Oh," she said, "it was all inside." The only explanation I have is that she had to keep going all the time. Had she stopped, had she started feeling sorry for herself, she would not have been able to continue.

ALICE: As we were growing up, I remember we used to tease. We used to say to my father, "When you took Mama out, did you used to kiss her?" Did you do this, did you do that—you know how little kids ask questions—and he'd say, "Oh, well, you know." He'd look at his feet. They were never affectionate with each other. I never saw them kiss or hug in front of us. I remember, once in a while, Papa would be sitting down in the rocking chair, and he'd grab her and make her sit down on his lap, but she'd get up in a hurry. She'd get all upset.

My father was very strict. He was so totally against going out with other nationalities that we would have been expelled from the family. Lorenzo continued that same strictness. He checked out who we went out with. We all did marry French Canadians, every one of us but the younger ones. It's changed with the younger ones. They are like a second generation. My brother married an Irish girl, and my last sister, Lucille, married an Irish boy. Her husband died, and she remarried. Her husband is Irish. My sister Yvette also married an Irish boy.

For us, though, it was understood that you married French. It came not only from the family but from the Church. They'd say, "First of all, if you don't marry in your own language, then you won't communicate as well; then, if you don't marry Catholic, you'll lose your religion. It's hard enough to get together when you're of the same religion and the same language; how much harder it will be if you're not. It's hard enough to be married, so try to get your own kind."

The Franco-Americans lived mostly on the West Side. We were almost segregated from them because we lived in the corporations. We were brought up much more American than Franco-American. We went to a French school—that's why we kept our French—but we were brought up with English-speaking people. We never had any relatives here; everybody was in Canada.

Everyone was working-class that we knew. We didn't know anybody middle-class or upper-class. Everybody that we knew, that we chummed with or went to church with, were all working in the mills or in the shoe shops. I don't think we thought about it. I felt very badly that I couldn't go to school, especially as my brothers grew more educated, and their friends were educated. I felt I didn't belong any more. I had been the one who had given the most, but I didn't belong.

My younger sisters are not as close to my mother as I am; there is forty years' difference between them, so when they go see her, they have nothing in common. I can understand what she says because I saw her live through all this, and I think that makes me very close to her. Not that I think she prefers me. On the contrary, I think she favors the others. She thinks they need her more, but I think she feels a lot closer to me because I'm the oldest. I was eighteen when my father died. I was left with her. I really helped to sustain her. The younger ones love her, but I think if it were left to them, they wouldn't be doing what we're doing for her.

In Quebec, older people used to live with their children. The old people had to break up housekeeping and go live with their son or daughter. But I didn't grow up with my grandparents. We lived in the corporations, where there weren't many Franco-Americans. I guess my grandmother, when she became old, went to live with one of her daughters. That's where she died.

When we were younger, when we were newly married, when we just had one child or two, we all used to see each other a lot because we used to go to my mother's a lot. But then all of a sudden, my mother got married again; and right away she made a rule that since she had twelve children, she would serve no more meals. She and her second husband had a chicken farm with five thousand chickens. She used to work from morning to dusk. She couldn't serve meals. We could go and visit, but nobody could eat there any more. One of my sisters was still there, and my brother Lorenzo had no home, so that was the only home that he had; but the rest of us all stayed home more. We all had more children. Now, it's just too

The Lacasse family, bottom to top, left to right: Maria Lacasse, Laurette Bouchard, Rita Bourque, Lorenzo Lacasse, and Alice Olivier, 1976

much for the family to get together. Too many children. God! My sister Laurette has eight children and nine grandchildren. We're all working people, and we just can't afford it! We're all too tired. We have enough with our own. My mother always thinks of me as young, but I'm sixty years old. I'm not young. She always says to me, "You're so young, you're so young." She thinks of me as a little kid, but after all, we're sixty, my husband and I. We're beginning to be the older people now.

► Marie Anne Senechal

Marie Anne Duchesne Senechal, eighty-one years old, worked in the mills all her life. She started work as a spinner in 1910 but spent most of her career in the Amoskeag as a weaver. Her mother died when Marie Anne was twenty; and as the oldest child in her family, she had to serve as a surrogate mother to her younger siblings.

Marie Anne raised all of them to adulthood, then continued to assist them, as well as to care for a chronically ill brother and a sister who lived with her. As a result, she postponed her marriage until she was sixty-seven, when she married her fiancé after forty years of courtship.

Widowed after five years of marriage, she continues to live in what was originally her husband's home. She shares her flat with her sister and brother-in-law and keeps another sister and brother-in-law in the one upstairs.

What can you do when you are the oldest? I went to work in the Amoskeag. I was lucky to get a job at all. When they were laying off people, the older ones stayed, and they put us out. So I kept changing around, taking care of the kids when my sister wasn't healthy. She had some kind of intestinal trouble. She couldn't work in the mills. So she took over and helped out at home. She was very good to the kids, but she wasn't a manager. She'd feed them ice cream and chocolate bars. Once we ran up a $50.00 bill in the store! That was an awful bill.

We were twelve, and we had to eat. Just my brother and

me were going to work; we were supporting all of them. My father was working, but he got into an accident. He cut one of his fingers in the bobbin shop, and they laid him off. That was the year that my mother died. So it was only me and my brother, and we got help from nobody. Nobody!

When my mother was still alive, she worked in the mill and I took care of the babies. At ten o'clock in the morning, my mother would go out and look across at our window to see if we were all right. We'd wave, and she'd wave. There was also an orphan girl who used to live with us. Her mother died, and my mother said, "We might as well take her in. She's a little orphan." So we took her in. She helped me out taking care of the kids. My mother always worked until the last minute before she had a baby. When she came out of the mill, I went in to work. The little my father made plus the little I made helped. All my life, until I retired, I got only one basket from the Salvation Army.

My younger brother had an accident when we were kids. He was thirteen. We were riding down the hill on a sled. On the way down, my brother got stuck on a branch, and I went flying. He didn't walk for seven years. At first, my mother carried him in her arms. Finally, he started walking, but he never worked until my mother died. Then he worked in the same mill, but not the same room, as I did. We had good bosses then. The boss would say, "When your brother can't come in, it's all right." Today, if you're retarded or anything, they send you to a special school, but then they just laughed at you. But the boss told me to bring him in, so I brought him in and got him a job. In the end he got $42.00 a month Social Security. He died when he was seventy years old. He lived all that time after his accident because I took care of him and let him do what he liked. When he'd feel pain, the boss would let him go home. He'd work three or four weeks straight sometimes, or more than that. But when they doubled up the shifts, they'd lay him off. So what could he do? Nothing but stay home. I had to feed him. You've got to feed your family; when they're home, you can't put them out.

I went to work in 1910, when my sister was born, because we were ten then. For my first job, I went into the spinning room and asked. At that time, you could go in on the floor, and

Marie Anne Senechal, ca. 1920

they would give you a job. If they thought you could do it, they'd just say, "You want to learn?" When they laid us off, I went to work in the shoe shops. But when I was eighteen, I went back to #10 Mill, and I worked there until the strike of 1922.

At the Amoskeag, the bosses were always playing favorites. If they liked your face, they gave you a job; if they didn't like your face, try and get it. And if you tried to stick up for your own people, they'd give you. . . . My father got fired once at the Amoskeag. He had made a mistake in the cloth, and my father said to the boss, "The hell with you," and walked out on him. The next day the boss said to me, "Tell your father to come back in." So this was a really good boss. The educated ones were the best ones; they were smarter than us. Swallow was well educated; Mike Ahern was an educated man. I went over and sat down with Mike Ahern many times when he wouldn't give me any work.

I was twenty when my mother died, and we had two babies in the house, one three years old and one a year and a half. The others were five, seven, nine, eleven, and fourteen. There was one more who died before that. My sister loved those kids, but she wouldn't wash a diaper. She'd say, "They smell. They look bad." So she would put them in a pail; and at night when I got home from work, I'd have to wash them out in the toilet.

One time my father said, "Marie, I've got a good mind to remarry." The woman he was seeing had money, but she was going to take in only the kids that were working. My father said he was going to put all the kids who weren't working in the St. Pierre's Orphanage. I said to Pa, "I don't blame you. You have a chance to marry a rich woman. Go and live with her, and come over to visit us any time, but I'm not going to put any kids or anybody else out. They're going to live with me as long as they want. I'm not going to give up the kids." They were just like my own children. They never went to my father. Whenever they needed anything, they always came to me, and I always gave it. He didn't marry her, though.

As we grew older, more of us went to work. My brother Henry went to work at sixteen. My oldest brother went to work at eighteen. That's how we kept going after my father's accident. But when my mother died, we were stuck. My brothers and sisters paid their board, but none of them gave their whole pay. I was the one who was running the money, paying the bills. My father had bought a house just before my mother died, but we lost it because we didn't have the money. We had to move out. We bought the house in September 1917; she died in January 1918. So where was he going to get the money to pay for the house? Today you can borrow thousands to put in a house. Then you couldn't borrow any money. Nobody had any.

When we came here to this side of Manchester, Henry and I worked to pay the rent. We were working for $6.00 a week to pay that rent. We always needed a big place because we were so many. With eleven people, you can't give them beds by themselves, so we had one room for four girls—two beds, two girls in each bed. When my sister got married, I slept with the other two girls because we were five girls and five boys and my father.

We used to eat anything. We'd have the same thing for dinner for three or four days. We'd eat cabbage, flapjacks, anything that was cheap. We used to drink a lot of milk, and we loved bread and milk. For supper, we'd put out a good meal of bread and milk. Today you never see anybody eating bread and milk for supper, but we always had plenty. I'd get paid on a Wednesday, and one of my sisters or brothers would come in to the mill to get my pay. They'd go right home and buy food for dinner. It was something to look forward to.

My father would go away to cut wood. Then he'd come back and work in the mills. When they'd send for him, I'd write to him and tell him to come home. They would tell us, "If you want to work when we need you, we'll send somebody for you." So when they'd send a man for him, I'd send a letter saying, "Be down for Monday." But he couldn't earn his own bread. He was only making $3.00 or $4.00 a week. He'd come home, and on Monday morning I'd go to the store with him, right at the corner, on West Hancock and Main. They used to eat salt pork in the woods, just cold salt pork. So we'd get bread, eggs, beans, all those things at the store, but it would go on the family's bill.

After my mother died, he lost all his courage. He didn't care if he lived or not. I think the farther away from home he was, the better he felt. When he'd come home on Saturday,

Marie Anne Senechal, 1976

he'd have some woman to go out with, to go to a show or to go play cards or something. That would keep him going. But he always liked the woods. I guess that's because my father was brought up on a big farm.

I didn't feel like getting married. I was having too hard a time bringing up a family. I took them to school even if they didn't care to go. They were just like any other kids—if they didn't like school, they didn't want to go. I took my sister [who now lives upstairs] to school when she was fourteen or fifteen years old. I had to take her to school every noon; she wouldn't go herself. She's a good woman, but she didn't like school. I wanted her to be educated. She could have graduated. But no, she wanted to work. She wanted to be big, just like the others, and bring in the money.

It's my fault that my sister got married. I should have told her not to. She was eighteen, and she was the one who was taking care of the house. She asked for my advice, and I said, "Well, an old maid doesn't have a very good name." You would have that going on all your life. You can hear that talk any time. An old maid is hateful; an old maid is like this; an old maid is like that. When we were young, we used to hear people say, "Oh, she's going to be an old maid. Isn't that awful?" At age twenty, if you're not married, you become an old maid. You couldn't get a fellow. Actually, it's so easy to get a fellow. But they thought you couldn't get one to like you.

My mother didn't push anybody. I had fellows before, and she'd say, "Mary, take your time. When you're old enough, you can get married and settled down, and then you'll be satisfied." That's what my mother used to tell me. But after she died, who was I going to ask about my sister? I couldn't ask my father. He wanted me to take care of the kids. So I pushed my sister to get married. She knew her husband from when she worked in the spinning room. He wrote to her from Buffalo or someplace and asked her to marry him. He never forgot her. She'd show me the letters.

My sister was eighteen, and I was twenty. She was very close to me. We always went out together. When she left with him, all of us were at the window. All the little kids. She never forgot our faces in the window. As long as she lived, she always said, "Marie Anne, why did I get married and leave you all by yourself?"

"You didn't leave me by myself," I said. "I had ten others" [laughs].

My father wanted the money when the kids started work. Not that he was bad, he just wanted the money. He thought the kids were going to work and expected they were going to give him the money, so they did. During this time, I put $500 of my own money in the bank. But I'd give him my rent and the household expenses. I never took a penny from my brothers and sisters. They gave $7.00 a week. The rest they could keep.

After the Amoskeag shut down, my father didn't go back to the mills because he was too old. He worked in the cemetery about ten or twelve years, but we never got a cent. He gave up [working] at eighty-seven years old. Eighty-seven years, with no pension, nothing. He had more ambition when he was older. He got a car. In the summer I would get $10.00 from him, but in the winter he wouldn't pay anything for board. He'd just keep his own money, whatever he had in his pocketbook. I never asked him for anything.

When my father died, he was ninety-four years old. He lived upstairs with my sister for two years, and he lived with me for twenty-three years, so I never was alone, to tell you the truth. I was alone only when my husband died, because that was after my sister got married.

The sister who helped me the most is the one that is living with me. She stayed unmarried, too. She had a fellow, but he died. She finally got married when she was fifty-four.

My husband and I waited forty years to get married. Forty years! The first year I met him, he was eighteen years old and I was six years older. I couldn't get married because I had to bring up a family, and he had to take care of his mother. When she died, she was ninety-four. He kept taking care of his mother, and I kept on bringing up my family. I thought I'd never marry. I was sixty-seven years old when I got married. And I'm seventy-nine now. It was too much of a wait, when I think of it now, because I would have been happier if I'd got married. But when you don't know, you just stay that way.

I met my husband when I was in the mill. He was a runner

boy. He took all the reports to the mills. After that, he filled up my batteries, or when he had any time, he'd come by. But the boss kicked him out of my looms a lot of times. He didn't want anybody to mingle with our work. He'd go at one o'clock for the report; he used to be watchman in the lunch hour.

When he was nineteen years old, he asked me to marry him. He said, "Marry me. We'll get out of town, get married, and come back." Just thinking of living with his mother, when I knew she didn't like me, was enough to make me not want to marry him. He asked me later many times. I got two diamonds from him. He gave me gifts all the time. He was very good-hearted.

When we were young, my fellow paid for the movies every night. When he was sixteen, he started work at the mill part-time. After that, he had the money to take me to the movies. It only cost 15¢ each then. That wasn't too much. Thirty cents isn't much to go out with a girl. I'd sleep through half the movie, I was always so tired. After I finished off the popcorn, I'd sleep. I was lucky that he stood me. If I took a fellow and he slept all night, I'd be mad. But he never got mad. I had a very good man.

All the years my husband and I were courting, he always went home to sleep, and he always went home to eat, even on holidays. He'd go home and please his mother by having his supper with her. But he'd take her back to my house for parties. We always took her out on Sunday afternoons. I tried to please him in that way for his mother, because his mother loved him. He was the only boy; and when you're the only boy, the mother never forgets. I knew that. I tried to please him in every other way but marrying him. I used to tell myself, "Oh, I'm never getting married, because I don't want any children. I've had enough." But it wasn't right of me, because I should have decided for my own self, and married and forgot about everybody else. I knew I wasn't living my own life, but I couldn't make up my mind. There are people like that. I couldn't make up my mind.

► *Anna Douville*

Anna Douville, seventy-one years old, was one of twelve children. She was born in Canada, but her family moved to Manchester when she was only a few months old. Virtually everyone in her family worked in the mills, and Anna herself went in as a doffer in 1924. She continued at the Amoskeag as a doffer and a spinner until the shutdown, and then she worked at the Chicopee until she reached retirement age, in 1972. Her career at the Chicopee is representative of those of many other workers who, having experienced the slower work pace of the Amoskeag, were unable to adapt to new demands for greater speed.

Oddly enough, although Anna is quite bitter about some of her family experiences while she was growing up, it is she who proudly keeps her family tree and record book.

Anna married in 1933 and lost her husband thirteen years later. They were not permitted to have children because of his poor health.

I went to Canada in 1927 and 1928 to visit relatives, but I didn't like it in Canada. I told my brother who drove us there, "Let's go back to Manchester. There's nothing like Manchester up here." In Canada, at eight or nine o'clock, they start to blow the lamp out; they're all ready to go to bed because they get up at three or four o'clock in the morning to milk cows and do the farm work. I hated it. In Manchester, we never go to bed before eleven or eleven thirty, and we get up in the morning at five thirty. In Canada, the minute it starts to get a little bit dark, they all start to yawn and get ready to go to bed.

My mother lost her mother when she was about six years old. There were five in her family. The oldest sister was nine years old, and she's the one who brought up the rest of the family so my grandfather could keep on working on the farm. The sisters and brothers brought each other up, really. My mother's job was to scrub the floors. (In Canada they didn't have any rugs or anything like that.) She had to scrub the floors every Saturday. One sister would do the washing and ironing, and another one would do the housework, wash the dishes. Imagine a kid nine years old baking bread and pastries and keeping the family going! My father and mother often talked about the hard times they had in Canada. They never went back.

In Canada, my father was a farmer. Sometimes he only earned 50¢ a day. My mother had twelve children. Ten were born in Canada, and the two youngest in the States, here in Manchester. My parents first came to Peterborough, New Hampshire, in 1908 because my mother's sister lived there. Then my father's brother said he could find him a job at the Amoskeag in the Coolidge Mill. I was their youngest one when they came to Manchester. I was four months old.

At the time they had children at home, not like today. Most of my mother's children were delivered by a midwife. My mother had a doctor at home only for those two that were born here in Manchester. My sister was born in 1900. My mother saw the doctor go and deliver a baby about two houses away from where they were living at the time, and she asked the doctor, "Will you be very far away today?" He said, "What for?" "Well," she said, "I started to have labor pains, and I was wondering if you could come." So he came down to the house, but she wasn't ready. He had to stay overnight, sitting next to my mother and waiting for the time to come to deliver my sister, Claire [laughs].

One day when I was about four years old, they sent me to school, saying that the Indians were coming by that morning and I had to leave the house. I cried all the time that I was in school because I figured somebody else was going to take my place [laughs].

When my parents came here, there was only my father and one child working, and they were getting paid every other week. It was very hard. I remember, we were so poor we'd go to bed hungry. All we had left in the house until my father got paid was bread and sugar, no butter. My mother used to wet the bread underneath the faucet and put a little sugar on it, and we'd have bread and sugar before we went to bed. When my father got his pay, they would buy butter and something else, like jam. When the oldest one started to work, it was much better. But I remember all the hard times we went through then. It must have been in 1909 or 1910, because I was just a baby.

Two of my sisters got married in 1924. That was the year that I had to support the rest of the family. They wanted to get out of the house and be on their own. When they had something in mind, they would get right on it. Even if we had to go on relief, they would have gotten married. I felt it in my bones, long before they talked about it. I said, "Well, I won't be able to finish grammar school." And I didn't. The teacher kept saying, "It's too bad they can't keep you in school. You only have two more grades to go and then you'll graduate, and at least you'll have your full diploma." I said, "What good's a diploma? We all have to go to work sometime anyway."

My mother had never worked Otherwise, my whole family was in the Amoskeag. My brothers and sisters worked there, too, except for my oldest brother, who got married. He was working as a meat cutter. Some of the others went to work in the shoe shops. It was still not enough to help anybody. We had to go on relief. We got our share.

I worked in the Amoskeag for twelve years, starting in 1924. Two of my sisters had already started to work—one at fourteen and the other at fifteen, but I started at sixteen because they had changed the law. You couldn't go to work before you reached sixteen. My father was not working at the time, and I was only in the sixth grade, because I had lost a lot of school on account of sickness. I was the weakest one in the family, always sick. But when I reached sixteen, I knew that I had to go to work. My sisters were sending out hints. Somebody had to go, and I knew I was the next one in line, so I started to work in #4 Mill as a spinner.

When I went in with my slip from the employment office and said I was coming in as a learner, they said, "Do you know anybody here?" I said I have two sisters. "What's their names?" I said, "Fregau." My sisters had told me to give a false name because they didn't want me bothering them while I was learning. They said "We don't have no Fregaus here," and told me to go see that lady there, and she'd show me how to spin. By the time I was sent upstairs, where my sisters were working, I knew how to spin, but I learned how to do it with a stranger.

They thought I would never marry because I was always with the nuns. It was when I was about fourteen or fifteen years old that I mentioned that I was in love with the nuns. "They're so nice to me," I said. "I wish some day, when I get older, I could join them." I wanted to go to the convent, but the whole family got after me. They told me I was too much of a coward to work like the rest of the family, so I was ashamed. I wanted to show them I was not afraid to work, so I gave the idea up. My mother would have liked it very much, but my father was against it, too. He said it was too private a life, that he would never have a chance to see me again if I locked myself into the convent. To make peace in the family, I said, "Forget it, I changed my mind. I'll go to work." So I went to work in the Amoskeag, and then I worked in the Chicopee for thirty-five years.

I was the only one in the family who had that crazy idea. I was raised in such a big family, with so much going on all the time, so many arguments, that I thought if I pick the convent, I'll be away from all that trouble. Some big families stay together, but it didn't work that way in our family. I think there were too many of us. I remember we used to wear long pigtails; and when my sisters wanted me to do something for them and I said no, one of them would pull my pigtails and say, "You're going to do it, or I'm going to pull your hair out." Sometimes I wished I had been born alone in the family instead of being one of a large family like that. We were always glad to see each other, but as soon as someone said something about one of the others, the arguments started.

Anna Douville

Even when I got older, my sisters were always picking on me. I would have to know how to spin right away or be smart like they were, even though they were much older than me. They jumped on me at home, in the mill, everywhere. If they were not supposed to do something, my mother gave me strict orders when she went out to tell her whatever they did. I used to tell my mother; and then, when I was left all alone with them again, they'd pick on me because I was a tattletale. But my mother loved me more than anybody else. She used to tell them to leave me alone because I was the smallest one. I was always sick, and they'd say, "She plays sick because she knows otherwise she'll have to get ready to go to work pretty soon." Things like that hurt you, even when you're a kid. I never had any trouble, though, with my brothers. They used to pity me because I was so sick, so tiny.

When I started to work in the Amoskeag, I wasn't strong enough to be like the rest of them. I passed out the first week I worked in the mill. That proved to my sisters that I was really sick, and they were kinder to me after that. In the morning, I was so tired, because all that work I had to do in the mill kept me awake all night long. So when I'd get up I'd get dizzy, and I passed out at home. I was already a spinner at that time. I was seventeen, and I didn't weigh more than eighty-nine pounds. I was only skin and bones.

In the Amoskeag village,* we had a six-room apartment. There were two rooms for the boys and two rooms for the girls. Three of the bedrooms were with double beds. Rita and I slept together, Alice and Bertha slept together, and Albertine and Claire slept together. The four boys had two little beds with two boys in each bed. My mother and father had their bedroom, and then we just had the kitchen and a little den they called a parlor. All the other rooms had to be used as bedrooms. We wouldn't have known then what it was to be independent, to have the life we have today. That's why I've been independent for so many years since my husband died. I don't want to mix with the family at all.

My youngest brother always took me roller skating. He was working at the skating rink, putting the skates on the girls and

---

* Amoskeag Village was the location of the earliest textile manufacturing establishment on the Merrimack River near the Amoskeag Falls. Originally a part of Goffstown, it was incorporated into Manchester in 1854.

the boys, so he could get me and my sister in free as long as we went in early with him. I met my husband at that skating rink, and we began to skate six times a week for a while. That's how we fell in love. Those were the happy days. I was working in the Amoskeag every day and skating at night.

I got married the oldest, in September, thirteen days after I turned twenty-five. My husband had turned twenty-six in April. I hated to leave my folks alone. I was the only one working, and I was the only one left single. All the others were married. The boys left home after the Amoskeag shut down and scattered all over to places like Wisconsin and Connecticut. When they lived at home, all the others just paid board, but I thought it was kind of mean to give only $5.00 board. I said to myself, "If I ever work, I'm going to try to be better than them. I'll give all my pay at home." So when I got my pay, I'd give it all to my mother. My mother had told the family, "The last one who stays with us will get my new sewing machine." I was that last one, so she gave it to me, which made hard feelings with the others. But she had promised.

When she saw that I had met the man I'd marry, she got me started on my hope chest. After the week's shopping was done and the bills were paid, we would take all the money that she had left to the store and buy me sheets and pillowcases. She bought me a dishpan, all my pots and pans, knives, and dishes. When I got married, we didn't have to buy a damn thing for years because I had all the things I needed. My mother thought I deserved it because I gave her all my pay to the last week that I worked. She never did that for the others, and they got jealous about it. They were on their own when they got married and had to buy all the stuff they needed themselves.

I had a lot of arguments about my fiancé. My sisters kept saying I shouldn't marry that man. I knew what they were up to. They were scheming to get me to support my folks until they died. But I had been going out with him for five years, and my mother told me, "Anna, don't wait too long. What if I die or your father dies? Then you'd insist on staying with me, and you'll lose your boyfriend. He's been waiting long enough. Get married while I'm still living." So I got married. My sisters said that I shouldn't marry that fellow because his father was a drunkard, but my husband was not a drunkard.

I lived two houses away from my mother after I got married. It was in my uncle's little furnished cottage. We lived there for two months, but I couldn't sleep. There were rats chasing each other between the partitions. The minute the lights were out and you were in bed, they started to get up and do their running around. I finally woke up my husband and said, "Gee, there's something running around the house, and I can't sleep." I could hear, "Eek, eek, eek." He said, "You're right! My God, how long have you been hearing that?" "Every night since we landed in this place." "Oh, my God!" he said. "We're gonna look for another place."

Somebody had to do something about my parents when I got married. They were on the city welfare. What a life that was! My mother felt nobody in the family was interested in her life except me. She used to come here and spend time with me, and I'd question her about different things in Canada. She told me about all the hard times. My father was working for 50¢ a day, cutting and baling hay. She had six children at the time. I said, "How could you live, Ma?" She said, "Well, we managed. Sometimes we had to take a bit of firewood and water, and then some butter, and make like a dough. We'd put that on the stove and fry it, and then butter it, so many for each kid." Oh, my God! So that's why, even with the hard times I had during my life, I never stopped for sympathy for myself, because I knew about my mother's life.

My mother never would have believed the washing machine I have. She had to scrub the clothes on a washboard. The whites went into a boiler, and you took them out with a stick and put them into a cold tub of water. All the little spots you could see, you washed by hand. My parents had never seen a TV in their lives. Sometimes, when I'm sitting here all alone, I wonder what Pa and Ma would do if they could come down and see all the funny things I'm watching all by myself. A lot of things go through your head when your folks are gone. You see how we get everything and have a good time, while they had nothing. You miss them after they're gone. You don't realize it when they are living. You want to live your own life; but when your folks are gone and you think of all the good things that you have today, you wish they could share them.

I was not going to support my husband's family. I told him,

"You supported your family as long as I supported my family. If you get any bills, let your mother pay them, because you always gave your pay at home like I did." He kept only his last few pays to buy his wedding suit and the things that he needed for our honeymoon. After I got married, his mother bought something for his brother and put it on Roland's account. I showed them that I wasn't dumb. I went to the store with that bill, and I told them, "My husband doesn't owe you a cent. If the old lady has a bill here for one of her sons, make her pay it. I have nothing to pay you." When his parents used to come and visit me and ask to borrow money while my husband and I were working, I said, "Listen, I don't go down to your house to bother you. I'm happy with my husband and get the hell out. Don't ever come here and try to borrow anything from him or from me." I put my foot down the first year that I got married, and my husband agreed with me. He said, "I'm glad that you can open up with them. I couldn't talk that way to my own family."

I said, "If we have bad luck and we need some help, I'll go to the priest. We always give money to the church, and if I need some support, we'll go to the priest and ask him for support." I wouldn't go to any of my family or any of his family either. We were independent. Even if we were starving to death, I wouldn't go and tell my mother we were having a hard time. And I never did. I slaved. I worked hard all my life to get what I wanted, but I never went and asked for help.

I didn't care for some of my husband's family. They weren't the same type as me. They wanted to play cards and gamble and go to nightclubs. That wasn't my social life. My life was to be with my husband, to be happy with him and to go out with him. We visited nice couples that we had been friends with when we were single. We were well liked because we were a respectable couple. They used to call us lovebirds. Every time they saw one, they saw the other. It's not very often that you see that in couples today. I had twelve happy years of life with him. We used to spend the evening playing cards at somebody else's house; then on Saturday they'd come down to our house, and we'd get a lunch ready. That was our good time. Quiet, no children around.

Part Six

Strike and Shutdown

The strike of 1922 not only was a cataclysmic event for all those associated with the Amoskeag, but it also had a profound effect on the economic and social life of the city of Manchester. For the Amoskeag workers in particular, the strike marked the end of their world as they had known it. Many of the interviewees identified events as having occurred either before or after the strike, as if they were referring to a natural disaster. "Things just were not the same after the strike" was the recurring comment. For them, the strike symbolized the end of an era of confidence and the beginning of an era of insecurity and mistrust.

At first glance, the strike seems to be an anomaly in the Amoskeag's history. Until it occurred, Manchester had been known as the strikeless city, a major corporation mill town which had avoided the kind of violent upheaval that had affected Paterson, Lawrence, and other textile cities. In 1911, the year of the great Lawrence strike, the Amoskeag Company commissioned the Burns Detective Agency of Boston to conduct a confidential survey of the attitudes of the Amoskeag employees toward their own jobs and toward the Company, to determine whether there was sufficient discontent to cause a strike. Although some evidence of minimal discontent was found, the survey report assured management that there was no danger of a strike.

For a variety of reasons, the Amoskeag Company seemed to have succeeded in advancing a step beyond other New England corporations toward that elusive dream of a stable, satis-

First parade of strikers, April 10, 1922

fied, and loyal community of workers. The root objective
underlying the principle of corporate paternalism seemed to be
paying off. Why, then, on February 13, 1922, did the twelve
thousand employees of the Amoskeag Company begin a siege
against the company to which they had hitherto appeared to be
so loyal?

The strike occurred after demobilization and the curtail-
ment of production that followed World War I. Having experienced a period of temporary prosperity, ample work, and
relatively high wages during the war years, the setbacks of
1920–1922 were particularly dramatic. The shrinking number
of jobs and the resultant layoffs and firings were further ag-
gravated by increases in work load and in speed. The records

of the adjustment board for the period 1918-1922 are replete with workers' complaints about speedups, ruthless firings, and "being worked to death." In 1919, William Parker Straw returned from the war to become full-time agent. Unfortunately, he lacked his father's unique ability to communicate with every level of the huge labor force, a factor that further shook the workers' confidence in the paternalistic system.

The announcement that sparked the strike came without any prior preparation for workers or overseers. On February 2, 1922, the following notice was posted in all the workrooms:

> Commencing Monday, February 13, 1922, a reduction of 20 percent will be made in all hour and piece rates in all departments of the Amoskeag. At the same time the running time of the mills will be increased from 48 to 54 hours per week, in accordance with the schedule posted herewith.
> —W. P. STRAW, Agent

The Amoskeag workers were faced with a decision about whether to accept this notice or to strike. One month earlier, fifteen thousand textile workers in Rhode Island had gone on strike to protest a similar 20 percent wage reduction and the introduction of a fifty-four-hour week. In Nashua, Dover, Newmarket, and Somersworth, workers confronted with comparable situations also went on strike, under the leadership of the UTW. By March, protest had spread to Lawrence and Lowell. In these communities, where, because of state law, there had been no attempt to restore the fifty-four-hour week, the major issue was wages.

Following the posting of the notice, the national headquarters of the UTW dispatched its vice-president, James Starr, to Manchester. Starr held a vote; and of the twelve thousand votes cast, 99 percent were reported to be in favor of the strike. Management announced that the mills would open as usual the next day, but very few workers crossed the picket line. The corporation was forced to close the mills "until further notice." Only maintenance work and the completion of jobs in progress continued; and the overseers, second hands, and office help were the only ones working, filling orders and salvaging materials.

During the first few months, suggestions for a compromise were made by Bishop Georges Albert Guertin of Manchester,

New Hampshire Governor Albert O. Brown, and the UTW itself. When both management and labor rejected Governor Brown's proposal for a fifty-one-hour work week and a 10 percent wage reduction, he recommended that the mills open one of their units "to afford employment to former employees who are out on account of the strike and who are needy, in some instances subsisting on charity, and desiring to work."[*]

The Amoskeag opened the Coolidge Mill on Monday morning, June 5, with the same wages and hours as posted on February 2. According to the newspapers, 113 workers returned to work. To enable the workers to enter the Coolidge without threats from the pickets, the court granted the Amoskeag a temporary injunction, which prohibited even peaceful picketing. One month later, the injunction was modified to allow two pickets at each gate. Initially, the number of workers returning to the Coolidge was insufficient to warrant the mill's operation, so the Amoskeag hired strikebreakers from other towns.

The opening of the Coolidge and later other mills presented many workers with difficult choices. As the strike progressed, most workers exhausted their savings but received very little assistance from the union. In August, the Bag Mill opened, and the police reported four thousand workers returned to the Amoskeag.

While the workers were beginning to succumb to deprivation, the Amoskeag, too, came under pressure. In August 1922, the strike in Lawrence, where the only issue was wages, was settled with the restoration of the old wage scale. Nine mills in Maine did the same. The reopening of these mills posed a new threat to the Amoskeag, since it began to experience difficulty in attracting strikebreakers in sufficient numbers. So, on September 10, the Amoskeag announced the restoration of the 20 percent wage cut.

Despite the strikers' continued insistence on the forty-eight-hour week, the number of workers returning to the mills increased steadily. By the middle of November, most of the mills were once again functioning with a partial labor force. Following an abortive attempt on the part of Bishop Guertin to propose an acceptable compromise, union leaders called off the

[*] *History of the Amoskeag Strike During the Year 1922* (Manchester, N.H.: Amoskeag Manufacturing Co., 1924), p. 75.

strike on November 25 on the grounds that "the real and permanent victory for the forty-eight-hour work week is not to be won in the offices of the textile corporations but in the legislative halls of the State House."*

From the workers' perspective, the strike had been a failure. After nine months of struggle, bitterness, and deprivation for them and their families, they had to return to a situation of partial employment, with the important issue of hours still unresolved. During the strike, the union provided little except flour and beans; and the Church gave only minimal assistance, hardly sufficient to make a dent. Most individuals were too embarrassed to turn to the city for relief, and the city's own resources were too strained to meet even this need. Some workers went to work in Lowell, Lawrence, or other textile communities that were not on strike. Others found temporary jobs as waitresses and chambermaids in resort hotels or took menial jobs wherever available. Many returned to Quebec, and some stayed there permanently.

In addition to draining the families' economic resources and destroying the job security of most workers, the strike also caused rifts in families between those who worked and those who chose to strike. Some relatives continued to avoid each other for decades afterwards. The strike also undermined the future employability of many of the strikers. At the termination of the strike, the Amoskeag ruled that first priority of re-employment would be given to those who had been working during the strike. Thus, temporary strikebreakers replaced permanent workers. Whenever workers applied for employment, their cards were checked against the employment office's blacklist. Many of those who had been on strike were rehired, provided they had not been active pickets or organizers; and their files were marked with an X for future reference.

The strike of 1922 represented a watershed for the corporation and the workers. It marked the breakdown of an unwritten social contract between the two, destroying a balance based upon internal corporate traditions, mutual respect, and the sense of identification with an abstract notion of "the Amoskeag" as an entity in itself separate from the people who owned

* *History of the Amoskeag Strike During the Year 1922*, p. 176.

it. For the first time, the traditional institutional structure of the corporation was stripped away; and the "absentee" owners, most notably the controversial treasurer, F. C. Dumaine, came into direct conflict with the large body of workers. Many interviewees, unaware that Dumaine had been in control of the Company before the onset of the strike, believed that it was his takeover of the Company that caused the strike and the subsequent decline of the Amoskeag. For the first time, F. C. Dumaine became a fixture on the Manchester scene.

To a large extent, the events surrounding the strike destroyed the spirit of the Amoskeag. They irretrievably undermined the workers' sense of pride, though an analysis of the situation preceding the strike shows that much of the good feeling had already been dampened by increased work loads, frequent wage reductions, and increases in hours. The strike, however, was so traumatic that, in the minds of former workers, it loomed much larger than memories of earlier dissatisfactions and disputes.

The strike also discredited the union, leaving the workers with the feeling that they had been betrayed. One reason for this is that leadership for the strike had come from outside the Amoskeag itself. The workers never fully identified with the strike leaders, such as Horace Rivière, a French-Canadian organizer sent to the Amoskeag by the UTW. In retrospect, Rivière was blamed by many former workers for much that went wrong.

Some of the interviewees even now attribute the union's failure to the ruthlessness and carelessness of its leaders, particularly Rivière. They feel that they were misled by the union organizers and sold down the river; that the union did not really care about what was happening to them; that they had been used and betrayed. The workers' own lack of understanding of the union, its organization and ideology, may be related to the fact that the UTW had made its first inroads into Manchester just three years before the strike. The strike's failure, coming before they had had the opportunity to understand the union's functions and its likely benefits to them, left the workers with a bitter memory that lasted for the remainder of their lives.

Given the failure of the strike, its bitter consequences, and the ensuing disillusionment, it is difficult to gauge the workers' earlier involvement in it. Even those who participated now claim that they did so because they had no choice. They did not want to be called scabs, and they were afraid of violence from the pickets. It is hard to reconstruct their level of commitment and to separate those who enthusiastically decided to go on strike from those who reluctantly stayed away from the Amoskeag out of fear. With few exceptions, the hundreds of former workers interviewed claimed that they either participated passively because they had no choice or that they had stayed on strike only as long as they were forced to and returned to work as soon as the Coolidge Mill reopened. It is possible, of course, that they took a different position at that time and are like those former student radicals of the thirties who, as they grew older, no longer wanted to acknowledge the "sins" of their youth.

In the workers' minds, the failure of the strike has become coupled with the Amoskeag's subsequent shutdown. This is not surprising, since, during the strike, F. C. Dumaine made the threat that "grass will grow on the streets of Manchester unless the workers agree to terms." And fourteen years later, the shutdown seemed to fulfill that prophecy. In reality, the strike was a consequence of the same forces that eventually led to the shutdown; but because of its cataclysmic character, it crystalized for some of the workers the collapse of their world. The passage of time also led many workers to confuse the strike of 1922, in which little violence occurred, with the two violent strikes of 1933 and 1934, which preceded the shutdown. In their minds, all strikes seemed to merge into one traumatic event.

Because the strike occurred during a time of slack demand, it actually had less of a negative economic impact on the Company than would otherwise have been the case. The 1921–1923 recession was but a prelude to a period of calamitous decline for New England's textile industry. Inevitably, this led to the closing, before World War II, of most of the large cotton mills in the region. A significant number of mills in Lowell, for instance, were either relocated in the South or simply liquidated during the 1920s; and few believed at that time that the New England cotton mills had a future. The question that might be asked, therefore, is why the Amoskeag continued to operate until 1935 rather than why it shut down when it did.

The Amoskeag's fluctuations and decline throughout the twenties and thirties were part of the New England textile industry's larger struggle with southern competition. As early as 1910, the South began to present a serious threat to northern plants. The growth of the industry in the South continued even during a national expansion of productivity that flooded domestic as well as foreign markets with more textiles than they were able to absorb. This problem was further intensified by the introduction of automatic looms, particularly in the South. The Amoskeag found it difficult to modernize in response to these developments because of the enormous costs that were entailed in retooling a plant of its size.

In response to these problems, the Boston office did take several steps which it deemed crucial to the continued operation of the Amoskeag mills. The most important step was the reorganization of 1925. After several years of increasingly large losses, Treasurer F. C. Dumaine moved to protect the $18 million cash reserve which the Company had accumulated during times of affluence. To accomplish this, he divided the Amoskeag Manufacturing Company into two companies: a holding company, called the Amoskeag Company; and the Amoskeag Manufacturing Company, which became a subsidiary of the holding company. The plant in Manchester and all of the stock in trade were transferred to the Amoskeag Manufacturing Company, while the liquid capital was almost entirely retained by the holding company.

With this one step, Dumaine effectively sealed the fate of the Manchester operation. By leaving the manufacturing company with insufficient cash for modernizing and properly maintaining the large plant, Dumaine made its eventual shutdown almost a certainty. At the same time, this corporate reorganization may be one reason why the mills continued to run for another decade rather than being suddenly closed and liquidated in an effort to get and distribute the large cash reserve. This reserve, now isolated in Dumaine's holding company and controlled by Dumaine himself, was safe from further losses in the manufacturing division.

In 1927, the Amoskeag Company warded off an attempt, by

a group of New York entrepreneurs, to purchase a controlling interest in it, with the object of liquidating both companies and distributing the assets, which were at that time of greater value than the market value of the stock. Instead, Dumaine devised a plan that allowed the disenchanted stockholders who wanted to sell to exchange their stock for twenty-year, 6 percent bonds, with the debt resting on the Amoskeag Manufacturing Company. This action consolidated Dumaine's personal control of the holding company; and, at the same time, it further crippled the manufacturing company by replacing the payment of dividends (which is done only when a profit is made) with the payment of 6 percent interest (which is a legal obligation). It was this bond debt which figured most prominently in the reorganization attempt prior to liquidation. Since the holding company held 31.6 percent of the bonds, the manufacturing company was, in effect, continuing to pay the holding company after its capital had been stripped away.

The meaning of this financial manipulation did not escape the attention of the Amoskeag workers. The $18 million withdrawn from the manufacturing company was, they claimed, a surplus created by their labor, funds that should be used to keep the plant running in hard times. When the management in Manchester was itself subsequently reorganized under a new agent, Henry Rauch, and he began to fire or lay off many of the older workers in an attempt to cut costs, feelings began to run high. As resentments intensified and workers began to feel the recurring pressure to vote their own wage cuts, several strikes erupted, one of which, in 1933, was sufficiently violent to necessitate the calling out of the state militia. As William Spencer reveals in his interview, the distrust and antagonism on the part of the workers were by then major obstacles to the continued running of the plant. Later, hearings investigating the closing of the mills had to be transferred to Boston because local hostility in Manchester was so intense. By then, the anger was directed at F. C. Dumaine.

Before the flood that devastated the Amoskeag in 1936, Dumaine made a final attempt to reorganize the Company under Chapter 77B of the Federal Bankruptcy Act and thus remove the burden of the interest payments on the bonds. The bonds would have been converted into stock at an appreciable loss in value to the bondholders. Dumaine proposed the plan and agreed to submit his bonds if the other bondholders would submit theirs. Many were reluctant, fearing that they would lose everything were the reorganized company unsuccessful. Nevertheless, a majority agreed to support the plan, but the flood then intervened and tipped the balance, forcing Dumaine and the Boston trustees to withdraw it.

As late as October 1935, Dumaine reportedly said that there would be no liquidation of the plant "as long as there is a breath in my body." However, on July 10, 1936, Arthur Black, the special master in the bankruptcy proceedings, recommended liquidation, and ten days later the federal judge ordered the plant liquidated. Following a U. S. Senate investigation into the financial structure of the Amoskeag Company, the special investigator announced that "the activities of the holding and manufacturing companies savor of nothing short of financial sabotage."[*] Later, his assistant was quoted in the October 2, 1937, *Manchester Leader* as saying:

> The evidence here shows . . . a willful disregard of the public moneys invested, to say nothing about what is happening to the mill employees and the community of Manchester.

Despite the evident signs of decline, repeated threats to shut down the plant, and the financial maneuvering, many of the workers appear not to have read the writing on the wall. In the week ending March 8, 1935, the Amoskeag employed 11,014 workers. In the course of that month, one thousand were laid off, followed by another thousand in April. By the end of June, the number of employees had been reduced to six thousand, and by September 15 to less than one thousand.

When all work stopped in 1935, the workers viewed the shutdown as a temporary condition. The Company had been operating for one hundred years; it was inconceivable that it would suddenly go out of business. Even when the flood of 1936 destroyed the river bridges and a great deal of the equipment, those working around the clock to rescue the machinery still expected the Amoskeag to reopen. On March 7, 1936, the Citizens' Committee of Manchester and the Manchester Textile

[*] *Manchester Leader*, September 17, 1936.

Council polled the Amoskeag employees who had been on the 1935 payroll, asking them whether they would be willing to work under reduced wages and conditions "which will present permanent and peaceful operations on a competitive cost basis as determined by the management and representatives of the workers." Of the 6,800 valid ballots, 54 percent were affirmative.

Similarly, a survey of the 931 residents in the corporation tenements, which was carried out by an Amoskeag representative in December 1935, reported that "the occupants of the tenements made the usual inquiries as to when the mills would reopen. 'Will they be closed all winter?' 'Are the unions to blame for the condition?' 'When they start, will it be longer hours?'" The investigators reported that "approximately 801 of those interviewed inquired as to when the mills would reopen." While some unemployed workers were filling their time repairing the tenements at their own expense, others "were indifferent as to what was in store for the future. . . . These persons are in debt, and their hope of ever getting out of the red is forlorn. They appeared to take the attitude of letting things take their course and drift along. All ambition in these families appeared to be gone."

The ranks of the unemployed continued to grow. In 1935, 6,272 workers registered with the State Employment Service. This number grew to 11,072 by 1938. Prior to the Amoskeag shutdown, the burden of relief had been greater on Manchester than on other New England industrial cities; after the shutdown, relief facilities were totally inadequate to cope with the staggering unemployment rates. By November 1935, 22.8 percent of Manchester's families were on relief. The Works Progress Administration established by President Roosevelt started employing people in the city that fall. By February 1936, 3,753 persons were employed on WPA projects and 3,160 were receiving general relief.

During the months following the shutdown, many left the city. Emigration from Manchester in 1936 exceeded by 53 percent the annual average of emigration over the preceding five years. Of those who left, 93 percent were former Amoskeag workers, most of whom sought jobs in neighboring New England towns or returned to Quebec.

Recovery after the shutdown was a slow process. In 1936, Arthur Moreau, the former mayor of Manchester, and a number of concerned citizens, including William Parker Straw, formed the Amoskeag Industries, a corporation designed to buy the Amoskeag properties and then to attract new companies to Manchester through the sale of mill space and machinery. From 1936 on, companies began to buy or rent space in the millyard and start new operations. In the ensuing years, the Amoskeag millyard became the site of a number of smaller textile mills and other businesses, most of which were short-lived. Many of these were branches of growing concerns located elsewhere; others were newly established small plants, such as dyeing mills, garment factories, shoe factories, a rayon knitting mill, a finishing plant for broom handles, and a casket company.

By 1938, there were seventeen companies functioning in the millyard. However, they employed a total of fewer than two thousand people. Some of these companies, which employed former Amoskeag workers, shut down again during the recession that year. Two more stable mills—the Chicopee, a branch of the Johnson & Johnson Company, which wove gauze; and the Waumbec, which specialized in synthetic fibers— became major employers of former Amoskeag workers.

Each time a new textile plant opened, former Amoskeag workers would rush to the gates, hoping that some of their former bosses would recognize them and hire them. Many got into a mill only to find themselves outside again. Lucille Bourque summarized the long history of uncertainty: "After the Amoskeag I went to the Raylaine and the Raylaine closed. I went to Textron, and that closed. So I went to Forest Hills. . . . Well, that closed. And then I quit. I used to go in and out. I'd quit and go back."

▶ *Paul Morin**

Seventy-six-year-old Paul Morin got his first job with a lumber company in Manchester at the age of eight, in 1909. Like his brothers and sisters, he followed his parents into the mills after leaving school at the age of sixteen. However, the mills were not Paul's whole life—he worked as a stereotypist for different newspapers in Manchester (including the French one), and again for the lumber company.

Paul's wife, Emelia, seventy-five, also went into the mills at the age of sixteen; and except for one year, she stayed at the Amoskeag until the shutdown. During her time in the mills, she was a spinner, spooler, spare hand, and winder.

Paul was interviewed in their second-floor apartment in a two-family building located on land that once belonged to the Amoskeag.

I started as a bobbin boy in the spinning room in 1917, and I ended up a cloth inspector in the weave room. I didn't try to be a loom fixer because the ones that had it wouldn't let it go. They died on the job. You might go ten years without getting that job. In order to learn, you had to get on with a loom fixer; they'd put you on as a spare, and you wouldn't get the regular pay, you'd get spare men's pay. As inspector, there was only a few dollars' difference with the loom fixers because you had quite a lot of responsibility.

When I worked in the weave room, they had a place where

° Fictitious name

you could sit down and eat. Some would bring hot dogs, and others bread, mustard and relish, and onions. The loom fixers had a steam box where they put the hot dogs; and when they were ready, they'd motion to us cloth inspectors to come and eat. If the weavers had a little time, they'd come over and have one, too. The boss never said anything. Of course, we didn't stay there all day; we just took our hot dog and got back to work.

I think I worked forty-eight hours a week. The salaries were $9.00 or $12.00. Then they went up to $15.00, which could go further then than a hundred today. You'd buy potatoes for 10¢ a peck, meat for 20¢, the best steak—a giant chunk of meat— for 40¢. Then the union came in, and they put the kibosh on that.

I never spoke to Herman Straw, but he would go around the mills. I can see him now, tall, well dressed. He'd smile at you, but he never would have anything to do with you. If there was anything he saw wrong, he'd tell the floor man. But I don't remember seeing anybody talk to him. When he went through the mills, the word would fly around, "Straw's on the floor." Then people stayed at their machines as much as they could.

He was well liked; but during the strike, the union guys turned against him. They turned the people against him, the ones that were crazy enough to listen to them. But he held on. He said he wouldn't give in, and he never did; but it killed him. He died right after, I guess.* He told the people he was sorry they hadn't stopped to realize what they had. People went on strike because they wanted a raise, and the Amoskeag said they couldn't afford it. The loom fixers started saying they wanted to get the ball rolling. [Horace] Rivière was the guy that stirred them up.

I worked with my sister in the union store. It was run by the union for the people who were out on strike. We'd fill bags with beans, sugar, rice, potatoes. Not anything fancy. It was twice a week on bread. Boy, if you think it wasn't a tough time! We'd collect the money before we even opened the door. You'd put your arm out in front of the door, and they'd break it. They were hungry. That's why I took the job, because I was in shape then from playing baseball. It was an experience for me.

* Actually, Herman Straw did not die until 1929.

I wasn't for the strike. I was mad about it. But what could you do? If you went in to work, you got your head bashed in. See, these guys that went in, they kept them in there, brought their food and everything. It was pretty hard for a while. The pickets were ready to break the windows and everything, but the police held them back. I was against that strike, but there was nothing I could do. These people that were starving had big families, and I said, "If I can help, I might as well do it," so I did.

After the strike, they told me I was blackballed because I had worked in the union store. I went up to the union office. Rivière and Beary were both there—I can see them now. They turned around and said, "There's nothing we can do about it." They washed their hands of it. They sold us like cows. There wasn't much talk about a strike beforehand, just for about a month or so. Then they started to enroll the people in the unions. You take twelve thousand people that pay their dues, and that's a hell of a lot of money.[*]

These two guys, Beary and Rivière, were on top of the world. After the strike they disappeared. Nobody ever heard of them after that. They got out of town. It was a good thing they did, because I nearly took a poke at them the day I went up and they said they couldn't do anything for me, after I worked in the union store. They didn't even want to bother. They said, "That's your hard luck." But before, when they needed me, they were down on their knees for me to go in and work there, help out the people. Rivière, the head man from the union, was running the whole thing. They had him to buffalo the French people. He was French, so naturally he had the French people in his hands. Then, when the strike was over, we got word that they had sold out to the Company! That strike accomplished nothing. We lost all our wages, and the Company went bankrupt. So everybody lost. It was never the same after we went back. The people were skeptical, kind of lost; and the Company just gave up. We didn't have anything to complain about before the strike, as far as I was concerned, because we had everything. If you got hurt, you were taken care of. They

---

[*] The union never enrolled all employees because the Amoskeag was an open shop. He is confusing the United Textile Workers of America with the company union, which was set up in 1923.

did so much for us, and then we went out on strike and cut our own throats.

The strike lasted nine months. The Amoskeag said that grass would grow on Elm Street, and it came damn near it. There were picket lines from one mill to another. It came near to violence at the end because people were getting hungry, and they were starting to go back in. The people that were outside were hotheaded. They didn't want to let them by. So they got the cops down there to help get them back in. After all, some of them had families, and nine months is a long time to eat beans. We got sick of salt pork, too.

The mills were always open to anyone who wanted to go in. They never closed down.* They got people from Lowell, and some of the Manchester people went in. They called them rats. The strikers were against the French paper, too. They called it *la tête de cochon* [pig's head] because the owner was with the Company.

When the strike ended, my boss, Herb Salls, asked my sister what I was doing. I was working at the lumberyard on the West Side, driving a double team. I never drove such big loads of lumber. He said, "I suppose he's making good money?" "No," she said. "Then why didn't he come back?" She said, "He was blackballed." So Mr. Salls said, "He was out for a cause, and I was in for a cause, so you tell him to come back in here." A guy from Lowell that broke the strike was on my machine; and when I came in, Herb told that guy, "From here on, you're his helper." So I went back to work in the mills.

---

* In fact, the mills were initially shut down; then the Coolidge Mill re-opened in June 1922. Several months later, some of the other mills reopened.

► *Cameron Stewart**

Cameron Stewart was still active at age seventy-eight when we interviewed him in 1974. After his career at the Amoskeag was cut short by the strike, he apprenticed himself as a bricklayer. Always ambitious, he managed to establish himself in the insurance business during the depths of the Depression. At the time of the interview, he was the general agent of an insurance company in Manchester and was serving on a variety of civic committees. He lives in a fine house in the North End, the upper-class section of Manchester. Like Colonel Jacobson, Cameron is a self-made man; however, unlike Jacobson, who had risen through the Amoskeag, Cameron, who initially intended to "learn the textile business," grew disillusioned with it and left, never to return.

Early in our interview, we showed Cameron his Amoskeag work record, which included the notation "agitator" next to his name. The surprise this caused him released a flood of sometimes bitter memories of mill life.

Heavens! They wrote in my record that I was an agitator! What would I agitate? The strike was coming on. I was in the spinning room learning the business; and if I was considered an agitator, it was because I was in sympathy with the workers. I had been brought up in a family where both mother and father worked in the mill. How could I be sympathetic with the Amoskeag?

The mills in the old days were just a place for someone to

* Fictitious name

go to work and make a living, but I didn't go around agitating
—I had no reason to. As a matter of fact, the help had gone out
on strike, and I still went in. I came out only because there
wasn't anybody there. I had nothing to do with the textile
union. I never went to the meetings. I'm surprised that they
put that on my record.

I might have said that I couldn't blame the people for going
out on strike; and, as a matter of fact, most of them had gone
out! When they finally walked out, quit, went on strike, I still
went in. For two or three days, if I recall. Then I said, "Well,
I'm not going. There's nothing for me to do." And I went home.
What the hell would I be agitating? I didn't even know—I'd
only been there a little while. I'm surprised they put that on
there. Oh, well, it doesn't bother me anyway.

You either bowed to the Amoskeag Manufacturing Company or you weren't in. Period! I know that. This is the history
of the Company and the thousands of people who worked
there. They had terrific storerooms where they would pile up
the material that they were going to ship out. When the people
became a little unrestful and they were afraid that they were
going to have a little trouble, they'd send them all home. Now,
those people didn't have any reserves. They didn't have any
money to live.

I would be willing to bet that when I worked there during
summer vacations when I was in high school, I was only getting $3.00 or $4.00, maybe $5.00 a week. I was getting 17¢ an
hour when I started. That was way back in 1915. My mother
and father used to go in around quarter of seven in the morning and come out around five o'clock at night, or even later.
They were putting in tremendous hours—ten hours was
nothing—and for practically nothing, too. Ten dollars. They
didn't pay any real wages.

I went to Boston to try and get through Boston University
in business administration. I got a job in a sweat shop in South
Boston for $8.00 a week and worked five days, plus Saturday
till noon. I worked for $8.00 a week and starved myself to
death and had to quit.

Having been brought up in Manchester and having seen
the mills all my life, I figured I could at least go back there, get
in, and learn the textile business. What else was there locally to

go into? For years the textile business had shut the shoe business out of Manchester. They didn't want the competition. It was later that the shoe business began to come in. When I went back, it was with the hope that I could work into a job at Amoskeag. The foremen made big money, and their jobs were not too bad. They had an overseer and what they called a second hand in the mills. The overseer was the top dog in the area, and the second hand was under him, supervising production. Fellows that I knew that were second hands were not too bad. The area on the other side of the Carpenter Hotel is where the overseers and the fellows that had the better positions lived. They paid very small rents. Down over the hill in some of those tenements is where some of the help lived.

The bulk of the people came from Canada. There were sixty thousand French people in the community. The Amoskeag agents went into Canada and imported the French people to work in the mills. It was long after that before the Greeks began to come in. I can remember when they came. Even as a youngster I was afraid of the Greeks. Of course, that prejudice eventually was overcome, but it was there. The immigrants were not educated, and this is how the Amoskeag kept control of the workers.

I would say perhaps some people in the mills worked themselves up into the overseer and second-hand positions. But they were so few in relation to the total number working in the mill that there really was very little opportunity. If you were in the spinning room, you stayed in the spinning room; if you were a weaver, you stayed a weaver. And, of course, the Amoskeag controlled not only the mills; they controlled the community. They bought the land. There's no question about it, they were a very powerful organization. Dumaine was the big owner, and I remember the Straws—Herman Straw, and then Parker Straw, who became president of the bank. Even when Straw was there, it was Dumaine who controlled the mills. It was his ownership. In 1922, when the government really began to attempt to do something with the mills, they were down about thirty-five hundred employees. When they finally liquidated the Amoskeag, those that had the money in it came out all right. They had the money piled up. But as far as way back, it was an outside control. The Straws themselves didn't really control it. They had ownership in it, but it's always been an outside control, as far as I know.

I think the problem of the Amoskeag was a production problem. The help would go in and produce the goods, but they were so far away from the management that it wasn't even funny. What could the management do for the employees? They could spread money around the community, where they felt it would keep people quiet. I can't recall them ever doing anything else for anybody, but I wasn't close enough. I was too young at the time. Later on I became a trustee of the savings bank here, and Mr. Straw was the president. One day I told him I thought the city of Manchester had suffered for years because of the one industry that we had in the city, in spite of the number of people employed there. How could people have accumulated anything? They couldn't. They were just working in an area, in an atmosphere, that was depressing. The interesting thing is that in any community like Manchester it's hard. You can select an industry like the Amoskeag, which was the predominant industry in the city, and you can ask what its value was to the community. You could say that fifteen thousand people got help, got work there, and so forth. But the community was stymied. I think the Amoskeag stymied the whole area. They built up this bureaucratic group in the city, and you were either inside that group or you were on the outside.

I'll give you an example: I was brought up in a family where we all worked in the mill. There were four of us boys. I sat down many a night to bread and molasses because that's all we had. As much as you don't dwell on these things, you never forget them. They're inbred. I graduated from high school as president of my class. I used to run on the track team; I ran in Hanover, at Dartmouth, and I ran in Boston. I went down to Harvard University and ran a quarter-mile at the stadium. I did fairly well. I had a chance to go to Dartmouth College. Even though I was offered part-time work up there, I still didn't know where to get the rest of the money. In those days, you couldn't go into a bank and borrow a hundred dollars. If I had gone in and asked for a hundred dollars, they would have thrown me out the door. There wasn't any such thing. I came out of high school, went to Boston University, and as I said, worked for $8.oo a week. I didn't even make enough money to get home. I stuck it out till spring, when my brother came down. When he saw what I looked like, he dragged me home. Now what was I going to do? I wasn't prepared for anything, so I went into the mills for a while. My brother was a carpenter, and he finally said, "Go learn a trade." So I learned a trade: I became a bricklayer.

When I was a bricklayer, people who lived in the North End wouldn't even say hello to me. That didn't bother me; I'm not bitter about it. And when I was a boy and I needed a job in the summertime, there would be kids from the North End, whose families had money, who would get the jobs I couldn't get. I'm sure a lot of people my age (I'm almost eighty years of age) who lived in that atmosphere had the same experience. I wish my mother had lived long enough to see that, maybe, in spite of the struggle, I would do something with my own life.

The people around here, like me, who did something with their lives, they didn't do it because of the mills; they did it in spite of them. There wasn't any help. There was no help in the old days for anybody. There used to be only about six or eight thousand Protestants in this town, yet they were in control. They were the controlling faction in the community, and for years the people were held down by this group.

The strike of 1922 was caused by dissatisfaction as a whole. There was terrific unrest among the workers. The damper was always down on them. I think when it happened, it was really unexpected, and the powers-that-be didn't think it would last; but when they shut them out, they stayed out. Most of the people, the workingmen, were uneducated; but back in 1921, 1922, they were becoming a little better informed, so there was a lot of discontent in the mills. They began to get labor unions and textile unions; they were beginning to get organized. So, I suppose, it's a result of all this that there was continuing agitation. But I'm surprised. I never knew that was on my record. I'd like to know why they put it there because, so help me God, I never had any reason to agitate.

When I was in the mills, I was young and the conditions didn't bother me. I did my job. I could see what was going on, but I did my job. I didn't think about it so much. I was a product of the mill life, put it that way.

▶ *Blanche Duval**

One of sixteen children, Blanche Duval was born in Quebec in 1896 and moved to Manchester with her family when she was a child. She began work in the Amoskeag, where she spent most of the next twenty-three years as a weaver. She left her last job when "work stopped." Most of the members of her family and her close friends were weavers as well.

We first interviewed Blanche in 1974, in her flat, which was located in a housing project for the elderly. A realistic woman, Blanche still carries strong feelings about her work experience and especially about the strike of 1922. Her first two husbands died; and eventually she married her very first boyfriend, who returned to her after he, too, had lost two spouses. He died in 1975.

My father had a sawmill in Canada with his brother, but it burned down and they didn't have insurance, so we found ourselves practically in the street. My mother had sixteen children, and my uncle had twenty-two. We didn't have much money for two such big families, so after the fire, my father sold out to his brother and came here to establish himself. I had another uncle, who worked at Amoskeag. He thought that it would be a good job for my father and a good place for my mother to raise the family, so my father went into the mill and my uncle showed him how to weave. My father worked for three or four months before he came back to Canada to get us.

* Fictitious name

My father was the one who showed me how to weave. He was a loom fixer. I didn't like weaving too much. It was difficult for me; I was too small. When I started to weave, I only weighed ninety-eight pounds. On that job, you had to stretch; and a person with long arms who is also big and tall would get less tired than me. Twelve hours a day tires a person. We didn't have much time to be bored, just tired. We were on piecework: the more we did, the more we got paid. It was left up to us. Mr. Grocock was our boss. There was no fooling around with him, but he was a good boss. He was fair, and everybody liked him and respected him. I can't say anything bad about our second hand either. If people didn't feel they were treated fairly, they could complain to the union.

There was no disagreement among the workers except where the strike was concerned. At the time of the strike, everyone made enemies. There were certain groups for the strike and certain groups for continuing work. It depended on your position. When you have a good job that pays well, you hate to abandon it. But during the strike, there were many who didn't want to go in. They called us all sorts of names if we went in. I loafed a long time before returning, but we had property, and we were going to lose it if we didn't go to work, despite the fact that it made enemies. I'd tell them, "We're not going to lose our property on account of that strike. As long as they're offering us work, we'll work. If you don't like us, then don't look at us. That's all." Those enemies became my best friends afterwards.

My husband was on the side of the strikers. At the time, I was married to another man. The husband I have now is one of my ex-boyfriends from when I was young. After I became a widow, he came and found me, and I married him. Those things happen in life [laughs]. He had a sister, who was a good friend of mine; but there was a short while when we weren't speaking to each other. You see, she was an old maid; and during the strike, she felt better loafing. Those whose parents supported them had nothing to lose. My first husband worked at a lumber company, so he was not involved in the strike. He kept on working, but he didn't earn big wages. I still remember he only earned $9.63 per week. We had two young

Picketing in front of the main millyard gate

children then, and it wasn't enough to keep a house and support a family.

I don't remember why they had the strike. I think it was because of the hours. The hours were too long. Groups of men and women who spoke against the bosses started the strike. When they went out, you'd see many of them breaking the warps and undoing and breaking the work to get revenge because they were mad. They invented songs to create hatred between the ones who worked and the ones who didn't work. There was one about Mr. Straw and Mr. Starr. I can sing it in French, but it's bad. It goes, "*Starr mange la bullshite et Straw mange la . . ."* [laughs]. That was the song they used to sing around the gates of the mill.

There were plenty that went in during the strike. They were like us—they needed the money, they had big families, they couldn't afford to stay out any longer. There were as many people going in as there were staying out. Those that stayed out had their parents to back them up, so they stuck it out. We belonged to the union, but we had to go in to work.

► *Joseph Debski*

(SEE ALSO PAGE 124.)

During the strike I was working in the employment office. I was on salary, doing whatever Mr. Swallow asked me to do. He'd say, "Take a walk, go down and talk with so-and-so (one of the bosses). Kill some time." They knew me, so I went right through the picket line. I never had any trouble with any of them.

Rivière and the big shots voted to go out on strike, so they all had to go on strike, but the union didn't live up to their part of the bargain. The whole nine months they were out on strike, people paid their dues, but the union never gave the families anything. They were promised $8.00 or $10.00 a week, all the time they were on strike. They got it for one or two weeks, and then they didn't get it any more. So why shouldn't they go down on the union? When the strike was over, they formed a company union.

I didn't see any major difference in the spirit of the Amoskeag after the strike. The difference wasn't in the pay; it was in the working hours. The Amoskeag couldn't compete—or that's what they claimed—with the southern mills if they had to work on a forty-hour-a-week basis, so they wanted the fifty-four. Just before the strike, I don't know what the occasion was, the workers asked for forty-eight hours, and management gave it to them. Then when the Amoskeag was going to cut their pay 22½ percent and put them on a fifty-four-hour week, they said, "We want a raise and stay at forty-eight hours," but the Amoskeag would not give in.

They reopened two or three different mills on a trial

basis during the strike because a lot of people kept writing in, saying they were despondent. They had nothing to eat, they couldn't pay their bills, and they wanted to go to work. We told them outright, "You know what you're up against if you go to work. You're going to be intimidated." They said, "We don't care. We got to go to work. We got to feed our families." So some of them did go to work, and there was an outburst.

The union kept saying that the Amoskeag would open up the mill, and the opening would fail because nobody would come. When the Coolidge Mill opened up, they had a lot of policemen around Canal Street and a lot of them by the mill itself. When the workers came out, one thing led to another, and the cops had to disperse the strikers. Then the workers would run for it. The people in the picket line scored there. They'd follow them all the way to their doors, call them scabs, call them this and call them that, call them everything. They would throw stones. They'd threaten those who were going to work. But some of them kept right on going, and they worked that way for about a month or so. Then around Labor Day, the strikers decided to accept the Amoskeag offer. It was agreed that if they went back to work for forty-eight instead of forty hours a week, the Amoskeag would dispense with the 22½ percent cut that they were going to give them. So they went back to work at the same rate of pay, but for the same number of hours as before the strike.

It was the older people with a family that wanted to work, people that owed so much money they couldn't get any more credit. They were desperate. The younger ones started all the trouble. They were single. They didn't care; they were living at home.

We used to have to put out warrants for strikers who were intimidating people. There's a law that you can go through a picket line, and you can have only so many people in the line. But the picket line didn't want to do that. They'd push them or they'd harass them, or something like that. So, they turned around and had the sheriff serve warrants on all these people before the court.

My wife doesn't even know, but some fellows who lived right above us on Canal Street called her a scab because I was working in the office. So I went up to see Charley Healey, the chief of police's son, and he told me he would take care of them. He sent someone down to have a talk with them, and this fellow said, "Don't say another word or I'll put you right behind bars." They never bothered her again. I wasn't bothered at all for the seven months that I was working there. I never heard anybody say anything. I'd go right through to the paymaster's office, across the street from the office where I worked, and they would stop picketing and let me through.

During the strike, the spinners had meetings one night, the weavers another, another night the electricians, and so forth. We had informants at every one of those meetings. We got a letter in the mail the first thing in the morning, so we knew what happened the night before. Those informants were not paid by the Amoskeag, but the Amoskeag took care of them. They saw that they got their jobs back when the strike ended, and they probably got a tenement. My boss was in charge of the tenements.

They had a watchman at every gate in the Amoskeag, and they had two detectives walking over the yard. They had two policemen to go along with the payrolls. We had a policeman (we called him a watchman) at the employment office to keep people in line and keep them orderly. The Amoskeag had their own detectives; they didn't hire any outsiders.

After the strike, they had a company union. On each company grievance committee, they'd have three people representing the Amoskeag, and they'd have three people for the people in the mills. The three committeemen from the mills would never give in to the Amoskeag. If there was any argument, the employees' representatives would get the best of it. They didn't have the odd vote there for the Company or against the Company. It was even all the time. And very, very seldom did the Amoskeag get a break. It was always the workers. I know. I used to have to write up those reports from the grievance committee. No matter what grievance came up, they would never give in and vote for the Company. Now that isn't right. You can't tell me the Company is 100 percent wrong on every grievance.

The overseers were members of the grievance committee. They didn't want the job any more than the man in the moon, but they had to take it; they were representing the Amoskeag.

Mr. Swallow would talk to W. P. Straw, look over the list of names, and tell him who to put on the committee.

People complained about most anything in a day's work. They wanted more wages, the conditions were this or that, they didn't like to work with this one or that one. A lot of it didn't make any sense at all, but still they'd argue the point. The employees on the committee could see only one side of anything. They were biased. They didn't have an open mind. How can you arbitrate with anything like that? And I'm not sticking up for the Amoskeag either. They were biased, too. Very much so.

► William McElroy

(SEE ALSO PAGE 98.)

During the First World War, the War Labor Board (I think that's what they called it) came in and shortened the hours at the Amoskeag. They brought them down to forty-eight. Before that they were working fifty-six or fifty-seven hours. They also did something about improving the pay.

Conditions were bad all over the country, particularly in textiles. There was a depression in about 1921, so Mr. Dumaine determined to increase the hours from forty-eight to fifty-four and at the same time cut the wages about 20 percent. He tried to tell the workers they were only losing about 10 percent of their wages because they would be working longer hours. Well, that didn't set well. They never had unions there up to that time, and they walked out almost the day the new hours and cuts were supposed to go into effect.* The people just wouldn't work. The people that worked were the overseers and second hands. In those days, anyone who was an overseer was in management, and they were supposed to carry out the instructions that were handed down to them, which they did. Of course, they were very upset about their own people, who they'd raised and everything, going out on strike. At that time, the workers had no great organization here.

I worked in the mill during the strike. I helped them salvage the stuff that was there. I worked in the Southern Division; that's the big mill just south of Granite Street. I worked in cotton goods, in worsted, and in the bleachery. Then I went up to #11 Mill and worked in the napping department. We were

* Actually, the United Textile Workers of America had been active since 1918.

salvaging stuff, not manufacturing new stuff. Otherwise, with all that worsted and wool, that place would have been ruined: there were thousands and thousands of dollars' worth of stuff in the plant. By taking it and finishing it up to a certain point, they could wrap it up and protect it against moths or other things. I was paid my regular pay—what I was getting at the payroll office. We'd be assigned to this job and that job, running looms or other things. It didn't take us long to learn how to run them.

The strikers didn't question me because they knew I was a paymaster; and, of course, the Amoskeag management had to protect the mills. They had about 250 overseers and second hands looking after the property. There was no trouble. My own brother was out on strike, and he'd pick me up at night or I'd pick him up, when they were picketing.

What we used to call the IWW's (the International Workers of the World, I think) were going strong down in Lawrence and Lowell, but they weren't strong up here. I think up to that time the workers in Manchester got better treatment on the management side because several generations of the Straw family had learned to work with these people. The workers weren't interested in the unions at all at that time. Of course, after they went on strike they joined the United Textile Workers of America.

The IWW's were a group that everybody thought were communistic. They were an entirely different type than the UTW, and they came up here to make trouble. They were in favor of breaking things up, starting fires, and beating up people, and they decided they'd take over the strike. They went to the police department and told Chief Healey that they wanted to hold meetings on Merrimack Common, to stir up the people. Chief Healey was a hard-boiled egg, and he said, "You're not holding any meetings here. You can go to the halls where the various workers have their own booths, but you're not having any public meetings stirring up trouble." Well, this particular IWW guy who came to see him said, "Then we'll have our meeting without your permission." Chief Healey replied, "I don't doubt you. Start your meeting; but if you do, you'll soon be carried out of this town, and you probably won't be able to come back." Well, they decided they wouldn't.

That was the IWW, and the local unions weren't in favor of them at that time because they were a very radical group. The IWW finally left because they had trouble enough on their hands—they were striking down in Lawrence and, I believe, Lowell at the same time, and down in Fall River. Anyway, I've always felt, though I don't know this, that the leaders of the UTW advised them to get out of town and stay out, because things were on the verge of being straightened out up here. They came in late and tried to start trouble, but there was very little trouble during that time, when you realize the workers were off for ten months.

I knew many of the overseers when I was working there. I'd been to school with some of these people. They were sick about the whole strike—to think that people they trained would strike against them, no matter what the occasion was. But the people that were out on the strike weren't sore at the overseers; as a matter of fact, they'd go over to the overseer and ask him how soon they were going to get back. They did come back, but of course they had to come back on fifty-four hours, and the spirit was gone. You could sense it. You can tell if a guy whistles at his work or is friendly with everybody, or if all the girls are joking about things. But that was all dead. After I'd been paying them off, I'd notice it in the way they walked. They did their work, but their hearts were broken—most of them.

► *Marie Anne Senechal*

(SEE ALSO PAGE 274.)

During the 1922 strike, I didn't scab; I stayed out. We were a year there without work, but I didn't stop working. I went to Lawrence and worked in the mills there. My sisters were grown, and they took care of the other ones.

After 1922, the mills weren't like they were in the best years. The last years they were bad. But in the old Amoskeag, when I first went to work in the spinning room, the work wasn't that hard because we had time to rest between jobs. We could read in the mill, and we could talk with the other girls. It was a different life. All you had to do was get next to your loom and watch your shuttle go.

They put me out of the Amoskeag because I was talking for the Amoskeag union. After the strike of 1922, they made a company union, and I was elected to go to the meetings. There were about ten or eleven of us who went to those meetings, and they said we had to go back and tell our weavers that their pay was going to be cut. Get on a chair there and tell them, "Boys and girls, you've got to work for $11.00 or $15.00 a week." I came back and told the people what was really going on at the meetings. The boss, Bert Molloy, didn't like it. I was telling the workers what to do. So he said, "I'm going to get rid of her." It wasn't fair. He wasn't using the weavers right.

I complained to [Fred] Meharg, the efficiency man, and Meharg said, "Get out. I'll talk for you at city hall. You might get $8.00 a week while you're not working." But I went out and got another job, in the box factory. When Meharg called me in,

I went back to the mill. The workers stopped all the looms downstairs, and they went to the boss and told him, "You got to put her to work." So they gave me another set of looms. They decided that I deserved my job. It was the boss that had made the mistake.

So I went back to work with Bert Molloy, but he never talked to me after that. He would have nothing to do with me. But I had to take it. I had to work, so I didn't say anything. He let me work till the end, until the shutdown, but he did give me a hard time. He gave me a lot of bad work.* But I liked weaving, and it was better than going out and working somewhere else, so I did the best I could.

At Arms Textile, where I worked from 1939 till 1962, I had to promise that I would never bother with the union. I wouldn't be interfering or even be thinking of it because I was working, and that was enough. When you're put out of a job, you think twice. If you want to work, you don't say anything.

* "Bad work" means faulty yarn, rotten warp, or colors that are hard on the eyes.

► *Henry Carignan*

Henry Carignan, eighty years old, came to Manchester when his parents' farm in Canada could no longer support him, and went to work in the Amoskeag. In 1921 he married Emelia Carignan (whose maiden name was the same, although they were not previously related), and they have been living in the same house ever since. Though both Henry and Emelia were mill workers, they wanted something more for their children. As a result, all of them received an education, and only their oldest children spent any time in the mills.

Henry, a second hand in the card room, worked cleaning up the mills after the flood and was one of the last persons employed by the Amoskeag before the liquidation.

I have five older brothers, and my father didn't have enough money to give every one of us a piece of land, so as soon as I was sixteen, I went to work in a paper mill in Trois Rivières. My brother John was living here, and I came to see him, not to work in the mill; but the first thing I knew, I had a job. John took me in to see the boss, Dave Ramsey. He turned to my brother and said, "If he wants a job, I can give him a job." That was May 5, 1916, and I was eighteen. It was about sixty years ago.

When I started, I worked in the card room. In the card room, the majority were Greeks, so I learned the Greek language with them [laughs]. After the strike, we didn't see many Greeks at all. I don't know what they did—I guess they went back to the old country. Anyway, after five or six months, Herbert Richardson, who was overseer, came over and told my boss, the second hand, to make me a fixer, although I had never fixed anything before. I did that many years, right up till after the strike.

My boss, Dave Ramsey, was stubborn sometimes, but I got along all right with him. Richardson, the overseer, never spoke much and he never smiled; but if you had something to say, he listened to you. He didn't pass the buck, so everybody respected him. But it was rare that we ever had to speak to the overseer; we'd settle all our business with the second hand.

When Richardson was named superintendent, they made [Arthur] Morrill* overseer in his place. Morrill jumped over the others because he was in politics a bit. I believe Richardson had put in a good word for him, but he also went out with the daughter of Chief Healey, the chief of police. Chief Healey and the Company were very close.

When the strike started, I got work in Epping, New Hampshire, making brick, but I didn't like it too much. I happened to come back to Manchester one day, and one of the superintendents saw me on the street. "Hey!" he yelled to me. "How'd you like to come work for me?" I said, "If you've got a job for me, all right." So I went back to work during the strike when they opened the Coolidge Mill.

A couple of days later Roberts, the superintendent, saw me over there. Then he went to the overseer of the Coolidge Mill and told him they needed me in the Southern Division worsted department. See, I knew how to run the machines, and they had nobody to run them. All they had were the second hands and section hands, but the fixers had all left and found other jobs. When I first got there, all those men were standing around. They didn't know what to do. I started to give them work; and in two or three days, I had it running. I stayed there a few months. In October they decided to call the strike off, so everybody went back in.

I was against the union. The union rejected me because I didn't follow instructions and went in to work. But nobody said a word against me. They never threw me in the river [laughs]. They called me scab or something like that, but I didn't pay

---

* This is not the same Arthur Morrill interviewed in this book.

any attention as long as they didn't hurt me. I kept quiet
[laughs]. You have to eat, so you say nothing. I voted for the
strike; but a few years later, when they had another election, I
voted against the union.

Even after the strike, people called me all kinds of names
because I was a second hand—especially when we had to divide the work. At one meeting, the overseer and everyone was
there, and one fellow said to me, "Excuse me, but you show
preference. You give the good work to certain people and the
bad work to other people." I stood up and said, "No! I try to
divide the work. I can't give you the good work all the time."
The superintendent said, "That thing is closed!" The fellow got
up and started to swear at me. I didn't fire him, but the superintendent did. He said, "You're done!" That's about the only
person I had to fire.

The union didn't want section hands and second hands. We
were management. Sometimes we got along all right with the
union people under us, but other times there was a little heat.
When it wasn't too bad, you tried to forget about it; but if it
went too far, you had to go to the overseer. He set his own
rules. As management, we didn't like the union coming in because it caused trouble all the time. The union representatives
were always against the Company. No matter what you do—
and you do what you can—you're always on the hot spot.

I remember I was an employee representative in 1926 when
the Company had set up a union by themselves. People were
elected from the different departments. So I went to the meetings, but it was just the routine stuff that always goes on in the
mill—people kicking. Nothing had improved. Nothing. I went
to two more meetings, and then I told the boss I didn't want to
go back. He said, "You have to. You've been elected." "Never
mind elected! I don't want it. Too many jealous people. They
want to have the best work all the time."

I don't know who had elected me to be representative, but
the first thing I knew, my name was on the list. If there was
someone who was not content with his work, he'd come to us,
but I never reported anything at the meetings. There were
some like that who never wanted to report anything because it
wasn't worth the trouble. We knew they [the management]
were crooked [laughs].

When Frederick Dumaine went in as treasurer of the Company, he pocketed everything and left nothing for the others. He looked out only for himself, he didn't look out for the good of the Company, so it couldn't last long being run like that. When only one is pocketing everything, the others suffer for it. Parker Straw would come around and speak to everybody. He knew how to talk. I guess he was a lawyer. But he wasn't good in the same way as his father. The old man, Herman Straw, understood the people and the people understood him. If it was too hot someplace, he tried to cool it down. That's the way old man Herman Straw was. I remember before the strike, he called me in. He was talking very nicely to his son, and he said, "Son, the union is kind of like a flood. If a flood is coming into the mill and you get a broom to try to push the water out, it won't do any good. It's the same thing with the union. You might want to try to sweep them out. Don't. You won't clean up anything that way." Old man Straw told us that.

During the years following the strike, they started cutting down on the number of people. There was a time when they'd put so many people out that the mills were practically not running. At one time, there were sweepers who'd pass by the machines, cleaning all the time; they took them all away. There were two men who filled the cards; they took one of them away. Another man filled the boxes—they got rid of him. The doublers, like I ran in the beginning, they scrapped them. They didn't run on those any more, they only ran it on gills. There were six men on the gills, and they cut them down to two. You had to be on the job all the time, all the time.

I worked up till 1935. I left two months before the mill stopped, in the month of August. Then the flood came in the spring, and I worked for a few months after that, cleaning all the machines. But it was terrible in 1935. From the month of July to the month of February, I earned a dollar! At the orphanage [St. Pierre's Orphanage], they had told people who weren't working that if they cut the lawn, they'd give them supper. That night, the nun who was supposed to cook for us got sick and she wasn't able to make us supper; so, instead of giving us supper, they gave us each a dollar. It's the only dollar that I earned from the month of July to the month of February.

► *Frederic C. Dumaine, Jr.*

(SEE ALSO PAGE 75.)

The Amoskeag started going downhill after the First World War. There was a recession in 1920, and all the box-loom companies of New England, plus some in the South, met to decide whether or not to form a U. S. Steel Corporation type of thing, a trust that would own all the box-loom mills in the United States. Everybody agreed that it ought to be done—but they all wanted to be treasurer.

At that time, if you compared the situation of the New England mills with that in the South, on the first problem—water power—we had them beat by a mile. Second, we had the best-quality product—everybody knew we'd always be there with an Amoskeag label. But on the third problem—transportation—we were at a handicap, because we were so much farther away from the raw material. Fourth, management had lost contact with its people, causing the strike of 1922 in Manchester. Fifth, was taxation, the New Hampshire inventory tax, which the South did not have. Sixth, we were behind the South on machine speeds and layouts. And seventh, the South's wages were well below the North's average. Everybody knew in the South they were paying no more than $12.00 a week for fifty or fifty-four hours.

The mills in the South were built fifty or a hundred years after we started, so they had the modern machines, and our machine layout and machine speeds were way behind those in the South. Beyond that, the textile-machine manufacturers were all northerners, but they couldn't sell the New England mills on the same deal as the southern mills. These textile-machine companies, like Draper, Crompton, and Saco-Lowell, could not sell enough machinery to us to keep their plants running, so they went to the South and financed a lot of the southern mills. They even took over some of the companies that were distributors of the southern mills' products. Then, with low rates of interest, the southern mills could borrow for almost nothing. The northern mills didn't take these advantages; and Amoskeag being rich, it didn't either. Instead of buying modern machinery and concentrating it all into one building, we put a little here to satisfy this superintendent and a little over there to satisfy that one; but when we got through, we didn't have one efficient mill. Of course, no one beat us in the quality of the products we had, like our ACA Ticking, 19,000-range gingham, and flannels.

The Amoskeag was a one-shift mill and didn't run in three shifts as in the South. The first time we started running three shifts was after Henry Rauch came to Manchester. In the South now we run on three shifts, seven days a week.* When the mills first started in the South, they brought these mountain and country people who had no industry except looking for honey and shooting bears down to company towns. They lived in company-owned houses at a dollar a month per room. Twelve dollars a year for your rent! Even the grocery store was owned by the company; they deducted the sales from the employees' pay. You had everything you wanted, and a good job; and you could save up, which was better than looking for honey! There were plenty of people to hire for any job.

Dad and J. P. Maguire bought the company houses from Marshall Field; they are still there. They're wooden buildings. Most of them had a two-holer out back. The runoff went right under the weave room of its Draper plant. There was no sewer system when we got there in 1953. We and the community finally got modern systems.

They didn't have any Catholic, Greek, or Italian help as we did in New England. Today we have a small percentage of Negroes, but there is a higher percentage of Negroes working

* The Amoskeag Company has controlling interest in Fieldcrest Mills, with plants in several North Carolina towns and other states. The Amoskeag Company under Dumaine acquired Fieldcrest in October 1953.

in the mills than the proportion of Negroes in the population of the towns. There were lots of what they call poor whites—and they were really poor. In the past, they would often bully the Negroes, causing the Negro problems in the South.

The Amoskeag grew big—it had a million square feet—but it failed to clear out the nonprofitable units that were inefficient and couldn't compete with the new modern layouts and high-speed equipment. The new mill, the Coolidge, did have the best machinery when it was built in 1909. Why, they could have produced the same goods by running three shifts in much less space, but nobody in the old days ever tore down mills. They didn't have to because before World War I, it was nothing to make 100 percent a year on capital. It was that profitable.

We were a seasonal business. We'd ship ginghams in the spring and flannels in the fall. There were over twenty-four thousand Crompton and Knowles gingham box looms running at one time. Marshall Field, Penny, and a number of others would come in and buy so many cases that David Jarvis, the selling agent, would have to allot the mill's output. When we didn't have any more work to do on ginghams, we would start on something else. I don't think the management under Parker Straw felt it had to meet competition. It didn't realize how big the southern manufacturers had grown. The management was living on Amoskeag's reputation. They were great in the past because they made the best products. They stuck to quality. You couldn't find any goods better than Amoskeag's, including the dyed goods. Down in the South, they don't even know how to dye fast colors. You can buy the best and still ruin the cloth if you don't know how to manufacture it. It's just like buying the best meat and spoiling it in the oven.

Amoskeag also had a big tax inventory problem. The state of New Hampshire was trying to keep up with Massachusetts by getting more tax money out of the industry, so they levied an inventory tax. Everything that you had—supplies, cotton, or coal—was taxed at its market value. The states in the South didn't do this; that was another advantage. Also, most of the companies which competed with us shipped their goods right to the wholesale outlets as these products were produced.

Amoskeag's historical pattern was to build up the gingham and chambray stocks all through the winter for spring delivery to the manufacturers. It cost Amoskeag a lot to build up enough inventory for spring delivery. We were at a handicap, even though we had the best power plant of any textile plant in the world.

Most of the other New England cotton manufacturing companies moved south or liquidated at that time. Those that moved did so because they could produce down there at lower costs. The companies had enough horse sense to make the most of the 10 or 20 percent difference in the wages paid per hour worked; but it was the increase in the inventory tax, plus one shift versus three shifts, that really raised our costs.

When we wanted to be competitive with the South and had cut wages, we had a twenty-four-month strike.° Every mill treasurer in the North agreed they all should cut wages. There were no anti-trust laws in those days. But this is what actually happened: all the treasurers went to a meeting with a pocketful of nickels; and when they came out, they went straight to the telephones and called their agents, telling them Amoskeag would be on strike, but they should keep on working and not cut wages or make any other move. When the Amoskeag strike was over, they'd settle on the basis of Amoskeag without ever losing a day.

The 1922 strike was when Horace Rivière, the labor leader, showed up. He was in his early twenties and French like myself—though I don't think he could have been more French than the Dumaines. Anyway, he was typically French: somewhat hotheaded yet very friendly with me. He suggested to Dad and I how the strike could be settled, while Dad and others were sitting around the table, working with Bishop Peterson. They wanted to get the people back to work, but they weren't getting anywhere. What did the bishop know about the textile industry? Very little, but he knew the people well.° °

Horace and I couldn't stand by while these people were not working, so Horace went out and made some suggestions for settling the strike, and the old man grabbed them. I hadn't even said a word to Dad; Horace didn't give in. He just got sick and tired of the employees being idle while all the other mills

° Actually, it was nine months.

° ° Dumaine has merged the strike of 1922 with the strikes of 1933 and 1934.

were running at Amoskeag's expense. The other mills had all agreed to cut wages 10 percent, and none of them did. They just didn't live up to what they had agreed. So Amoskeag settled: they agreed to give a little and take a little. We had no reason for staying out except that we couldn't make any money!

The Boston office, through its treasurer, controlled all operations, while the agent was supposed to take care of employee relations—the hiring and firing—the running of the mills, the quality of the goods, all that sort of thing; and report to the old man. Herman Straw had the greatest relationship with the employees, but in 1920 he wanted to retire. The old man had great respect for Herman Straw and wanted to please him, so he insisted on his son, Parker, taking the job. I knew Mr. Straw didn't want Parker to take the job as agent since he was very shy and didn't mix easily. He didn't come by it naturally the way his father did, and the labor unions resented it. In any case, Parker Straw didn't have IT. The dictionary doesn't describe what IT is, but Tom Burke, our cotton buyer, had cotton IT; and Mr. Patton, the buyer of wool, had wool IT. He could look at a pile of raw wool and tell you what kind of quality it was and how many pounds there were in it.

Police Chief Healey, Michael Ahern, and a fellow by the name of Welsh (a plainclothesman) I remember were very close to Dad. Dad and Chief Healey were like that [shows two fingers intertwined] all the time. Dad had known him a long time. I can remember going into the police station with Dad, just dropping in, at least twice a year. Or they'd telephone back and forth.

Chief Healey had a very good lieutenant in the police department, an Irishman, Jim O'Neil, who became head of the American Legion. Chief Healey and Lieutenant O'Neil and Welsh were close to Dad. Parker Straw, in his shy way, was rarely seen with those people. Herman Straw worked closely with them and they respected one another. He always helped Chief Healey keep things under control. They had a firm hand on local affairs. Whenever a train came in, there was a plainclothesman down at the station to see who was getting off.

The average worker didn't want to strike. He wanted to work, just work, under good conditions. Wages were low, awfully low, in this country, but then money was worth something. You could buy a lot for a $10.00 bill. And don't forget, there were as many as four or five people in a family working and pooling their funds.

Of course, some of the workers did want the strike. There was full employment through the First World War; after, they went down to only part of one shift, and half of the people weren't working. But they still needed money, and the cost of living had gone up. When a fellow came with a glib voice and dared to speak, why shouldn't they listen to him? Free world. So they wanted more wages? The South didn't care if our wages went up as long as their nonunion people worked for less pay and produced more work than in the North.

The southern mills were built on private land, not in cities. They knew what the plants in Amoskeag and Lawrence and Lowell and New Bedford and Fall River were paying. So they put in better plants, new machinery, and better layout, and they paid lower wages. There were always plenty of people to hire for any job.

One company, I remember, had a large private property just like Amoskeag. It was fenced in. They had their own personal police. The owner was a pilot in the First World War, and he had his own little airstrips. When Frank Gorman [the labor leader] came with his so-called mobile strikers, the owner would send a message by airplane from the mill office that Gorman was headed for such-and-such a mill. He'd follow him in his airplane, get in ahead, and have the gates closed. He had his own millwrights equipped with guns and other police equipment. And down there, the unionists didn't dare go on private property. It wasn't like in Lowell and Lawrence, where all the cities and streets were public.

Amoskeag's problem began when they lost touch with labor. In the 1920s, between the time Herman Straw retired and the time Henry Rauch took over Parker Straw's job, the management had lost all contact with their people. Parker Straw may not have given the superintendents enough authority; and the superintendents didn't pass authority down through the assistant superintendents, the foremen, and the assistant foremen. The union may have lost some of its power

after the strike. After so many months of strikes, employees
held back from paying dues, while the rest of the textile community kept working.

The worst trouble didn't come until the strike in 1922,
when the state had to call in the National Guard.° There was
no violence. Dad used to drive up during the strike and go
right through the picket lines without any trouble, but women
were getting beat up by goon gangs while their husbands were
working on jobs such as keeping the fires going in the winter so
that the pipes wouldn't freeze. Chief Healey asked the state for
help because his men were worn out. The governor sent in a
company of National Guardsmen and put them in the armory
up River Road. They would patrol along with the police. The
Guard would come back at night and go to bed, but the strikers
would surround the building and keep them awake, yelling and
screaming and beating drums, tin pans, and so forth. Finally,
the National Guard got quite touchy and posted armed men on
the roof.

The colonel in charge was a Manchester man. He had been
a superintendent in the mills. He and the chief met, and the
chief argued, "You can't handle a local strike this way. All
you're doing is making things worse. The friction's growing."
The colonel said, "What do you suggest? Do you want me to
stop?" Chief Healey said, "Listen, Colonel, Fred Dumaine will
put your men up in one of the big warehouses. You stack your
arms—your guns and bayonets—and I'll supply them with two-
handed billies." So they laid out a plan. The colonel thought it
was a pretty good idea. The first thing you learn is never hit a
woman or a man on the head or any bone or joint. If you lay a
two-handed billy across the thigh or back, you bruise him, and
you make a martyr out of him. You have to hit him right across
the butt. This way, every time a fellow moved at night, he'd
wake up and be reminded of being in the wrong place.

Chief Healey, with his snow-white hair, and the colonel,
with only a pistol, marched up to the rioters on Elm Street.
Behind them was that big company of men, carefully spaced
out, stretching as far as the eye could see; yet it was still only

° The records show that the National Guard was called during the strike of
1933, not 1922.

Manchester police, date unknown

one company. One could see the street full of troops and the
strikers coming from the other direction. The chief was right
there in front. Everybody knew him. I remember he saw the
daughter of one of his friends in the front line and he said,
"Mary, what are you doing here?" The chief told the people
the governor had sent these men here and that he wasn't going
to tolerate any more disturbances, so they should disperse.
Then the brick bats started coming, not from the front ranks
but always from the rear.

The troops with their billies raised faced the crowd, and
everyone in the front rank turned around, trying to get to the
rear. Then they hit them right across their rears in a good, soft

place. The more smacks you heard, the more the people in the front started pushing toward the rear. The people just dispersed. Not one shot was ever fired in Manchester, New Hampshire.

The leaders of this country still haven't learned that lesson. You cannot treat a strike with bayonets. The chief could do it because he knew how to handle "his people," as he used to call them. After fifty-six years it makes you kind of sick to realize our leaders today still don't know how to police school and civil strikes in South Boston or anywhere else. They haven't learned how to handle the people under strike conditions.

In 1920, we were having a recession, and everybody was demanding more wages and higher dividends. We weren't running one half of the plant. The investors had made up their minds that manufacturing in Manchester was endangered like all the other mills in New England. Dad didn't want to go south; he knew the conditions of the southern mills. And he was right, absolutely right. The South had already grown so big that he didn't want to move out of New Hampshire.

In 1925, Dad decided to keep the old company charter and at the same time form a separate, new Amoskeag manufacturing division. The $14 million in bonds [which he transferred to] the manufacturing division was equivalent to its inventory only. In addition to all the machinery, land, and water power, it was a pretty good setup for the manufacturing division. Its downfall, in 1936, came because of poor labor relations, the inventory tax, and finally the flood of 1936.

Some outside stockholders wanted out in 1927. A large percentage of those that got out were New Hampshire people. They didn't like the way Amoskeag was going. The directors said, "Well, we have a lot of surplus money here." So they offered the stockholders a choice of staying with the old Amoskeag Company common stock or taking cash and the new manufacturing company stocks and bonds. Those who took the new Amoskeag stocks and bonds turned in their old Amoskeag common stocks, which had sold in 1927 for around $90.00 a share. For each share of the old company stock, they got $52.00 in cash, a $40.00 gold bond redeemable in 1948 and bearing 6 percent interest, plus a share of common stock in the new manufacturing company. It added up to about a hundred dollars per share, at market.

We didn't close the mills until 1936. In 1934 we had applied for [voluntary] bankruptcy—for reorganization under Section 77. We thought we had an agreement with the people of New Hampshire. A group chaired by ex-Governor Brown, the head of the Amoskeag Savings Bank, agreed with Dad to recommend to the people of New Hampshire and other bondholders and investors that they accept the new plan, stating that the Amoskeag Company would turn in its Amoskeag Manufacturing Company bonds for the new plan.* It had been well planned. Three weeks later, Dad went back to Manchester on a Sunday and met with ten or fifteen of them in the Amoskeag Savings Bank. I wasn't in the room, but I remember some of the fellows that were there, like Arthur Franks, Arthur Moreau, Frank Solloway, Norwin Bean, and Arthur Heard. The ex-governor's advisor said, "Well, we didn't say we *would* recommend; we said we *might*, if you would." Dad said, "That isn't what you said at all." They had quite a row. This fellow [ex-Governor Brown's aide] was a bit of a loud-mouth, and Dad wouldn't stand for it. He got up and said, "I'm sorry, gentlemen. I've done my job, and you failed to do what you said you would do." He was so mad and hurt he couldn't see straight. He hated a liar.

The next morning, Monday, there was an emergency board meeting at nine o'clock in the Boston office, and it was decided that the Amoskeag Company would withdraw its bonds from the plan of reorganization. There had been a power play between those who wanted to control the Amoskeag money and those who really controlled it outside New Hampshire. Soon after the court opened, the judge presiding over the bankruptcy proceedings ordered the Amoskeag Manufacturing Company liquidated—practically from the bench, as I recall it. I was there.

Dad wanted to see the mill run, but he wasn't surprised. I think he anticipated the situation. The plan they had worked

---

* "Amoskeag" here refers to the Amoskeag Company, the holding company under Dumaine's leadership. The bonds of the Amoskeag Manufacturing Company were intended to be wiped out in the new financial plan to keep the mill in town.

out for us was a good plan. If everybody turned their bonds in, there wouldn't be the debt on the mill. The mistake was in putting that debt on the mill in the first place in 1927, a prosperous year. It was just done in order to let out some of the disenchanted stockholders, mostly from New Hampshire, who wanted their money. The board didn't put the debt on to raise money. Some of them didn't sell their bonds between 1927 and 1935, before the reorganization plan came out. During the Depression in this country, some owners sold their bonds at very depressed values.

The fact was that the mill couldn't make money in the 1930s, in the Depression. Amoskeag Manufacturing had a hard time making any money, except in 1929. In this one year, they paid a one-dollar dividend. But what dragged us down was the bond debt and no sales volume. Six percent on the $14 million in bonds amounted to over $800,000 a year in interest. This was a big burden they had, plus local taxes. The manufacturing costs were higher than in the South; the selling prices were only equal to what the South would sell their products for. So there you are, you're in the squeeze.

Only Mr. Frank P. Carpenter and myself voted against liquidation. It was ten to two for liquidation. Dad said, "Why'd you do that?" And I said, "Because I think by cutting the Amoskeag down in size and taking out the best of the undamaged machinery, we could have kept something going." We were running only about seven thousand people at the time we closed, and we could operate on three shifts with more people employed, with free water power—we'd have done pretty damn well. You couldn't replace Amoskeag's fixed assets for $50 million.

We didn't close the Amoskeag; we applied for reorganization. Everything done was done justifiably, but the results were way beyond our control. We could not have stopped the flood. We know over $3,600,000 worth of machinery was destroyed, and it cost a lot of money to put what was left back in shape. What we did put back in shape from flood damage cost a lot. Even then they wouldn't reorganize, so the community bought for $5,500,000 all the fixed assets. The New Hampshire Public Service Company paid $2,500,000 for the water power rights and the hydroelectric plant and steam plants.

The liquidation didn't hurt Dad and the other Amoskeag Company stockholders financially, but it broke his heart. There was no one who loved the people who worked in the mill more than my father. He had always worked as hard as anyone for a living, from office boy to treasurer, advanced by Mr. Coolidge to run the Amoskeag Company in 1904.

► William Spencer*

William Spencer was born in 1899. He was educated at Harvard College. His progression in the textile business is characteristic of his generation of textile management men. He started out as an apprentice at the Nashua Manufacturing Company in Nashua, New Hampshire, learning the entire operation of a textile mill. At the same time, he took evening courses at the Lowell Textile School. At a young age, he became treasurer and general manager of the Oconee Manufacturing Company in Whitehall, Georgia, a mill in a small, isolated company town.

In January 1934 he was asked by F. C. Dumaine, Jr., to work as his special representative in the Amoskeag. This major assignment as a troubleshooter while the Amoskeag was already in its death throes lasted only ten months—"the shortest job I ever had." He resigned when he felt that "there was nothing more I could do for them, because the union was making heavy demands and I knew I couldn't meet them without Dumaine's support."

William subsequently worked as vice-president and general manager of the Warwick Mills in Warwick, Rhode Island, and after that at the Monument Mills in Housatonic, New York. The last job in his distinguished textile career was as head of Textile Specifications for contracts for the United States Army.

I was hired in 1934 as a public relations man to sell the name of Dumaine in Manchester. Buck Dumaine came over to

* Fictitious name

see me sometime in March and said that there was a man who had done a very good job overcoming the labor troubles at the B. B. & R. mills in Rhode Island; and that because of my personality, he felt that I could do the same thing in Manchester. I was out of a job at the time—it was during the Depression—so I said I'd be glad to try it out. One reason I was selected for the job was that I had intensive training in textile engineering. I knew what work loads were in the mills, how many spindles a spinner should take care of, and how many looms a weaver should handle.

Buck Dumaine took me up to Manchester and introduced me to the department heads at the Amoskeag. The head man [agent] at that time was a man by the name of Henry Rauch. Rauch had been to the Bentley College and was a splendid accountant, but he was a hard-boiled, frozen-faced guy who believed that the figures gave the answers: "Never mind how the workers feel; my figures are these." He had gone with young Dumaine to liquidate the Hamilton Mill in Lowell. That was a rather unpleasant job because the old man would call up from Boston and say, "I want that payroll down to so much by Friday night." Young Dumaine would slam the receiver down and say, "That man is the most impossible man in this world!" Then Rauch would have to go around to these overseers and say, "You're done, and you're done." He'd have to cut the payroll every Friday night.

When I came, the NRA° had just been declared; and although the mill was shut down, it was about to be started up again. Dumaine came up and spoke to all the workers. He stood on an elevated platform, and all the workers were down in the yard. He made a speech, saying that everybody was to be taken back and no more hard feelings. He said something to the effect that: "Never has anyone refused to do what I've asked, and I'm sure you'll cooperate with me from now on." Bygones were to be bygones. Well, the history of Amoskeag had been pretty bad, so that sort of a statement was a complete about-face.

Right after this speech—it was practically my first day on the job—one of the press came up to me and asked if I would have the smoke coming out of the chimneys. In order to give

° National Recovery Act

the impression that the mill was going to go back on full time, I went up to one of the operators in the boiler room and asked him to open up the draft and let the black smoke curl out in the sky, while the photographer took pictures. Well, the superintendent of the boiler room gave me the devil. He wanted to know what basis I had for authorizing them to open up the draft. I said, "Mr. Dumaine told me that I could do whatever I wanted to." But it was a waste of money. The smoke was coming out of the chimney all right, but it was because the oil wasn't burning properly.

I was to go down to the employment office every morning to interview the applicants for jobs. The personnel manager would bring me in a card that they kept on each individual; the individuals would sit about two or three feet apart at the table in front of me, and I would read the card. It had the date they were hired, who they worked for, if they shifted from one department to another, how long they worked in each department, and then what they did during the strike. If there was something like "This person threw flares through the window of the Coolidge Mill" or "Threw rocks through windows," it would also say, "Do not hire under any circumstances." The wool sorters were particularly bad. Every time I hired one of these people that had "Do not hire under any circumstances" written on his card, I knew that the overseer wouldn't be very pleased to have a fellow come back in who had been a troublemaker. Still, I hired them because Mr. Dumaine had made the statement in front of the whole crowd that bygones were to be bygones.

I had the prerogative of going to see and talk to anybody I wanted in order to get an idea of what was wrong. Dumaine, Sr., wanted a letter written to him in Boston, every night, so I would dictate a letter at the end of the day and forward it to him. I was caught in the middle. I was trying to satisfy labor and also satisfy management, which included, in a way, the New York office, where the selling agents were.

Labor knew as much about accounting as anybody else. The workers' argument to me was: "My grandmother and my grandfather worked hard to establish this surplus. We really earned it for the Amoskeag Manufacturing Company. Now, in the Depression, why can't they at least pay me a living wage and keep the mill operating? That surplus is really ours, but they've taken it away." I would tell them that I would discuss the matter with the executives, and I would let them know through the union, the following week, what I could do.

Another part of the job was to meet with a fellow by the name of Horace Rivière, who was the head of the union. Rivière supposedly got his job because he had saved the life of a higher labor leader during a strike in Nashua a couple of years before. The other man was about to be clubbed over the head, and the story is that Rivière threw his arm up in the air and deflected the club. So he was head of that whole area, and being a French Canadian, he spoke the language of most of the people. Every Monday, I met with the grievance committee. Rivière sat at one end of the table, and I sat at the other end. There were about eight other members. They presented the grievances to me, and I had until the following Monday to answer them.

One of the grievances I remember was that the ends were breaking in the roving process, which is the last process before the yarn goes into the spinning. With my textile experience, I knew that you have to run with a certain percentage of humidity or the ends break and get very brittle. So it was obvious that there was no humidity, or not enough. The humidifying system had been installed by Amoskeag itself, and it was a very crude one. It was merely pipes with little nozzles, spaced every so often, and regulators that they made themselves. I talked with the employees in the carding department, where the roving is done; and they told me that when Mr. Straw was there, he had said four machines were too many to run and three were not quite enough. They were being forced to run four. It was obvious that the room was too dry, so they couldn't run the number of frames that Rauch, through the overseer, had told them they had to run. I wrote to Mr. Dumaine, saying that each worker could run four frames if they had proper conditions; but I gathered that Dumaine and the New York office didn't like that type of thing—they didn't want me to concede that labor was right, even in that one respect. Management had one idea of what they could do, and labor had another idea. If Dumaine could have afforded to pay higher wages, maybe the workers would have turned out more. But because he was so penurious, they would do just enough to hold on to their jobs. This was the era of what they called sit-down strikes. They would sit down on the job and wouldn't go back to work until somebody came and listened to their complaint.

Every noontime Henry Rauch had a lunch meeting in the accounting room for all the superintendents and overseers. Mr. Rauch would sit at the head of the table. It was just like a lumber camp: nobody talked. At the end of the meal, he would read off all the notices and discuss what was going on. I wrote a letter to Boston, telling Dumaine I thought that at noontime the men should go out and relax, forget about the mill a little bit. I thought it was a bad idea to have to listen to bad news on top of a full meal. Some of the overseers agreed with me, but I had to act pretty much alone.

Mr. Dumaine had a lot of tricks that were so old-fashioned they would be obvious to modern management, or to anyone, for that matter. The workers were all French Canadians and didn't have much education, but they weren't fooled. He used tricks such as storing cotton in the Billerica car shop, because he was the director of the Boston and Maine Railroad. Then instead of unloading it in Manchester all at once, they would haul the cotton by truck from Billerica, a truckload at a time. The theory was that labor would see just a little bit of cotton coming in and would think that they were running out of orders. He did the same thing with wool. It was to give the workers the impression that the mill was in bad straits and was just barely getting by, so they better not cause any disturbance or the mills would have to close. He'd buy a brand-new Sanforizer, which was just coming into its own at that time, to try to kid them into thinking that he was going to install some new machinery to keep the mill running. But it was a machine that could be liquidated if the mill folded up, so he would get back just as much money, or more.

The management had taken a big chunk of money, something like $16 million, out of the Amoskeag Manufacturing Company and put it into the Amoskeag Company, a holding company separated from the manufacturing division in 1925. The Coolidges and a number of the old Boston families were trustees of the holding company. The people that sat around the table with me on the grievance committee knew just as much about accounting as I think Mr. Dumaine or anybody else did. One of them had been with the Carmen's Union, and another one had been with one of the utilities, and they knew exactly what the purpose of that move was: if they couldn't operate and had to liquidate, no one could touch any of that money because it was no longer Amoskeag Manufacturing Company money.

I knew from my textile background that it would have taken an enormous amount of money to have put that mill into good operating condition, with proper humidity and proper lighting, just the fundamentals. Some of the lower floors were merely lighted with old-fashioned kerosene lamps. They used to make black roving; and in order to thread the roving down through the trumpet, you need good lighting. It was so dark and dingy that they couldn't see to thread the machine. In the spinning room, I saw a spinning frame with only half of the spindles running. My impression was that the mill was on the downgrade; but when you speak of Amoskeag, you're really talking about ten mills. Some of the new mills were pretty good, well lighted and well humidified, with modern machinery. But the old mills didn't stand a chance of operating in the North with labor the way it was.

I went to see Bishop Peterson at the church, and I asked him why the people felt the way they did toward the Dumaines. He answered me, "These people are speaking from an empty plate." The plate was empty because they didn't get even three days of work a week, and that's what they were complaining about. They had nowhere to turn if the Dumaines didn't provide the payroll. The whole city was dependent on that payroll.

When I look back on it now, I think the workers in Manchester were the most courteous lot, because every morning, when they came down there to get a job and I had to tell them that there were no more jobs, they believed me. By being perfectly frank and honest with them, I think I got well treated. I would listen to them and try to correct whatever they said was wrong, but the number of things that I *could* correct in the mills was practically nil.

Instead of figuring out what it cost to produce a piece of cloth and then adding something as profit, Rauch took the selling price, what they could get for it on the New York market, and deducted the operating overhead to get a total manufacturing cost. Then he would proportion a certain amount of that cost to each superintendent and overseer, so that if a person needed a hundred people in their department, his cost would tell him he couldn't pay a hundred people. He'd given the men x number of dollars, and you'd have to turn out y amount of cotton for those dollars. The cost was always figured backwards. The workers weren't getting enough money, but Rauch wouldn't accept anything I might recommend that could increase his costs. To me, he was a cold accountant.

Of course, Rauch was trying to keep the mill operating with what was left in Amoskeag Manufacturing after all that money was taken out. Every time the mill had a strike, they lost the market for one of their big fabrics. When I went to work in 1934, I think they employed fifteen thousand people. When they were running full, they were one of the largest mills in the world under one roof. The people felt the Amoskeag should break even. But eventually anybody who knew anything about textiles knew that it would have to be liquidated, because the South at that time was putting in mill after mill, with the most modern machinery and the most modern mill layouts.

My feeling was that even if Dumaine turned the Amoskeag over to someone else, it couldn't have continued indefinitely, even without that flood in 1936. The flood was enough to kill the mill right then and there. Dumaine must have been making money or he would have liquidated earlier; but how much he was making, probably only Rauch knew. And as long as labor would stay quiet and not ask for more money, he felt that he could still operate.

I do think one should give Dumaine credit, that he felt he had a moral obligation to run that mill. If he'd thrown eight thousand people out of work, all those businessmen in Manchester would have been on his neck. Dumping all that labor on the city would have affected all of them, all of their businesses. And he had a lot of pride. I think he got a lot of pats on the back from the Coolidges and the other directors in Boston. I think they just thought he was God, the way he operated the thing. He had the ability to make money, and in better days they probably received good dividends.

I remember Mr. Dumaine had asked me to come and see him one Saturday at noontime. I had a classmate in Manchester who was a judge, and on Friday I had dinner with him and his wife. After dinner he really let his hair down and told me that Mr. Dumaine couldn't operate that mill because the hatred for him in Manchester was too much to overcome. The next day I went to Dumaine's home in Groton. I sat in a chair in the little den, and he stood with his back to the fireplace. He asked the man to bring in some mint juleps; it was a warm day. After we had the juleps, he said, "Well, what's the story?" I said, "Mr. Dumaine, I'm not an old man and I'm not a young man, and I've been around quite a bit. I think that as long as you are the operating head of the Amoskeag mills, they cannot function. If you're willing to hand over the reins to somebody else, you might be able to pull through." Tears started running down his cheeks, and he quoted some poet: "Once in a lifetime a man reaches his zenith." Then he said, "Maybe I've reached mine."

I thought I was doing all right, that I had got my point across, when suddenly he started raging like a tiger. He turned and said, "No! I'll blow the God damn place to pieces before I see somebody else operate that mill!" Then he said, "Young man, did you ever read *The Romance of Old Sandwich Glass?*" I said, "No, sir, I never did." He went to his bookshelf and brought me a copy. He said, "Now, I want you to take that home and read the next-to-last chapter." Well, the inference was obvious. The book says the Boston management did not deny that labor had the right to strike, but they were fed up with being told how to operate the factory. The smoke ceased to come out of the chimney, the ivy grew around the window, and that was the end of the Sandwich glass industry.

The next day I went over to see Buck Dumaine and told him that we'd reached an impasse and that I couldn't go any further. I had done all that I could. They very nicely gave me my salary for the next few months, so I have the highest regard for Mr. Dumaine. In spite of everything, he had a difficult job; and, of course, a year from the day I told him this, the dam gave way and they started to liquidate.

He knew Blackstone's *Commentaries* from A to Z, so that it didn't just happen that Mr. Dumaine got where he did. He really studied. And in spite of the fact that he had this cold outside, he was very warm inside. He had developed that mill; he'd hired all the people in there; he had set up the New York office. It was his life. He really ran it. He had a very strong personality, and there wasn't much arguing with him. I look back and I feel that I had a lot of courage at thirty-five to tell him what I did.

► Thomas Smith and Virginia Erskine

(SEE ALSO PAGE 219.)

VIRGINIA: You can't imagine the impact that the shutdown had on a community like Manchester. Complete families —fathers, sisters, everyone—were all out. There was nobody that you could turn to. I don't think before the Amoskeag closed I ever knew anyone that was on welfare during the Depression. People were proud, very proud. If you were in trouble and didn't have any income, someone always would say, "Well, come live with us for a while." That's the way it happened. Like in the Amoskeag, it would be friends that you worked with or ethnic friends or your relatives.

TOMMY: I remember my old grandfather lived with my mother and father, and then with my aunt and uncle, and then back again. Today he would have been in a nursing home for ten or fifteen years.

VIRGINIA: Of course, they didn't have any Social Security at that time; there was nothing to fall back on. So we just took it for granted that if you didn't have anything, somebody else would provide for you. But this all stopped when the Amoskeag closed and the Depression came. I can remember when my father was without a job. Then Roosevelt put in the WPA;° and, of course, it was a real godsend. Half the town was out of work. The only thing was, you couldn't get a WPA job unless you were on welfare first. It was a terrible thing to an awful lot of people to be forced to go on welfare to earn money to feed

° Works Progress Administration

their families. I can remember my mother pleading with my
father to go on welfare: "It will only be for a couple of weeks,
then you'll get a job." We had no income. He said, "Never, I'll
die before I go on welfare." He went to Lawrence and found a
job working nights. He didn't have a car, so he had to take the
limousine down there. Sometimes he'd get down there and
there'd be no work, and he had already paid for the limousine.
Oftentimes during the week he'd pay more money than he
earned. But he wouldn't go on welfare.

The year I graduated from high school, the mills finally
closed down. That was the last of it. I had wanted to go to
college, but you couldn't even find jobs. It took me two years to
find one. At the place where I got the job, I discovered there
was a job that my father could have. One of my bosses got it
for him. That's the way we climbed out of it.

So he never worked for WPA. He ended up getting a job at
the Chicopee Mill as a watchman, and he worked there for
many years. About the time of the war, my father got sick, so
my mother went to work at Chicopee, too.

TOMMY: I was all right after the shutdown. First I got a job
in Providence, then in Philadelphia, and finally in Lewiston,
Maine. Even at that time, a dyer was in pretty good demand.

When I came out, I bummed around for six or seven
months; this was a time when they were thinking of opening
half of the mill again. Dumaine was there, and they called in
all the top men. They wanted us to go in as watchmen on three
shifts, and they would pay us $16.00 a week. I didn't want to
do it, but they persuaded me to go in. I worked one winter as a
watchman. The mills were all shut down. It was just to keep
things going. When I got out of that, I went down to Providence and went to work for the biggest yarn dyers in the world
at that time. They had the same machines for dyeing yarn to
put into packages that we had at Amoskeag.

VIRGINIA: Not many people had as much education as
Tommy then. Most people didn't have a full high school education; a grammar school diploma was about the highest they
had. There weren't many university graduates at that time,
because people couldn't afford to send the children. There was

no way to get loans, like you can now. So people couldn't go to the universities unless they were rich.

There's one good thing that happened when the Amoskeag closed. We were living in the Amoskeag tenements; and for months after the closing, nobody paid any rent. You had to repair all your own houses, but you did have the free rent, because it was all from the Amoskeag.

TOMMY: You were supposed to be making the payments all the time, only they didn't force you. They just let it slide. We had to pay it all back in the end, though [laughs]. They didn't get after us for back rent until after they sold the block to Amoskeag Industries. We could continue living there afterwards, but the rents weren't the same, and you had to fix the houses on your own. The new landlords didn't keep them up anywhere near as well as the Amoskeag did.

Personally, I was astounded when the Amoskeag closed down. The superintendent of dyeing and bleaching—I was his assistant—told me that it would be two or three years before there would be any sign of it but that that was eventually what would happen. I always thought he was off-color on that. I didn't think it could ever happen, but they started closing very systematically, one department after the other.

Mr. Dumaine tried to buy the whole thing out at 10¢ on the dollar, but there was a minority group of stockholders who hadn't had any dividends for quite a few years. They got provoked at that, organized, and got attorneys in there. They forced Dumaine to liquidate, forced them into bankruptcy. Dumaine would have picked out what was efficient—what he could make money on. He'd have done it.

In fact, we had a meeting before the final shutdown. We were going to open up some of the very profitable lines (ginghams, flannels, cloth) on a partial basis and operate half the mill on those fabrics. They were to be last efforts, but then the flood came along and ruined everything. I think they would have done it, too, if it hadn't been for the flood. We had weave rooms, like in the bag mill up there—you know how tall a weave room is—and after the floods subsided, you could go in there and not see many looms. Nothing but a sea of mud that completely covered the looms. The flood was the climax. The

Eleven interviewees who participated in the filming of a documentary on the Amoskeag for public television. They were photographed while gathered in the now empty mill, December 10, 1977.

biggest thing before that was the financial shenanigans of Mr. Dumaine. He was a ruthless man. He was in control. I think that's why he was finagling around with it—to get absolute 100 percent control. But the minority stockholders forced him into a bankruptcy. On the stand in court, he said he didn't even know what his own salary was. Now, you can judge a man by that. Anybody who ever read about it knows he wrecked Waltham Watch and Eastern Steamship; but he wasn't the cause of the shutdown [of the Amoskeag], because if he could have brought it off [the reorganization], I think perhaps he would have.

Of course, at that time rayon was coming in and orlon was coming in. There was going to be a changeover. It was a really hard thing. Most of the workers couldn't go for other jobs. They didn't have the ability, and a lot of them were very old. I don't know what the percentage would be in age, but it was terrifically high. A lot died of broken hearts. I don't know whether any committed suicide or not, but it was a terrible situation. In those days there was no relief; there was no welfare. Nowadays, a man can go out, and if he can show proper reason why he can't get a job, he can live better on welfare than he might working in some jobs.

Part Seven

Child of
the Shutdown

► *Lottie Sargent*

Lottie Sargent was born in Manchester in 1924. Her father's side of the family consisted of a long line of mill workers, his maternal grandparents having come over from Scotland to work in Manchester. Lottie still cherishes the paisley shawl that her great-grandmother brought with her to New Hampshire.

Lottie's mother died when Lottie was still an infant; and after her father's remarriage, she spent an unhappy childhood in her stepmother's household. Her childhood suffering was intensified by the shutdown of the Amoskeag and the Depression. Her subsequent story is one of survival and pulling herself up. She worked on a variety of jobs until she reached age seventeen, when she started to work in the Chicopee Mill, where she spent the next twenty-five years. In addition to her mill job, she held a night job as a salesperson for many years in order to help support her children.

Lottie lost her job when the Chicopee shut down in 1975.* Like several hundred of the Chicopee workers, she relived the shutdown of the Amoskeag as a result. She is now working again in a textile mill in Suncook, New Hampshire. She has a remarkable mineral collection, and both she and her husband restore Model-T Fords and participate in antique car rallies in costume.

---

* The Chicopee Mill opened in 1937 in the old Coolidge Mill. It was owned by the Johnson & Johnson Company and was shut down in 1975.

I really hoped that my children would be something better. Nobody wants their child to go back in the mill. *Nobody*. It's no life; it's just survival. If you're something like a teacher, you have prestige, you have money, you have a decent place to live. When you're a peasant, it's a roof over your head, and bread and butter, and lots of beer if you can afford it.

Probably 99 percent of us went back into the mills because there was nothing else. I wanted to go into nursing, but I got married [laughs]. So I went back to the mills instead of becoming a nurse. But I'm still a nurse. You can't take it away from me. I took all the courses; I can still do everything. I didn't work as a nurse because I didn't finish my training. You can't have a husband and children and be in training; it takes three years.

My husband and three kids and I lived on a farm with his mother. We didn't have a car, so for fourteen years I had to walk to the bus to get to work. He was gone in the service almost ten years, and I was all alone with the family. We had all kinds of animals, and I had to take care of everything. I had a milk route and sold eggs. I made all my daughter's clothes and canned [the produce from] our three-acre garden. We all had to work. We cut wood—I'd split a cord of wood an hour. Then when we needed money and he was out of work, I worked at Chicopee.

My father's family were mill workers from Scotland. My mother's parents disowned her when she married my father, mainly because he was part Indian and not so much because he was a mill worker, although people looked down their noses at mill workers. My grandfather Fisher was an Indian, and Indians were not supposed to work; that's why my grandmother ran a boardinghouse for the mill workers on Merrimack Street. My father says he never remembers his father ever doing a day's work. My father was the youngest of four brothers, and there were three daughters that were younger than him. As soon as they got to be teenagers, everybody left. My father is the only one that stayed and took care of everything. When he was nine, he went to work in the mills in Canada; and when he was twelve, they came back to Manchester. In those days there was no border. Everybody just walked across into the United States. So my father lived in the corporations as a youngster. He grew up there, and he worked in the mills from the time he was twelve. He also delivered lunches when he wasn't working.

My mother died when I was nine months old. My older brother was sixteen or seventeen years older than me, and at the time he quit school and went to work. My brother next to me was put in the children's home, but I was too young. I think you had to be three. The only people my father knew were people that patronized clubs and bars, so he would have women he met there—bar ladies—come over and babysit for me; and when he came back from work, he would find me down in some bar, climbing around or curled up in a chair sound asleep. They were the only babysitters my father could afford. They were supposedly taking care of me, but they didn't know what to do with me, so I spent the main portion of the time when I was really small going from barroom to barroom with these ladies. They weren't prostitutes, but everyone had to make a buck somehow; there was no money.

When I was old enough, they put me into the Webster Street Children's Home, and I stayed there until I was seven. I was a very lonely little girl and a very naughty little girl—very sassy, very fresh, very smart. If I could antagonize anybody to get attention, I would. So I ended up having a room of my own. I didn't have any mother, and without a mother you don't have very much. My father worked, and on weekends he wanted a good time, so he didn't see his children too much. Besides, the people at the orphanage would press him for money.

My father and my brother George, between the two of them, were making $18.00 a week. They were buying their own food, paying for their room, plus they were paying $7.00 apiece for my brother and me in the children's home. That's how much it was at the home in those days—$7.00 a week apiece. When you add it up, it was almost impossible for anyone to do anything.

Some of the matrons were nice, but we had one lady by the name of Miss Wyman who was terrible. She used to beat us. She hated kids. If we were sick and heaved on the floor, she would take the mop and put it in our faces. No matter what was wrong with you, they gave you castor oil, and that made you sick all over again. Somewhere along the line I learned how to swear. I don't know where, probably from the bar ladies. I knew every word in the book apparently, because I used to get my mouth washed out with brown soap.

I was too young to go to school, but they still made us work, doing things like sorting clothes from the laundry and dusting. In the morning before school, the older kids had to form lines. One was for washing faces, one was for washing hands, and one was for combing hair. I would have to take a comb and stand on a chair and comb somebody else's hair.

My father met my stepmother in the orphanage. She had two children there, too. I can remember asking her, "Are you going to be my mother?" when she came to visit her boys. I knew she was going out with my father. When there was no one there for me, I'd go over and stand near her, and Miss Wyman would say, "Get away from her! Get away from her!" I would say, "She's going to be my mother." "Oh, no, she isn't. Get away from her!" So I was quite happy when my father and stepmother first got married, but afterwards I wasn't quite so happy about it. It didn't turn out the way I thought it was going to. I was the only girl, so naturally I did the housework, and I did the washing, and I did this, and I did that. I worked in the garden, took care of the kids, took care of the neighbors' kids. Anytime anybody wanted anything, it was "Lottie will do it." It's still the same way today. That's why I ended up with my brother. Finally he said, "Well, enough is enough! You'll go to school and take care of my kids." At least I had a roof over my head. He was like a father; and even though they had their differences, his wife was always good to me. Then I got married, the best thing I ever did for myself.

When I was a child, my father worked in #4 Mill. I used to take lunches into the mills and spend the whole day there. Some of the other kids would come, too; and we'd walk the whole two miles through the mills, through the overpasses, the underpasses, and everywhere. Number 10 Mill is where we particularly liked to go, because we could look down and see the brownies swimming in the mill canal. The brownies are the strong young men that go swimming all year-round, and in the summertime they swam down there with no clothes. In those days, you just didn't do those things. Today, of course, it's nothing.

My father worked most of his life in the cloth room. Everybody in my family was a cloth inspector. Way back they came from Scotland to be wool sorters and inspectors. My brother worked downstairs in the card room. The card room was a terrible job, filthy; the cloth room was always nice, although they didn't pay as much because it was a cleaner job. It was fantastic to walk into the cloth room. They had all different colors of toweling, and it traveled on rollers, all the way up. The whole ceiling, the whole room, was just floating in cloth. Eventually, it probably ended up being steamed and put on smaller rollers and cut, but I never saw that operation. All I could see was mile after mile of cloth, going over and under rollers, all over the room.

There is no way to describe a full-blown weave room going. The whole place shakes back and forth in rhythm. The noise is something you've never heard before. I tried to get my son a job in Chicopee once, and they went through the cloth room where I worked and opened the door to the weave room. My son walked in and turned around and walked back out. He said, "You don't work in noise like that." The noise scares you. And here I was, a little seven-year-old, walking mile after mile through all these weave rooms. You can't even converse; you learn how to read lips. When thousands of looms are going, there's no noise like it.

They had overhead passages, and they had underneath passages between the mills, but they still allowed us kids to go in. Of course, half the kids in there were working anyway, so they didn't think anything of it. My father would buy me a little carton of milk, a half-pint of milk. I don't know how much it cost him, but it was my reward for doing all his work. Milk was for babies. Otherwise you didn't know what milk was. In the summertime we'd probably have bread and milk for supper, but for drinking, no. When you outgrew your babyhood, you weren't allowed milk. Nobody could afford it.

Times were very, very hard. When my father married my stepmother, she had two kids and he had three, and then they had two themselves. My brother got married the year after my father did and had a family, plus there was an old man who worked with my father; and we were all living together. Actually, the man wasn't that old, but he was older than my father, and he was alone. He had no place to go, so my father took him in, and he lived with my father free until he died. My father took in everybody—everybody lived off him.

In order to survive, my father practically lived in a club. He used to sell numbers tickets, and I was one of the runners [laughter]. This was a good many years ago; my father is long dead. I had to learn the back streets of Manchester. My husband has never heard of anyone who knows the back streets like I do. A man would come and give my father tickets, and he would divide them up into little bags. Then he would send me at night through the back streets to deliver them, thinking that nobody would catch me. I was terrified! Who would think of a little girl using the back streets? And I could really run.

It was the worst part of the Depression, and nobody had anything. In 1936 the mills went out, and the world stopped for everybody. A lot of our neighbors, a lot of the men, committed suicide. There was nothing. There was no food. I really don't know how we made it.

We lived in the corporations, and we had corporation parties. Everybody helped everybody else. Families lived together. My father belonged to all the old Amoskeag clubs. The men in those days didn't stay home much. They all congregated somewhere, and . . . [laughs]. They talked and drank, even though there wasn't any money. I don't know how they managed to do this.

When the Amoskeag shut down, everybody had to do everything they could. I was ten or twelve, and they sent me out to work. I took care of kids, I did housework. When I went to work at Chicopee, I found all these mill workers' children that I babysat for. I was only a couple of years older than they were. Women had to work whenever they could. I would go and stay with the kids and do the housework, do the cooking, and everything else, and they would probably give me 25¢ a week, which I had to put into the house. The Carnivalware glass here is worth $85.00 now [laughs]. We used to get it at the movies. The neighbors used to give me a dime to go into the movies for them. For a dime, I'd see the movie plus I'd get a dish. Nobody had dishes then. Nobody had anything. Nobody could buy things. I also worked in the gardens. We had to sell the produce in order to get enough money to live on.

The corporations on West Merrimack Street, looking down toward
the mills, 1969

At one time when they were working in the mills, they were
making pretty good money. After World War I, though, they
started cutting down; then they had a couple of strikes, and
that's when my father went on the police force. There were a
lot of hard feelings. Apparently the Amoskeag couldn't afford,
or didn't want to afford, higher pay. I think it was a lot of
mismanagement. You can't just cut your workers. The mill was
the only thing in Manchester. There was nothing else; and
when it closed, everybody was desperate. One of the men who

committed suicide lived two doors up from me. He was from Sweden, and there were five children. They had left the old gaslights in the corporation tenements, and he went up to the attic and gassed himself.

I was never home that much because they put me out to work. I more or less supported myself all my life, until I got married. I even worked my way through high school. There was no money before World War II. They paid me $2.00 or $3.00 a week, but I had to buy all my clothes, my food, my lunches, anything I needed. Everybody married young, and everybody got out on their own just as soon as they possibly could. My stepbrother married my high school chum, and I married my high school chum's cousin [laughs]. We live so much better today. We have so much compared with what we used to have, but we aren't any happier, because people were very close then.

Manchester was all nationalities; each place had its little group. When we lived in the corporations, we had gang wars; it was just something you did. But they didn't have knives in those days. Nobody could afford a knife. My brother was always a fighter. Poor boy, he just died in January. He had a family of eight. Girls didn't even watch fights. We knew better. The Greeks would come down to fight the Upper Corporation, and whoever won would fight the Lower Corporation. The Greeks didn't live in the corporations, but the Polish and French did. My brother wore glasses from the time he was young, and he had more broken glasses. My father always had to scrounge and sell a few more tickets and do a little more gambling on the side to buy him new glasses.

They had curfew in those days. The whistle used to blow at eight o'clock or eight thirty; and when the whistle blew, we all had to be home. If we weren't, Father would go out with a big, long shaving strap. He would put his two fingers in his teeth and blow, real shrill; and when the boys heard that, they would head home down the back streets, trying to beat him. If they made it, they could say, "Well, we were here. You just left when we came." But if they didn't make it, they got the razor strap, and that didn't tickle. I never got it very much. I was a little hellion but not so that I would get the strap.

My brothers were the Marble Kings. They had bags and

bags of glassies, all different sizes. Nobody ever bought a glassie; nobody could afford to. You borrowed one, and you played marbles. Boys used to play poppies, and girls used to play bunny in the hole. Now, today, if you ever find anybody playing glassies or marbles, they play bunny in the hole, not poppies. In poppies, the kids would make a little hole in the ground, and you'd sit down with your legs straddling it. You'd measure off so many feet and draw a line, and this is where the contestants stood. The guy that was sitting at the hole would put his marble down, and the others would try to hit it. My brothers were terrific at it. When they got too old to play, they used to lean out the windows and pop glassies at everybody that passed by. The girls played bunny in the hole. We didn't pop at them, we just pushed them in the hole with our finger, and whoever got the most in won the pot. The boys had real tournaments, playing poppies. It was quite a thing. The marbles were smaller than glassies. They were little and tan-colored. I don't know what they were made out of, some kind of pottery. But the glassies were all with figurines, and they came in different sizes. They came in onesies, twosies, fivesies . . . [laughs].

Besides marbles or glassies, we played games together. We played run, chief, run, or hide-and-seek. During the summer months, it was so hot that everybody stayed up late. There was no sex; it was just boys and girls playing. It's not like it is today. When you were ten or twelve, even if you had a boy-friend or girlfriend, you just played. We lived on the second floor, and in the wintertime the boys would make a great big pile of snow and would jump off the second-floor porch; or if it was a very bad winter, they would jump off the roof down into the snow. The snow was deeper than it is now, much more so.

My father felt terrible at Christmastime. He cried because he couldn't give us what he would have liked to give us, but usually he tried very hard, doing some extra gambling. One year I remember I wanted a pair of skates, and I got the skates. We would go to the Amoskeag playground. They flooded it in the wintertime, and we used to skate there. One brother had the hat, another one had the mittens, and the other one had the coat. I was the only girl. If my brother wanted to go skating

The children's playground, ca. 1920

and I couldn't go because I had a lot of housework, I would loan him my skates, and the other brother would loan him the mittens, and the other would loan him the coat. Nobody had a complete outfit of clothing to go out in the winter with. We used to get sample shoes because they were a lot cheaper, and we went barefoot all summer long.

There is hardly more than a year's difference between my brother Bob's son and my son and my half-brothers. We all had a baby practically the same year. My stepmother was in her thirties and my father was in his forties when they got married. She never worked too much, although when my father married her, she was working as a cook and governess for a lawyer in Manchester. I can't say that my father defended his own kids, because my stepmother used to beat me. I ran away from home two or three times. My father was never home; he liked to play cards and play pool and go to the clubs and drink. If there was a club, my father belonged to it. He belonged to the Redmen, an Indian organization; and the British-Americans, which is a social club in Manchester. He was a social bustler. We always asked him whether he would like to take his bed to the club with him.

There wasn't any money, but everybody was drinking. My father used to make home-brew in the house. When it is fermenting, it smells terrible. Everybody made home-brew in those days. Nobody went out and bought bottled beer or bottled wine. We would make root beer in the summertime, and sometimes all the bottles would pop and there would be root beer all over the place. We were too poor to afford anything like lemonade, so my stepmother would mix vinegar and water and sugar; it was very tasty.

They had a Coathouse factory in Manchester that used to make clothing; and while I was going to high school, I wore Coathouse clothing. It was like a sewing project, a WPA for women. A lot of women didn't have any husbands and had to support themselves, and they did that instead of being on welfare. Their styles were terrible, so you always knew who had Coathouse clothes, but they made quilts which were nice and warm. I was only making $3.00 per week, and I had to support myself on that, so I had no choice anyway.

My stepmother was a good cook. My father used to help her sometimes because we were a big family. They made the bread together. We were on WPA, and we got surplus food besides. A truck would come to the area, and everybody would go and get eggs and butter. (This is what I can't understand about America: people who work eat margarine, and people who don't work eat butter.) I think they had canned meat then that was horrible, just like they have canned meat now that is horrible. It was like parboiled beef. I knew someone who had a

hard time getting surplus food five years ago, before they had
food stamps; and they got some of this canned meat and even
their dog wouldn't eat it. Back in those days, you ate it.

We kids didn't get many heavy meat meals. One thing that
all of us resented: my stepmother and father used to have steak
and pork chops at night after we went to bed. It's not that we
didn't have enough to eat; we did. It's that they had the better
life after we went to bed. We used to sit on the stairs and look
down. After all, you can't help smelling steak and pork chops.
But the man that worked was supposed to get the best. I
wouldn't ever do that with my family, but many times I gave
my husband all the meat. I guess I ended up doing that because it was expected of me. He didn't know it then, but he
knows it now. He wouldn't have allowed it; he would have
given me half of what he had. I used to just give it to him and
tell him that I wasn't too hungry, and all the time I was starving. That's the place of the mother: you give and don't take.
Women are getting away from that now; with each age group
it gets better, but I'm still old-fashioned.

I studied paleontology, and I'm a mineralogist. As you go
back in the history of mankind, women don't exist. They were
thrown the bones that were left over; and in this century, we
are standing up and saying, "We're hungry, too. We don't just
want the bones; we want half of your steak."

It was terrible, trying to support yourself when the mills
went out. My brother went to work for Chicopee in 1938. I was
living with him then. He was working in the cloth room. Then
my father and my other brothers went in, and finally I went in.
My father was fit to be tied. "You don't want to work in the
mill," he said. "There are other jobs. You can do something
else." But it was before World War II, and there wasn't anything else, unless you wanted to go to the shoe shop. I had a
family by then. My husband was gone in the service, and we
needed bread and butter. I was alone with my children.

I've worked all the shifts. My husband wasn't home when I
was working the night shift because he went back into the
service after I had my third baby. I got him out when the
Korean War started. I wrote a letter to his commanding officer:
"To Whom It May Concern: Please send my husband home."

He was fit to be tied, but they did send him home [laughs]. I just couldn't stand it any longer.

My father made sure that I got into the cloth room because there was a better atmosphere there. I was a quality inspector all those years. If you asked me how to do the job, I could never tell you; you just know. My father was the same way. I just feel cloth and I know, or I just look at cloth and I know. I love cloth, and I do a lot of sewing. It's one of those things that some of us just seem to have the ability to do.

During World War II, I went to work making fifteen-millimeter bullets. The bullets come out of the screw machine that makes them, and they drop into a bin of hot oil. You hurry and scoop them up, boiling hot, and put them in the basket, and then you inspect them again by fingertip. You had to have fingernails to inspect them. My brother that I lived with got killed in World War II at the Belgium Bulge. He never came home. I was so very nervous; it was terrible. What if I didn't do it right, and my husband got this bullet, and it didn't go off when he needed it? It was so nerve-racking that I had to quit. I couldn't stand it any more.

Finally, I went back to Chicopee, but they didn't treat you very well there years ago. It had a very bad reputation. It ended up that nobody would send anybody there to get a job because of their terrible reputation. You were afraid to say boo; you just did what they told you. You were dirt, let's face it. I was sick one day, and I was told I had to come in. I was too sick to come, so I lost my job. Then I worked at Manchester Knitted Fabrics, right across the street; but the minute my father told me there was an opening at Chicopee, I went right back in again.

All the former Amoskeag workers worked in the Chicopee. They used to work a good many hours in the Amoskeag, but from what I ever heard or observed, they never really worked that hard. At Chicopee they had to work hard. They were always under pressure. The Amoskeag was not a piecework place. The Chicopee was all piecework; and when you're on piecework, you're nothing but a machine.

When the Amoskeag closed, there was nothing in Manchester until the Chicopee came; and when they first opened, they ran two four- or six-hour shifts. They didn't run any eight-hour shifts. It took a while for them to get going and get all those people in there. After working all those years for $14.00 a week for WPA, when you did have a job, you were so grateful that they could do anything to you. Because there was no place to go, we couldn't leave, we couldn't quit. And during World War II, there still were not that many places to work. It was either Chicopee or the shoe shops. I'm not condemning the shoe shops because I never worked in one, but they didn't have a good reputation. The people were on a lower plane than the mill workers.

One of the managers of the Chicopee, the man on top who was supposed to listen to our complaints, just walked through every day and insulted everybody. He thought if you were a woman and you were in the mill, *you were dirt! And then some!* He swore, he said anything he wanted in the presence of women. He'd make fun of you, and you had to take it. There were no other jobs.

When the southerners [from one of Johnson & Johnson's southern plants] came in, we had quite a turnover of management. They treated women better. They were gentlemen. They claimed they didn't discriminate against women in pay, that women doing the same jobs as men did not get paid less. I never dwelt on it that much. When you work that hard, you don't know how much anybody else is making, because you really have to push to make your own.

Every now and then I ran piecework to prove to the guys that I could do their work. I would never tell anybody else their work was no good unless I could do it myself. I figure if the women can do it every now and then, the men should be able to do it all the time. It was all heavy lifting. During World War II, they had women do inspecting; and when I inspected, I had to put the heavy frames on the machine by myself and take them off, six hundred pounds. But I had more muscle when I was skinny [laughs]. You grow with the job. If you have a baby, if you pick it up every day, when it's six years old, it's tripled in size, but you can still pick it up. It works that way with almost everything.

I worked at Chicopee three years, four months, and five days the first time, and I went back in 1949. When I came out again, I had two years and about ten months. Altogether, it seemed like ten years, but it wasn't ten, it was something like six. It was forever, anyway. I stayed at Chicopee for so many years because it fit my schedule. I was home when the kids were home; I never had to leave them.

At Chicopee, we didn't work only with our hands. I did statistical analysis. It puts you in a different position. I worked out of the standards office, measuring faults in the cloth. I kept track of mistakes, the statistics of the cloth. I was hated. I told men that their work was no good, that they'd made a mistake, and they reacted normally—they hated me. My father worked in the same room as me in the Chicopee, and I did statistics on his work. If his work was no good, I told him so, just like anybody else, and my father didn't like me either [laughs]. But that's how I am. You have to do your job.

I was checking the inspectors, which involved the whole mill. The inspector running the cloth has to know how to grade each one of those pieces and what he can let pass. When I first started, the rolls were probably five hundred yards, but when I left, they were thirteen thousand yards. I grew with the machine. We all had to grow with it. For a good many years the cloth at Chicopee was running at two hundred yards per minute. Now, this is a moving object at two hundred yards per minute, so you don't see it per se. You feel that a certain thing is there. But if you're operating the machine, and the stuff is going by almost too fast for the eye to see a specific thing unless it's as big as your head, you can't stop it in time. It would probably go on for so many yards; and by the time you saw it and shut the machine off, it's way over there in the machine somewhere, and you have to pull it all back and cut it all off. Now, if you're an inspector, you have to earn a living, so if it has gone by, you say, "Well, nobody is looking for the mistakes, they don't check it, nobody'll know."

This is where I came in. Every day they'd take one piece from this man, one from that. Nobody knew who I was going to take it from or when I was going to take it. I'd say, "All right, give it to me," and I'd have a chart. I'd have all these things written down; and as the cloth went through I wouldn't run it as fast as the men do, so I could see it. It takes a trained eye.

All I need is to see a little twist here or a little lump or a little something there, and I'll know. I know automatically. It's long gone by the time you put a little mark on the paper.

Everybody has a trademark. Everybody does a certain thing a certain way when they work. They used to complain, "It's mine and you don't like me, so you're being hard on me." They'd try to fool me; they'd say, "We won't put anybody's operator's numbers on the rolls or anything." I'd still tell the boss, "That's so-and-so's bolt in there." "How did you know?" "Because he did such-and-such." After doing it so many years for certain people, I simply could tell.

I had worked twenty-five years when they closed. When the Chicopee shut down, I was one of the first ones to leave. I was a pencil pusher, so they didn't need me. I kept telling the guys, "I'll be the first one." "Oh, no," they'd say, "they got to keep you." But they were wrong, and now they're not any better off than I am, because they haven't got any jobs either.

It's terrible trying to find another job now. You would think that being on the same job twenty-five years, they would say, "You must be good; you must be a nice, steady person." But it's not that way at all. If I had had fifteen or twenty-five jobs during that time, they'd say, "Gee, if you do all this stuff, we'll take you." This way they say, "If this is the only thing you know how to do, we don't want you." I keep telling them, it's not the only thing; I'm a very versatile person. Maybe I don't know how to do it now; show me how, and I will. There's no reason why I can't do something else. But at fifty years old, they figure you're dead. I keep telling them I'm not, but they don't believe me.

Part Eight

Eulogy

► *Bette Skrzyszowski*

Bette Skrzyszowski, who is fifty-two years old, works in Manchester's last surviving textile mill, the Waumbec Mill, as a battery hand on the night shift. Born in Baltimore to parents native to New England, she came to Manchester in the late thirties and married Mitchell Skrzyszowski, who was working at the time as a smash piecer in the Waumbec Mill.

Bette worked as a battery hand in the Chicopee Mill until its shutdown in February 1975. She raised her three sons while working the night shift by sharing child care with her husband, who worked the day shift. She is now so accustomed to working the night shift that she is unable to sleep at night when she is not working.

We visited Bette immediately following the shutdown of the Chicopee. The statement that follows is her eulogy to the world of work of which she had become a part. She and her fellow workers in the Chicopee, many of whom had worked in the Amoskeag, were reliving the Amoskeag's shutdown as a result of the Chicopee's closing.

You've worked all this time, and now you see it shutting down. You go up the aisle and see one loom running here, back and forth, and then stop, all empty.

I've always worked in the weave room. Suddenly they said they had to be shut down by the twenty-eighth of February. We'll be working just another week. The empty cans are lying across the back, the beams are taken off, and everything's been picked up and trucked away. The other day they had ten trailers backed up in there, taking cards. The cards will be gone this weekend. They're sold. But the looms—I don't know where they could sell them. But they have to be out of the mill. All the machinery is going. You can't get parts for some of the looms any more because they're so old, so I imagine they'll junk them or maybe sell them to a small mill which can use them for spare parts.

When I first started, all of the looms were run on belts. Now the ones upstairs are the only ones on the belts. In the weave room downstairs, there's a shaft on the ceiling, and the belts used to run from there down to the looms. It was like walking through a forest, it was so dark, because of all those belts. Every loom had a belt. I never liked that.

There were two thousand looms in one weave room, about four or five thousand looms altogether. They always have the looms running in opposite directions. Some will go this way and some will go that way, to allow for the weight on the floors. Upstairs it's just the reverse. I've seen the floors come away from the walls when the looms were running. It would leave a sizable hole; you could see it. You had two thousand looms running at one time—that's a lot of machinery going.

Everything is so quiet in there now. Only about three hundred looms are going. You can hear some noise, but you can imagine what it was like when all of them were running. What a noise it would make!

This week some workers were laid off Tuesday, and some were laid off today. Next week there'll be a layoff in mid-week, and then another one on Friday. They let you know a day ahead of time exactly when you'll finish, but actually they can't tell how fast the warps will run out. A warp usually takes four or five weeks to run out, but they may have a smash or a weaver that's goofing off.

They go around every day taking a count of how many looms are going and how many warps are coming out. On most of the warps now there are only two sets running, and they're running a good two weeks because they're big warps, almost full. They're running three shifts—two sets and three shifts. Otherwise, they would never run them out.

Sometimes a loom is stopped all day; sometimes it's stopped for two or three hours; sometimes it's stopped half a day, if they have a smash. There are any number of reasons why the looms stop. If they ran just one shift, they would have to run it twenty-four hours a day and never stop. If a loom breaks down now, they just take the warp out and put it on another loom to keep it going instead of bothering to wait for the fixer to fix the loom. They have to shut the loom off and let it go, but they keep the warps running because they have to be done on the twenty-eighth. They have to keep them going until they all run out.

It's hard now. This week especially, I've had it pretty rough. I'm very tired, because as the looms stop, they cut down on the help. Before, a battery hand would have all the looms in one place. Now, you might have only one loom going here, with maybe four or five on the other end, maybe three in the other row, four or five over there. You run all over the place, but you have to keep filling them till they run out. I must have walked fifty miles this week. I even missed a couple of them. The weaver today told me that I forgot two looms over there. The darn batteries were empty. You try to conserve steps, you try to see where the looms are running, and sometimes you go down the aisle too far and miss one or two.

You go up and down the aisle, and you say, "I used to have all these looms to fill." Now you don't have anything. Now it's so empty, you can almost hear the stillness come across the room. You go through a section where a lot of them are running, and then you come to where it's awful quiet. Only a few are running. And it's a lot colder, too.

People don't say very much when they're leaving. They're sad, and a lot of them cry. It's a bad thing when there are no jobs to be had. If only you could say, "Well, the heck with it. I'll go out and get another job." But there's just no place to go. After you put that many years into a place, it's like a second home. You go every day, you know how much time it's going to take you, and you come home at a certain time. Just a nice

The weave room in the Coolidge Mill when it opened in 1909. This room and the one above contained 2,000 looms.

routine. You knew what to do and how to do it, and you knew how long it would take you. Nobody bothered you.

You knew you had a job to go to. It was a good feeling. Now you know your time has come, and you feel lost. You just have no place to turn. I've spent half my life in the mill, really, because I'm fifty years old, and I'm going on twenty-three

The same room, now part of the Chicopee Manufacturing Company, seventy years later, photographed just prior to the junking of the looms after the closing of the mill in 1975

years in the mill. If there were other mills, you could say, "I'll go to another mill. That mill is just as good." But there are no other mills to go to.

There's no more weaving. There are no more old looms any more. Everything today is modern. I don't know how to explain it, but you're connected with the machinery. It's a part of you;

it's your life. I love the mills, I love to work, I loved being a battery hand. I always liked it. I used to complain a lot, but if I had my choice, I would stay here until I retired. And three quarters of the people here would have stayed here for life. It was a good mill to work in; they were good people. We were the old reliable help. There was always a big changeover, new ones coming in and going out, but there was the old steady help, too. The bosses never bothered you if you did your work. They didn't care if you went for a break. They were never on your back, saying, "Now we've got to get this done." We all worked together as one. Everybody had their work to do, everybody knew what to do, and they did it. There were no fights, no bickering. It was a good life. I think everybody in Chicopee would tell you the same thing.

I'll miss the people I worked with, I'll miss the mill itself. The day they close will be the saddest day I've ever seen. Three quarters of us who are still left won't believe it until we are out the door. It's just something you don't accept. A lot of us keep hoping for a miracle, that somebody will come in and say, "Forget it, we're gonna start up again." What a celebration that would be! But it's really too far gone for that.

They put money into the mill. They bought new machines. They hired a guy from Monsanto, the chief engineer. When they hired him—I'd say he's been here less than a year—they told him they wanted a man who would stay with the company at least twenty years. He's only thirty-two, so he had a good future ahead of him. Now he's out of a job, and he had a good job with Monsanto, too.

The only suspicion we had about their planning a change was when they brought that plant manager up. It must have been before vacation. They told us he was the northern plants manager and that he was supposed to make sure everything was all right; but as soon as he came through that door, we said, "Something is in the wind." No other plant manager had come to visit here before, in all the years I had been here.

The day they told us, all the supers and the managers had a meeting. When the meeting was over, the boss came around and told us they wanted to see us downstairs right after work. The afternoon shift was coming in, and they wanted the whole mill, 450 people. We all suspected something. They stopped the looms. They had to because they kept us there a good three quarters of an hour, explaining everything. We had expected a two-month layoff, because when they bought these new carding machines, they said they were going to put them in during the month of February. They were still delivering the new carding machines and their parts. One of the girls said, "I saw the big Skyline truck here just yesterday when we were going out." The very next day, they told us the plant was closing.

At Chicopee, it was just one big, happy family. We were always running into somebody from the card room or the spinning room or the spool room, or one of the slashers. Everybody knew everybody, and we always spoke to one another. For a place that big, for as many employees as they had, and for the ethnic groups that they had, the different people really got along beautifully. There were people in there that couldn't speak English. They could only speak Greek, or they could only speak Puerto Rican Spanish or Colombian Spanish or French. But we always made out, and everybody always got along with everybody else. The Puerto Ricans could talk to the darker people from Colombia. You could talk to the higher-ups, too—the super of the weave room, the manager—whoever you wanted to go see about whatever treatment you felt wasn't right. There really weren't that many grievances, because I don't remember anyone going over the bosses.

They usually had a twenty-five-year dinner every September. Anybody who'd been there twenty-five years was invited to the supper and could bring a guest. They would give you a gold watch with your name and "Chicopee 25 years" inscribed on the back. At one time Chicopee had a rule that at sixty-five you had to retire. Not any more, though; you could retire whenever you wanted.

Three quarters of the time the mill has been here, there's been a big turnover of help. That is the main reason for the low production. The young people, they come in the mill, and they're there for that week's pay. They're not in there for an honest day's work. The old people like us knew that that job was our bread and butter. We knew we had to put out an honest day's work, because if we didn't, we were going to lose our jobs. But the young people don't look at it that way. They were in there for their week's pay and the heck with it. There'd be bobbins on the floor, making for dirty filling. We weren't supposed to put dirty filling in the batteries, because if it's dirty, it's going to be dirty when it weaves. Our type wouldn't do it, but the young people would throw the bobbins any old way. That hurt Chicopee. They couldn't care less whether they did their work or didn't do their work. They'd say, "I'm going to get my pay the same as you next week, so why kill myself?" That's an awfully poor attitude when you're working. A place isn't going to stay open that long with people like that.

The old crew, the old reliables, were mostly on the day shift. I worked nights for sixteen years, for the simple reason that when Frankie [her son] was small, my husband worked one shift and I worked the other. We didn't have to pay a babysitter. Why work and pay the babysitter? We worked a split shift. He worked the afternoon and I worked the night. I slept in the morning, after I came in, till probably twelve or one o'clock, and then I'd get up and do my housework. The kids would come home from school and do their schoolwork, and I'd fix supper. Then I'd go lay down for a couple of hours before I went to work. I did that until seven years ago, when I had a chance to go on the day shift.

Chicopee was a good-paying mill. "Protect our workers," they said. Of course, textile workers are not the highest-paid people, but Chicopee kept up with the union mills, and we got good fringe benefits. Textiles is not a $7.00 or $8.00 an hour job, but we were the highest-paid textile workers around.

You always heard that Chicopee was a slave shop, that it was a hard place to work. The workroom was big; but once you got to know the work, if you were an honest or a hard worker, you didn't mind it. I know, I worked in the Waumbec Mill across the river. I had forty batteries to fill in Waumbec; when I started in Chicopee, I had 161. It was cotton, and in cotton the bobbins run fast. I used to tell the girls [at Waumbec], and they couldn't believe it. How could I fill that many? When I first went there, I said, "Oh, my God, how will I ever do all that?" But once you got into it, you had no problems at all.

My job was secure, I was working. If this was a year ago and I really needed a car, I might have thought of buying one. Who saw this coming? A lot of people bought houses here

Bette Skrzyszowski

eight or ten years ago. They still have a way to go on the mortgage, a twenty-year mortgage at best. And they have children, a lot of them have schoolchildren. With us, it's just my husband and me. Our home is paid for, our car is paid for. I'm not rich, but I'm thankful for what I have. Very thankful. I look around and see people with a lot worse problems than I have, so I'm not hurting that much.

Chicopee was like the city hall. You thought it would always be there. Many times people quit Chicopee, but they always came back. They'd quit and say, "I'll never come back," and in a year they'd be back. I could name dozens. There was always work then. We worked six days a week, steady, three shifts. Who would ever conceive that it would close?

We were talking to the bosses a couple of weeks ago in the cafeteria. The big bosses from New Brunswick told them a year ago that this plant would never close: Manchester, New Hampshire, would never lose its plant. Within a year it closed; nobody foresaw this coming. Even the bosses were surprised.

Why did they buy those cards if they were going to close? You talk to people, and they say, "This is a big decision for a big company to make." I guess it is. But to me it must have been an overnight decision. Otherwise, why would they invest so much? There's an awful lot of money invested in that mill. An awful lot. Why on earth would they buy new cards? Just to bring them up here and ship them south again? They could have stayed south in the first place.

Last year they completely changed all the offices, some upstairs and some downstairs. Everybody got new offices, with all new paneling, air conditioning, and wall-to-wall carpeting. The ladies' rooms and the men's rooms are all tiled with brand-new tile. They must have been thinking of something. Why invest all that money in a place you're going to shut down?

I don't know any other type of work. That's the sad part. And I'm not the only one. Most of the reliable help have been there anywhere from fifteen to twenty-five years. So we're all forty years old or over: we're not spring chickens. We can't say, "I don't like this job," and go find something else. We're fast, but how many jobs are there for battery hands?

If you gave me my choice, if you said today, "Which would

The Stark Mill in the Amoskeag millyard, photographed in the late afternoon of the day before it was demolished in 1968

you rather have, a thousand dollars right here or the mills starting up tomorrow?" I'd rather have the mills start up. I'd feel secure then; I'd have a job. I'd know what I was going to do. I'd know that I could handle it. This way, I've got to go out and start over.

BATTERY   the device on a loom designed to change the filling bobbin in the shuttle automatically without stopping the loom. This invention, which came into use around 1900, revolutionized work in the weave room. (*See also* handloom.)

BOBBIN   the wooden spool on which the roving or yarn is wound. Bobbins come in different shapes and sizes depending on the use.

BOBBIN WINDER   a machine designed to transfer the yarn onto small filling bobbins; for use in the shuttle

BURLING   picking the burrs or burls (as well as knots caused in spinning, dressing, or weaving) from the surface of the cloth; done primarily on woolen cloth. The process is carried out with a needle resembling a crochet hook.

CARD   a large machine with drums covered with wire teeth used for disentangling and laying parallel the fibers of wool or cotton; preparatory to spinning

COMBING   the process designed for producing especially fine yarns in which the fiber is combed before it is spun

COUNTS OF YARN   the number given to a thread to indicate the number of yards that weigh one pound; this will indicate the fineness of the yarn

DOBBY LOOM   a loom designed to produce more elaborate weaves by having a greater control of the raising of the warp threads

DOFFING   the process of removing filled bobbins from spindles in spinning

DOUBLING   the combination of two or more slivers or threads

DRAWING   the process by which the carded sliver is stretched to make the fibers parallel and uniform

DRAWING-IN   threading the warp threads into the loom harnesses

DRESSER   a machine in which the warps are prepared for weaving. The yarn gets covered with chemicals to protect it.

END   a single strand of sliver, roving, or yarn

FILLING   the threads running crosswise in a fabric

GILL BOX   a machine used in the process of worsted spinning for elongating and leveling the sliver either before or after combing

GINGHAM   a cotton fabric made of yarn and dyed before being woven. The name was introduced into England from India; and the manufacture first started in Glasgow, the seat of the gingham trade, in 1786. Gingham was the Amoskeag's largest volume product.

GREY GOODS   yarns or fabrics in an undyed or unbleached state

HANDLOOM   As used in the book, this means a power loom in which the filling bobbins must be inserted into the shuttle by hand.

HANK   a skein of yarn of a fixed length

HARNESS   a frame containing the heddles through which the warp threads are drawn-in prior to weaving

HEDDLES   the long, slender part of the loom harness having an eye near its center through which one or more warps pass

LONG CHAIN SYSTEM   a system of dyeing in which the finished yarn is dyed before it is put on the warp. To accomplish this, the yarn is tied into a long rope and put through the dyer.

MANUFACTURE   "Derived from *manus*, the hand, and *factura*, a making. In its etymological sense it means any system or objects of industry executed by hands, but in the vicissitudes of language it has now come to signify every extensive product of art which is made of machinery, with little or no aid of the human hand, so that the most perfect manufacture is that which dispenses entirely with manual labor." (*Structure of Fibres, Yarns and Fabrics*, 1890)

NAP   the wooly substance on the surface of cloth. The ends of fibers extending fur-like, outside a thread, are found most predominantly in woolen yarn.

NAPPING   raising the nap on the cloth by machine, especially for flannel goods

PICK   a single throw of the shuttle in the loom, inserting a filling thread in the cloth

PIECE GOODS   goods bought by the piece; the set unit containing from 24–100 yards

ROVING   the process preceding spinning which introduces a twist to the sliver

SHUTTLE   the bullet-shaped device for carrying the filling yarn back and forth through the warp in the loom

SIZING   the procedure of coating warp with a thin layer of starch to strengthen the yarn so that it will have less tendency to break in weaving

SLIVER   a long ribbon of cotton, wool, etc., drawn out by means of carding, combing, or drawing and run into a can. The sliver has no twist and clings together by the natural crimps of the fibers.

SMASH   the term for the damage that occurs in weaving when the timing of the pick is off and the shuttle tears the warp threads

SPINNING FRAME   the machine for spinning the roving into yarn

TICKING   the striped cotton material traditionally used for covering mattresses. Amoskeag's most famous original product was ACA Ticking.

TYING OVER   the process by which the warp is threaded through the harness and the reeds on the loom, and is then tied. This operation is done on the warping machine.

TWISTING   the process by which two or more threads are twisted into a single thread

WARP   the threads running lengthwise in a cloth

WEFT   the British term for filling

WORSTED   fabrics made of yarn combed straight and smooth in their process of manufacture; distinct from woolens, which are woven from yarns crossed and roughed in the carding and spinning processes

WRONG DRAW   an error in warping when the end of the yarn is placed in the wrong end of the reed of the loom, thus upsetting the pattern

YARD GOODS   cloth sold by the yard or fraction thereof

YARN TESTER   a worker who tests the strength and size of skeins of yarn. This is usually done with an instrument.

SOURCE: E. A. Posselt, *Structure of Fibers, Yarns and Fabrics* (Philadelphia: E. A. Posselt Co., 1890).

► *Photograph Credits*

About the Authors

TAMARA K. HAREVEN is Unidel Professor of Family Studies and History at the University of Delaware and Visiting Scholar at the Sociology Department at Harvard University. A social historian and one of the foremost leaders in the field of family history, the life course, and aging, she has organized international conferences and workshops and founded the *Journal of Family History*, for which she is the editor. Professor Hareven received her B.A. from the Hebrew University in Jerusalem in 1961, her M.A. from the University of Cincinnati in 1962, and her Ph.D. from Ohio State University in 1965. She is author of *Family Time and Industrial Time* (1982); *Transitions: The Family and the Life Course in Historical Perspective* (1978); *Aging and the Life Course in Interdisciplinary and Cross-Cultural Perspective* (1982); and *Aging and Generational Relations: An Historical and Life Course Perspective* (1995), as well as numerous articles and edited collections. She has completed a comparative study on Japan, to be published in her book *The Silk Weavers of Kyoto: Family and Work in a Changing Traditional History*, and is currently writing a book entitled *Generations in Historical Time*. Professor Hareven has been the recipient of grants from the Ford Foundation, Rockefeller Foundation, National Endowment for the Humanities, the National Institute on Aging, and the Social Science Research Council, and she received the Radcliffe Graduate Society Medal in 1992. She is currently President of the Social Science History Association.

RANDOLPH LANGENBACH is a designer, architectural historian, and photographer. His documentation of, and historical research on, nineteenth-century industrial cities have become well known in both the United States and Great Britain. His articles and photographs have been published in numerous books and magazines; and his book, *A Future From the Past*, was published by the U.S. Department of Housing and Urban Development. He has produced an exhibition in London on British industrial towns, and was actively involved in planning the new national park in Manchester's sister city, Lowell, Massachusetts.

UNIVERSITY PRESS OF NEW ENGLAND publishes books under its own imprint and is the publisher for Brandeis University Press, Dartmouth College, Middlebury College Press, University of New Hampshire, University of Rhode Island, Tufts University, University of Vermont, Wesleyan University Press, and Salzburg Seminar.

Library of Congress Cataloging-in-Publication Data

Hareven, Tamara K.
    Amoskeag : life and work in an American factory-city / Tamara K. Hareven and Randolph Langenbach
       p.   cm.
    Originally published: New York : Pantheon Books, © 1978, in series: Pantheon village series.
    ISBN 0-87451-736-2 (pbk. : alk. paper)
    1. Textile workers—New Hampshire—Manchester—Biography. 2. Amoskeag Manufacturing Company—History. 3. Manchester (N.H.)—History. I. Langenbach, Randolph, 1945– . II. Title.
HD8039.T42U648 1995
338.7'677'0097428—dc20   95-34264
♾